Population

AN INTRODUCTION

Population

AN INTRODUCTION

JOHANNES OVERBEEK

University of Maine at Orono

HARCOURT BRACE JOVANOVICH, INC.

New York   San Diego   Chicago   San Francisco   Atlanta
London   Sydney   Toronto

ISBN: 0-15-543488-8

Library of Congress Catalog Card Number: 82-81687

Printed in the United States of America

Preface

Human populations have been investigated for centuries, yet it is only in recent years that demography—the systematic study of population—has come into full bloom. Changes in population affect us all. Increased immigration may change the kind of neighborhood in which we live. The aging of a population may affect tax rates and social security systems. The increasing youthfulness of populations in less developed countries may make economic development more difficult to achieve. *Population: An Introduction* examines these and other major issues of the study of population through its presentation of the principles of formal demography and the socioeconomic causes and consequences of population change.

This book is intended mainly for students of sociology, economics, and geography. It emphasizes the minimum of technical competency in formal demography necessary to unravel population-related problems. For students who have not taken a course in statistics, Chapter 2, "Analytics," describes the basic statistical concepts and techniques needed to read and understand the graphs, charts, and tables that present demographic data.

v

Other features include a generous treatment of migration in three chapters, including the theory of migration (Chapter 8), international migration (Chapter 9), and internal migration (Chapter 10). Chapter 9 focuses on increased immigration as a source of American population growth, and Chapter 10 examines the redistribution of the American population, as evidenced in particular in the growth of the sunbelt. Chapter 12, "The Socioeconomic Effects of Population Change," contrasts the growth of an aging population in the Western nations to the explosion of a younger population in the developing countries. In Chapter 12 and throughout the book, data are drawn from Europe, Canada, and the Third World, as well as from the United States.

Both the University of Guelph in Canada and the University of Maine at Orono were instrumental in encouraging and indirectly sponsoring this book. Their facilities were generously provided, and for these I am grateful. Colleagues Bill Soule, Tom Duchesneau, and Dave Prescott contributed comments and suggestions so gracefully that I felt greatly encouraged. To Faye Welock and Donna Rog thanks are due for dedicated secretarial service. Lastly I would like to thank my wife, Chantal, for being the kind of person who makes a book like this possible.

J. O.

Contents

1

The Nature
of Population Study

Demography is destiny. Between 1946 and 1961 a bumper crop of almost seventy million children was born—by far the largest generation in American history. Today they constitute almost one-third of the American population. Their problems are the nation's problems. In the 1950s they transformed the United States into a child-oriented society of new schools, suburbs, and station wagons. In the 1960s they rocked the nation with their troubled youth. By the 1970s and early 1980s they were facing the problems of finding work and shelter. Hereafter they will reach their peak spending years. When, after the year 2010, they begin to retire, because of their numbers alone they will once again pose unprecedented problems for the nation. The baby boom will be long remembered in American history, if only as a magnificent illustration of the fact that almost all socioeconomic issues have a demographic component.

POPULATIONS

Populations are the subject matter of demography and population analysis. There are basically two kinds of populations. A *demographic population* consists of a number of people inhabiting a geographic area that may be a nation, a province, a county, a city, and the like. But in statistical theory the concept of a *statistical population* is used to signify the total collection or complete set of persons, objects, or events, in which the researcher is interested. The term *universe* is also used to designate a statistical population. A statistical population, then, comprises the entire group of observations under study, and is a totality of individuals or things that have a common characteristic. If the researcher is interested in the marital status of female college students at the University of Maine, his or her statistical population would consist of those students. But the term *statistical population* does not necessarily refer to a collection of human beings or living organisms. If the researcher is interested in the annual sales of supermarkets in a given area, then the yearly sales of those supermarkets constitute the population. All the factories in a particular region could likewise make up a statistical population.

SAMPLES

Any portion drawn from a demographic population or any part of a statistical population is known as a *sample*. The sample is any subset of persons, objects or items selected from the population. A good sample faithfully represents the population from which it is drawn. Samples allow the researcher to work with relatively small quantities, thus making possible economies of time and resources. The information obtained from a representative sample can then be generalized in terms of the larger population or universe. If, for instance, researchers want to know how many people in San Francisco contribute to the Humane Society, they might interview only a sample of 2,000 people instead of the entire population. Figure 1–1 illustrates the relationship of samples to populations they represent.

FORMAL DEMOGRAPHY AND POPULATION ANALYSIS

It has been customary to differentiate between formal demography and population analysis. *Formal demography* refers to the statistical description and analysis of human populations; it aims at statistical measurement of a given population and its evolution. Population statistics have a logic

FIGURE 1–1

Relationship of a Sample to Its Population

of their own: if a population grows, it may be because the number of births exceeds the number of deaths, or because the number of immigrants exceeds the number of emigrants. Demographers, therefore, study not only the current state of a population but also its evolution, and sometimes they predict its future course. The numerical portrayal of a human population is like a photograph, whereas the study of changes taking place over time is like a movie. The formal demographer is interested in both kinds of analysis. Formal demography is essentially a quantitative discipline; numbers and measurement are its very basis.

While formal demography limits itself to the study of such subjects as the size and composition of a population, as well as its fertility and mortality, *population analysis* leaves the realm of statistical measurement and seeks to explain the determinants and consequences of observed population trends. Population analysis is therefore related to all the social sciences and is by definition interdisciplinary. The population analyst may attempt to examine the impact of fast population growth on economic development, or investigate the determinants of a decline in fertility, which may be social, economic, psychological, and so on. Population study uses the data of formal demography, but relates them to the other social sciences. Hauser and Duncan have argued that population study transcends formal demography, devoting itself to the relationships between population changes and social, economic, political, geographical, and psychological variables.[1]

At present not everybody wholeheartedly accepts the above-mentioned distinction between formal demography and population analysis. In his presidential address at the annual meeting of the Population Association of America in 1979, social demographer C. B. Nam maintained that although this widely accepted distinction has proved its usefulness, it could also be said to have "unwittingly contributed to professional schizophrenia and marginality."[2] According to Nam (and the author agrees), the narrow

[1] P. M. Hauser and O. D. Duncan, "Overview and Conclusions," in P. M. Hauser and O. D. Duncan, *The Study of Population* (Chicago: University of Chicago Press, 1964), pp. 2–3.
[2] C. B. Nam, "The Progress of Demography as a Scientific Discipline," *Demography* 16 November 1979): 487.

view of "demography" should be abandoned. Demography as a discipline should be understood to include the study of the internal dynamics of populations as well as "the broader societal determinants and consequences" of those dynamics. According to Nam, "understanding and explaining population phenomena is what demography is all about."[3] But the demographic profession has not as yet accepted this more complete and integrated definition.

CONCEPTS FOR REVIEW

Demographic population
Statistical population
Universe

Sample
Formal demography
Population analysis

QUESTIONS FOR DISCUSSION

1. Analyze the differences between a demographic population and a statistical population.
2. What is meant by the statement "formal demography is essentially a quantitative discipline"?
3. Describe the difference between formal demography and population analysis.

BIBLIOGRAPHY

Hauser, P. M., and O. D. Duncan. *The Study of Population.* Chicago: University of Chicago Press, 1964.
Nam, C. B. "The Progress of Demography as a Scientific Discipline." *Demography* 16 (November 1979).
Thompson, W. S., and D. T. Lewis. *Population Problems.* 5th ed. New York: McGraw-Hill, 1965.

[3] Nam, pp. 488, 491.

2

Analytics

The purpose of this chapter is to familiarize you with some of the basic quantitative principles underlying much of the demographic research that follows. Most of these raw materials belong to the domain of *descriptive statistics,* which can be defined as procedures for collecting, summarizing, presenting, and describing facts and data; as such, it is concerned largely with summary calculations, tabular and graphical displays. Statistics can also be useful in generalizing from past experience: *inferential statistics* seeks to make inferences (statements or conclusions) from collected data. Usually such generalizations are made about a population by investigating only a portion of it referred to as a sample. In this book, however, inferential statistics will concern us very little.

Many people find quantitative thinking difficult and approach statistics with prejudice. Such need not be the case. This chapter is designed to help you understand much of the statistical reasoning behind elementary formal demography. It provides the clay without which the bricks cannot be made. Little mathematics is required for a good understanding of the basic concepts introduced here.

DEMOGRAPHIC RESEARCH IN ACTION

When we start an investigation, say, of the number of children under 15 years of age per married mother in a Hawaiian village, we must first define the units to be investigated. The elementary units, subjects, or individuals are the married mothers of children under 15. For each case or subject (each married mother) a selected *characteristic* (her fertility) is observed. As we note the selected characteristic—the number of children under 15— we can group our observations (the mothers) in different *classes* or *categories*. All married mothers with 2 children are a class. Those with 3 children are another class, and so on. Here we are using the measured quantity—the number of children under 15—as a measure of fertility or reproductive performance; we have constructed a *fertility index.* In all likelihood this characteristic will not have the same value for all mothers. A specific trait or characteristic such as fertility, income, level of education, age, racial origin, or marital status which varies among people is called a *variable.*

VARIABLES

A variable can take on a range of values. A single variable is usually symbolized by the letter X. Two variables are often symbolized by the letters X and Y. Variables have three properties: (1) they are traits of objects or persons, (2) they are observable, (3) they differ from observation to observation.

Scales

To record the variable, we use *scales. Scaling* consists of placing the values of a variable on a scale, which may or may not be numerical. In our type of society, for example, the variable "age" is normally scaled in years. Once we have a scale, we can record the values of a variable (fertility, age, and so on), a process called *measurement.* We now observe the degree in which the variable varies and obtain information about it. That information, often numerical, consists of *data.* A plural Latin word meaning facts or figures, data are the end result of measurement and the starting point of statistical analysis. Once data have been gathered, the next step is to present them in tabular or graphic form. In measuring variables, four important types of scales are common.

FIGURE 2–1

A Nominal Scale Representing Marital Status

Nominal Scales. Nominal measurement is *categorization*—the most elementary form of measurement. It results from a classification of objects into categories on the basis of attributes such as sex, race, religion, and so on. Suppose we are observing the sex of immigrants. If any observation is assigned the value "male," it means that the subject simply falls into this category, and not that he has more or less of the attribute in question. All the males will be classified in the category "male" and all the females in the category "female." Usually classes have categorical names, but sometimes, as for manipulation by computer, numbers can be used instead. Thus we can give the class "male" the number 1 and the class "female" the number 2. Such numbers, however, are mere labels and do not permit arithmetical operations. Other numbers so used—to identify rather than to measure—can include those designating highways, hockey players, social security cards, houses on a street, and so on. Figure 2–1, a circle graph, shows a nominal scale of marital status.

Ordinal Scales. In some cases the observations can be ordered so as to indicate that one observation represents more of a given variable than another. Ordinal scales rank individuals in terms of some quality such as health, prestige, beauty, or academic achievement (Figure 2–2). The ranks— that is, the numbers used for identification—do not indicate how much more or less of the property each observation has, but only that they have "more" or "less." If in a beauty contest there are three winners to whom the numbers 1, 2, and 3 are assigned, we imply only that 1 has more of the variable "beauty" than 2, while 2 is prettier than 3. Other examples would be a list of preferred states of destination of foreign immigrants, or a hierarchy of social classes. When the social scientists measure social class

FIGURE 2–2

An Ordinal Scale Representing Health

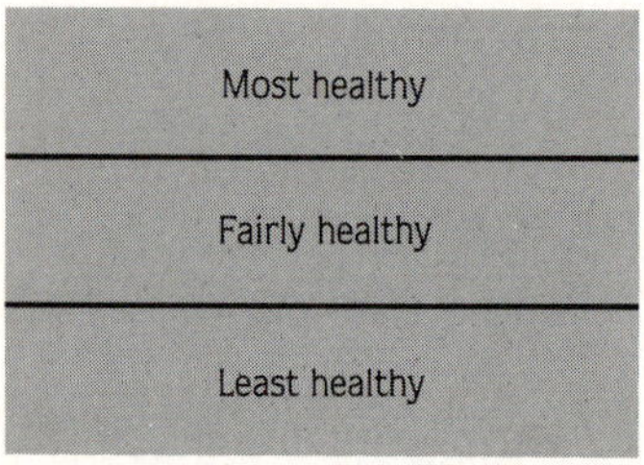

| Most healthy |
| Fairly healthy |
| Least healthy |

on an ordinal scale, it enables them to speak in terms of "higher than" and "lower than," but never to answer how much higher or lower.

Interval Scales. Observations on such scales are recorded numerically. The numbers not only order the observations but also convey meaningful information with regard to the distance or degree of difference between all observations.

Interval numbers have magnitudes, for they are based on a common unit of measurement; therefore, the distance from one integer (whole number) to its adjacent integer is equal to the distance from any other integer to its adjacent integer. The distance between 3 and 4 is the same as that between 8 and 9. Arithmetical operations are now possible. We can add a number to or subtract a number from each of the values and still maintain the essential properties of the scale. However, we do not know where true zero is on the scale, so we cannot make multiplicative statements about it. The Fahrenheit thermometer is an interval scale (Figure 2–3). There are equal units along the scale, but zero on the thermometer does not signify an absence of all heat. If the temperature rises from 40°F in the morning to 80°F in the afternoon, we cannot say that there is twice as much temperature in the afternoon as in the morning.[1]

Ratio Scales. In addition to the properties of the interval scale, the ratio scale has an absolute zero point that represents an absence of the measured quality. This is the most sophisticated level of measurement.

---

[1] In the early eighteenth century Gabriel Daniel Fahrenheit, a German instrument maker, invented a thermometer consisting of a column of mercury in glass. In devising a scale for this thermometer, Fahrenheit defined it in terms of the lowest temperature he could obtain by mixing common salt and ice. He chose this point as his zero point. The freezing point of pure water was measured as 32°. Normal body temperature was 98.6° on his scale, while 212° registered when pure water boiled. The range between the freezing and boiling points was 180°.

FIGURE 2–3

The Fahrenheit Scale

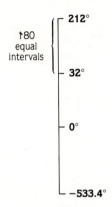

Measures such as speed, fertility, weight, and income have absolute zero points: 0 income, for instance, is no income at all. The centimeter scale is a good example of a ratio scale (Figure 2–4). The origin on this scale (0) corresponds to no length at all. On such a scale, ratios between any two given values of a variable can be computed. An object that is 8 centimeters long is twice as long as an object measuring 4 centimeters. The ratio between the two scores is 8/4 or 2/1.[2] Some social scientists treat ratio scales as a subcategory of interval scales, so there is no need to be concerned with the distinction between them.

   Discrete and Continuous Variables. Variables measured on an interval or ratio scale are commonly classified as either discrete or continuous. *Discrete variables* can take values only at certain discrete (separate, discontinuous) points on a scale. Thus a discrete variable can only achieve scores that may be represented as isolated points on a scale. We usually encounter discrete variables as integer variables derived from counting, as for example the number of cars in a garage, the number of children in a family, or the number of books in a library (Figure 2–5). There cannot be 2.4

FIGURE 2–4

The Centimeter Scale

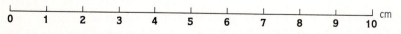

[2] Ratios are discussed on pages 31–32.

FIGURE 2–5

Variables by Scale Continuity

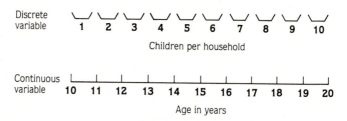

children in a family; if there are more than two, there must be at least three.

Conversely, *continuous variables* are able to take any value (integral or nonintegral) within a certain range. They have values at every point on a continuous scale; given any two distinct points or values on the scale, we can always think of another value that would fall somewhere between. Distance, weight, temperature, and age are obvious examples. Age is commonly reported in years, but changes between the reported values in fact pass through a continuous scale; for the continuous variable of age there exists an infinity of possible measurements (Figure 2–5). Even so, the United States Bureau of the Census reports age in years "as of last birthday," so that the number 18 represents all ages from 18 up to but not including 19. Persons who have just passed their eighteenth birthday belong to category 18, as do others who are on the verge of their nineteenth. Keep in mind that measurements are limited by the precision of the available measuring instruments and the number system. If between ages 18 and 19 there are an infinity of possible measurements, for practical purposes they cannot all be measured.

Independent and Dependent Variables. Researchers choose their variables. How they choose them depends on what aspect of the world around them they want to study. Depending on the use of variables made in research, they can be divided into two types: independent and dependent.

The *independent variable* is the variable being manipulated in experimental situations, or the one from which predictions are made in nonexperimental settings. The effect of the independent variable is observed in changes in the *dependent variable*. The independent variable has an impact on the dependent variable that can be thought of as the "to be explained" phenomenon. If, for instance, we investigate the effect of someone's exercise on his or her weight, the exercise is the independent variable and the weight the dependent variable. Graphs often display an independent and a dependent variable and the actual results of an experiment on the relation between them.

Functions

When two or more variables are related, the relationship between them is called a *function*. A function is the mathematical expression of the dependent variable in terms of the independent variable(s). To every value of the independent variable there corresponds one value of the dependent variable. If income and savings are related in a cause-and-effect manner in the sense that to every value of income there corresponds a value of savings, we have found a functional relationship between the two. Income is the independent variable, savings the dependent variable. To say that savings is a function of income means that the magnitude of savings depends on, or is conditioned by, the magnitude of income. Functional relationships are often written in algebraic notation, as for example, $Y = f(X)$, in which Y is the dependent variable and X the independent variable. In the case of $Y = f(X_1, X_2)$, Y is conditioned by the two independent variables X_1 and X_2.

GRAPHICAL ANALYSIS

The functional relationship between two variables can be illustrated graphically. When two variables are plotted together, the result is a *bivariate graph*. Here we can distinguish between two major types of graphic figures, functional relationships and line graphs.

Functional Relationships

To give a picture of the *functional relationship* between two variables, a rectangular coordinate system is used. We draw two lines perpendicular to each other. The horizontal axis is called the X-axis, the vertical axis the Y-axis. The point of intersection of the two lines is called the origin, 0. The two lines partition the graph into four quadrants that are identified by numbering them counterclockwise, starting with the upper right-hand corner. The axis can now be numbered in each direction from the origin. Along the horizontal axis we lay out the values of the independent variable, with the positive values to the right and the negative values to the left of the origin. Scores of the dependent variable are indicated on the Y-axis; those above the origin are positive, while those below are negative.

FIGURE 2–6

A Rectangular Coordinate System

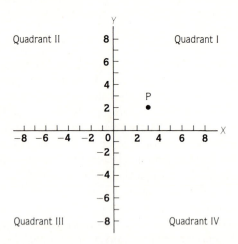

Because so many social measurements are marked on scales extending from 0 in a positive direction, quadrant 1 is often the only one used. The other three quadrants are omitted.

We are now ready to locate any point on the graph (say, P) with two numbers, one for X and one for Y. These two numbers are called the *coordinates* of the point P. It is conventional to represent the X coordinate first and the Y coordinate second. For example, the point P in Figure 2–6 has coordinates 3,2.

Suppose we have five pairs of values in a table showing savings as a function of income. We can regard the pairs of values as the coordinates of the points A, B, C, D, and E. Subsequently, we can draw a picture of the functional relationship, using the five points:

X	2	4	6	8	10
Y	1	2	3	4	5

The table shows that we have used the formula $X = 0.5Y$. The graph of $X = 0.5Y$ is shown in Figure 2–7. This graph can now be used to find the amount of savings for any level of income shown on the graph. The scales used on the horizontal and vertical axes may vary to suit the purpose of the researcher, but the point of origin should always be zero.

Direct and Inverse Variations.   The primary function of a graph is to illustrate the relationship between two variables. The relationship $X = 0.5Y$ is an example of *direct variation* or a *positive relationship*. Increasing val-

FIGURE 2–7

Savings as a Function of Income

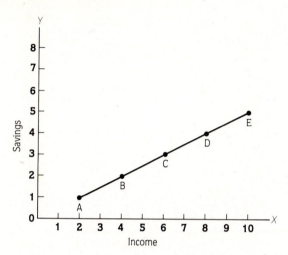

ues along the X-axis are associated with increasing values on the Y-axis, indicating that more income is associated with more savings (Figure 2–8). With *inverse variation* or a *negative relationship,* one variable increases as the other decreases (Figure 2–8). If, for instance, the number of deaths increases, then—other things equal—the total population will fall. The more deaths, the smaller the population.

FIGURE 2–8

Direct and Inverse Variation

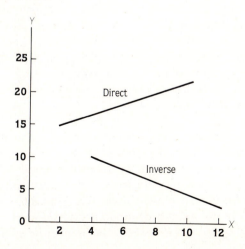

FIGURE 2–9

Linear and Curvilinear Relationship

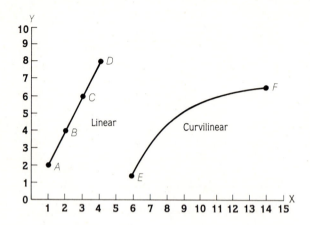

Linear and Curvilinear Relationships. Another useful distinction may be made between linear and curvilinear relationships. *Linear relationships* imply that equal changes on the horizontal axis are always associated with matching changes on the Y-axis. Suppose that one-unit increases, starting at 1, in the variable X are always associated with two-unit increments in the variable Y, starting at 2. We then obtain points A, B, C, and D, which can be connected with a straight line (Figure 2–9). The slope of line AD shows the change in Y for any given change in X. Since a straight line has the same slope everywhere, it corresponds to a function for which a given change in X is always associated with the same change in Y. For linear relationships the lines are always straight.

The relationship between two variables can also be curvilinear. *Curvilinear relationships* imply that graph lines do not have the same slope throughout. The lines are continuously changing direction, which indicates that equal changes in X are associated with changing increments or decrements in Y. The relationship between income and age is curvilinear in nature. The line EF in Figure 2–9 shows a curvilinear relationship between the two variables X and Y.

Line Graphs. *Line graphs* are commonly used in demographically oriented publications to show data relationships in graphic form. The main purpose of all graphs is to picture relationships among various kinds of data and to allow the viewer to discern at a glance relationships that might remain unnoticed in tabular presentations. Line graphs are often used when the variable on the X-axis is a continuous interval-level variable such as time or age. Suppose we want to show the number of immigrants for suc-

FIGURE 2–10

Immigration (Canada, 1851–1971)

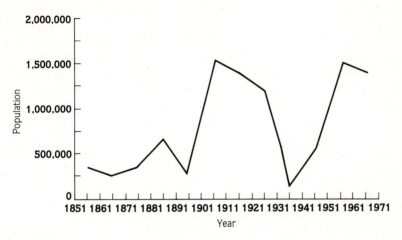

Source: W. E. Kalbach, W. W. McVey, *The Demographic Basis of Canadian Society* (Toronto: McGraw-Hill, 1979), p. 55.

cessive years in a given country. With such a line chart, time is plotted from left to right on the horizontal axis, while the number of immigrants is measured along the vertical axis. Such line graphs, which present the different values of a variable at successive points of time, are called *time series*. Time must be plotted at even intervals of, say, six months or one year. The numbering on the Y-axis must also be equally spaced. Once we have constructed the horizontal and vertical scales, we plot the pairs of values as points and then connect the points by a continuous line. The resulting time series shows how the number of immigrants varies over time. A time-series line is merely a stringing together of measurements of the same variable; the values charted do not have a functional relationship (Figure 2–10).

MODELS

Social phenomena are extremely complex—it is impossible to describe all the variables of a social system and their interaction. Therefore social scientists build logical structures or models that capture only the essentials of a process, theory, phenomenon, or system, while omitting details whose net effect is thought to be insignificant. A useful model is concise and presents a minimum of information to be assimilated. Models are usually presented in verbal form, or as charts or equations. The generality and simplicity of models help us to think efficiently about actual problems. By isolating the most relevant variables and their interrelations, a good model will cast light on the more complex (and sometimes confusing) world of reality it represents.

The writers C. A. Lave and J. G. March have defined a model as "a simplified picture of a part of the real world. It has some characteristics of the real world, but not all of them. It is a set of interrelated guesses about the world. Like all pictures, a model is simpler than the phenomena it is supposed to represent or explain."[3] The better the data and the more precise the measurement procedures, the easier it is to build a good model. However, measurements and observations are not enough. One must have the insight to perceive structure in a mass of data in order to develop an effective model.

Explanatory and Predictive Models

Models can be divided into various types or categories. One such distinction is between explanatory and predictive models. An *explanatory model* describes a process or system in terms of its components and their interrelationships. The description is formulated to explain some observed properties of the process. We should be able to test an explanatory model against the actual facts. A *predictive model,* on the other hand, makes it possible to predict the occurrence of certain future events in the system. Many models are both explanatory and predictive.

Another classification is between *simple models* and *complex models.* A very simple model may focus on one aspect of a given population, such as the relationship between family income and fertility. Only two variables are involved, a dependent variable and an independent. explanatory variable. Some relationship between the two variables is then hypothesized. More ambitious models pick out a larger number of strategic variables that are still logically manageable and arrive at conclusions that claim to mirror the course of events in the real world. Some complex models even specify a set of assumptions and then reason how an entire population or society would react to the modification of a key variable. This was the sort of work done in *The Limits of Growth,* a well-known book which emphasizes that continued exponential growth of population and production would eventually result in planetary disaster.[4]

---

[3] C. A. Lave and J. G. March, *An Introduction to Models in the Social Sciences* (New York: Harper & Row, 1975), p. 3.
[4] D. H. Meadows et al., *The Limits of Growth* (New York: Universe Books, 1972).

Historical, Institutional, and Theoretical Models

Another distinction is that between historical, institutional, and theoretical models. One particular model we will encounter later in the text—the demographic transition model—is an illustration of a *historical model.* Such a model generalizes from past experience. In the past, for example, modernization and economic development in countries like Great Britain and the United States have initially depressed mortality levels, thereby inducing a population increase. Actually, a decline in both mortality and fertility levels resulted, but the decline in fertility occurred with a lag.

Institutional and Theoretical Models

Institutional models emphasize social, economic, political, and cultural institutions and state a relationship between one of them and another variable. The social institution of the extended family in traditional societies, for instance, helps to keep the variable fertility at high levels because the procreating couple does not bear the full cost of raising the children; other family members share in the responsibility.

Theoretical models imply a tight application of logical reasoning, as in this example: "Suppose that in a low-income country per capita incomes begin to rise. This will allow people to buy more and better food. Other things being equal, their mortality will drop. Population will then grow faster. The population/resources ratio will tend to deteriorate, productivity will fall, and per capita incomes will drop to their previous low level." This theoretical model, the "Malthusian trap model," will be explained and illustrated in Chapter 12.

FREQUENCY DISTRIBUTIONS

We mentioned earlier that descriptive statistics includes techniques to organize data, make summary statements about them, and show how they are distributed in value. Most of the data that researchers encounter consist of scattered observations on the variable they are interested in. The investigator faces the problem of organizing and summarizing the data in a meaningful way. The *frequency distribution,* a common technique in demography, shows how a collection of observations is distributed among the various individuals or categories. Usually a set of mutually exclusive classes is established. Each observation (specific value of a variable) is placed in one of the classes or categories. The number of items in each class is called a *frequency*, which can be defined as the number of times a given value occurs.

In many frequency distributions only one variable, such as fertility, is observed. When recorded data involve a single variable, we refer to a *univariate* (one-variable) *distribution*. An example would be a study of the number of children born to 50 married mothers. Only one variable, the number of children, is observed. *Bivariate analysis* deals with two variables at a time and focuses on relationships between them. Suppose that we obtain two variables, the number of children and age, from the same 50 women. Each observation now consists of a pair of numbers and is therefore a bivariate (two-variable) observation. *Multivariate data* involve more than two variables—for example fertility, age, and income.

Consider the previous example of a univariate distribution, namely that of the number of children under 15 years of age per married mother in a small Hawaiian village, in which we supposedly carried out a demographic survey in 1980. We counted 50 married mothers each having a certain number of children under age 15. Obviously we have 50 observations of a variable, namely, the number of children under 15 per married mother. Our categories or classes are: 0 children, 1 child, 2 children, and so forth. A frequency distribution must show how many mothers out of 50 have 0 children, 1 child, and so on. So a frequency is a count: it consists of the number of times we observe something. Here frequencies are symbolized by the letter f, while the sum of the frequencies—that is, the total number of observations—is denoted by the letter N. Here $N = 50$. In graphic presentations of a frequency distribution, some characteristic appears on the X-axis while the number, percentage, or proportion of cases (the frequency) appears on the Y-axis. There are three well-known graphic presentations of a frequency distribution: bar graphs, frequency histograms, and polygons (pp. 21–27).

The Frequency Table

Returning to the example of our Hawaiian village, suppose that our survey yielded the following results regarding the number of children under 15 years of age per married mother.

2	3	9	3	7	8	2	6	3	8
3	1	10	2	4	10	3	4	6	12
5	4	8	1	3	5	5	5	4	5
1	6	5	3	5	4	4	2	4	6
9	7	4	4	2	2	7	2	7	11

Among the observations listed above (we have 50 mothers and 246 children), some values occur more frequently than others. For instance, the value 12 occurs only once, while the value 2 occurs seven times meaning that only one mother had 12 children but seven mothers had two children under age 15. The question arises: how can we present the above data in a more meaningful way?

The first step is to calculate the *range*. The range summarizes the numerical observations. It is an index of the spread of values stated in the frequency table, providing information about the dispersion or variability of the observations. The limits in Table 2–1 are 1 and 12. Subtracting the lowest from the highest value, we find the range: $12 - 1 = 11$.

Tallying. As some observations or scores appear more frequently than others, we can determine the frequency with which each observation occurs by making a *tally sheet* that lists all possible categories (here the number of children under 15 per mother) within the range of observed values. We then tally (record) each of our observations on the appropriate line of the tally sheet. The frequency distribution is then obtained by counting the tally marks in each category. The *cumulative frequency* is obtained by adding the frequency of observations in the first class to those in the second.

TABLE 2–1

Distribution of Children Below
Age 15 in Hawaiiana, an Imaginary Village (1980)

Category (number of children below 15 per mother)	Tally	Frequency (f) (number of mothers with number of children stated in category)	Cumulative Frequency
1	111	3	3
2	1111 11	7	10
3	1111 11	7	17
4	1111 1111	9	26
5	1111 11	7	32
6	1111	4	37
7	1111	4	41
8	111	3	44
9	11	2	46
10	11	2	48
11	1	1	49
12	1	1	50
		$N = 50$	

Then those in the first and second are added to those in the third, and so forth. Instead of showing the number of scores in each category, the cumulative frequency shows the number of scores in or below each class.

The table we have now is a frequency distribution. Three mothers had one child below 15, 7 mothers had 2 children below 15, and so on. N denotes the number of scores in the entire distribution.

Grouping. When, unlike the example just given, there are many observations falling in numerous categories, the number of categories can be reduced by *grouping:* single measurements are collapsed into groups into which each frequency will fall. The example below illustrates this idea as applied to the Hawaiian village.

Interval (Number of Children)	Frequency (Number of Mothers)
1–3	17
4–6	20
7–9	9
10–12	4
	50

The single values have been brought together into a number of groups or blocks each containing an equal number of score values. These groups of numerals 1–3, 4–6, and so on, are called "class intervals" or simply "intervals." The number of score units (1, 2, 3) included within an interval such as 1–3 is called the *interval width,* symbolized by the letter i. Here $i = 3$.

Class Limits. The above groups or classes each have an upper and a lower limit, which are the values at both ends. Four and 6 are the recorded lower and upper limits respectively of the class 4–6. But we now observe that there is a gap between such classes as 4–6 and 7–9. Had we dealt with a continuous ratio variable such as distance or weight, the fractional value of, say, 6.4 could not have been assigned to either of the two classes and would have to be excluded. Therefore we must distinguish between apparent and real limits. The numbers 4 and 6 are the *apparent* or *expressed limits* of class 4–6. The *real* or *true limits* are always a half unit above and below the apparent limits. Thus the real limits of class 4–6 are 3.5–6.5, while the real limits of 7–9 are 6.5–9.5. Now the gaps between adjacent class intervals have been closed.

An Exception: Age. The continuous variable age is not measured as explained in the previous section. People tend to state their age as of the last birthday rather than the next one, even if the next one is nearer. We consider a person to be 10 years old after his or her tenth birthday, and to remain 10 years old until the eleventh birthday. Strictly speaking, the value 10 now means 10 up to but excluding 11, but it is commonly stated as the interval 10–11. For wider intervals the same holds true. When age is scaled, a five-year interval such as 5–9 (including ages 5, 6, 7, 8, 9) extends from 5 up to but excluding 10. In such cases it is legitimate to use 10 as the dividing line between age categories 5–9 and 10–14, as in the example below.

5-9	10-14	15-19	20-24

5   10   15   20   25

The Midpoint. Another characteristic of any group interval is its *midpoint,* which can be defined as the middlemost score value in the class interval. One way of finding the midpoint is to average the apparent limits of a class, that is, to add up those limits and divide them by 2.[5] For the class 4–6 we obtain

$$\frac{4+6}{2}=5.$$

With age classes we average the real, not the apparent, limits.

GRAPHICAL PRESENTATION OF FREQUENCY DISTRIBUTIONS

In tabular form, frequency distributions lack visual appeal. Also, they do not call attention to the outstanding features of the distribution. But graphs do. They come in a number of forms, one of which is the *bar graph*.

Bar Graphs

Bar graphs are used for data at all levels of measurement. The left-hand vertical axis shows the frequency of people who exhibit the characteristic described on the horizontal axis. The bars are separate, each one representing the abundance of observations of the variable.

Suppose we want to present graphically the number of immigrants into Hawaii. At the same time we wish to make visible the difference between the immigrants from the United States mainland and those from elsewhere. We would place the years of immigration on the X-axis and the number (frequency) on the Y-axis (Figure 2–11). In other words, the Y-

[5] Various methods of averaging are explained on pages 27–30.

FIGURE 2-11

Bar Graph Showing Immigrants from
the United States Mainland and Other Nations
to Hawaii, 1955–75

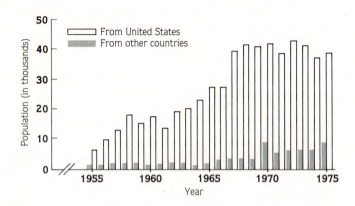

Source: E. C. Nordyke, *The Peopling of Hawaii* (Honolulu: University Press of Hawaii, 1977), p. 81.

axis shows the frequency of the characteristic described on the X-axis. We take the period 1955–75. The jagged line indicates that there is no interest in the values that lie to the left of the break.

Histograms and Polygons

To picture ordinal level and interval level data, we use *histograms* and *polygons*. A histogram is like a bar graph, except that the bars touch. On the horizontal axis we present the categories of the variable, and on the vertical axis the frequencies. For some problems it will be more convenient to let the vertical axis represent relative frequencies or percentages (pp. 33–35). The classes on the X-axis are represented by a scale line which is laid off to show the real limits of the class intervals. The use of real limits eliminates the spaces between the bars and produces a solid appearance (Figure 2–12). On the vertical axis we present the frequencies of the individual classes or intervals laid off on the horizontal axis. For both the histogram and polygon it is customary that the vertical axis be about two-thirds the length of the horizontal axis. If we scale the X-axis as stated above, the bars that represent the frequencies can be drawn adjacent to one another. The horizontal axis should as a rule be divided into equal, regularly spaced units. If we mark off the real limits of each interval along the horizontal scale, we can easily find the midpoint of each interval. We

FIGURE 2–12

A Histogram Representing the Number of Children
under Age 15 per Mother (Hawaiiana, 1980)

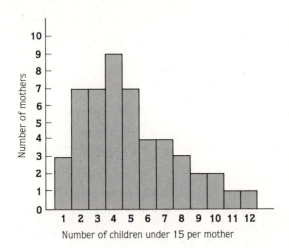

Number of children under 15 per mother

then construct rectangles centered on the midpoint of the interval and drawn
to the width of the interval. The height of each rectangle equals the frequency of scores in the interval. In Figure 2–12, an example of a histogram, we return to Table 2–1 (p. 19), presenting the number of children
below age 15 for each of 50 mothers.

Suppose that in Hawaiiana we also surveyed the age distribution of
the 50 mothers and found that all those mothers were between ages 20
and 49. In a presentation of the age distribution (Table 2–2), we indicate
the characteristic being tabulated (age of mother) in the first column. Un-
derneath we list the categories or classes, 20–24, 25–29, and so on. In the
second column we state the number of cases, that is, the frequency for
each category.

We have added a third column that states the *relative frequencies,* a
common practice in demographic literature. We find the relative frequency
or proportion for each value by dividing the frequency (say, 12) by the
total number of cases (50). For the first column we have: 12/50 = 0.24.[6]
The sum of all proportions must always be 1. A histogram using relative
instead of absolute frequencies will have the same shape as the one using
absolute frequencies. Only the scale on the vertical axis will change. Data
from Table 2–2 appear in the histogram shown in Figure 2–13 (relative
frequencies are not included). All the bars of this histogram touch, empha-
sizing that age varies continuously on a time scale. The total area inside

---

[6] Proportions are discussed on pages 32–33.

TABLE 2–2

Age Distribution of Mothers of Children
Below Age 15 in Hawaiiana, 1980

Age of Mother	Number of Mothers (f)	Proportion of Mothers (relative frequency)
20–24	12	0.24
25–29	7	0.14
30–34	10	0.20
35–39	15	0.30
40–44	4	0.08
45–49	2	0.04
	50	

all the rectangles of the histogram represents the total set of mothers of children below 15. The area inside each rectangle is proportional to the frequency of mothers within the corresponding interval. One defect of histograms presenting grouped data is that they show frequencies as identical for each subinterval in the grouping, whereas this may not be the case. Usually, however, the histogram gives a fair and useful idea of the distribution.

An alternative way to portray a frequency distribution is the *frequency polygon,* which pictures the same data as a histogram. The easiest way to draw a polygon (Figure 2–14) is to connect by straight lines the midpoints of the top of each rectangle of a histogram. The ends of the line

FIGURE 2–13

A Histogram Representing the Age Distribution
of Mothers of Children under Age 15 (Hawaiiana, 1980)

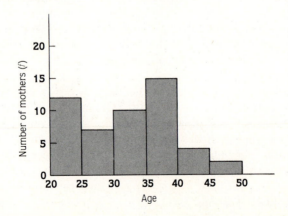

FIGURE 2–14

A Frequency Polygon Representing the Age Distribution
of Mothers with Children under 15 (Hawaiiana, 1980)

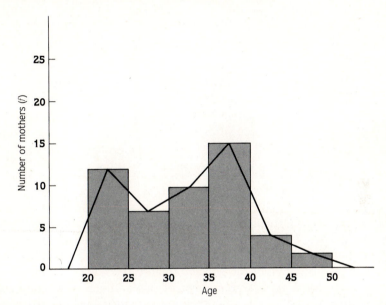

in a polygon can be left unattached to the horizontal axis, or they can be joined to it by adding classes with zero frequencies at both ends. Either a solid or a broken line can be used to complete the polygon.

A second method does not require a histogram at all. First we place dots directly above the midpoints of each category, with the height of the dot corresponding to the frequency of the class. The dots are then connected in sequence. The figure can be closed by dropping the lines to the X-axis at either end. The resulting frequency polygon emphasizes the continuity of the data and draws attention to the overall shape of the distribution.

Frequency Curves

As stated earlier, histograms suggest that the frequencies are distributed evenly throughout each particular interval, which may not be the case. Frequency polygons, on the other hand, suggest that all frequencies within a particular interval occur at the midpoint of the class interval. This also is generally not true, but errors introduced by these assumptions are usually tolerable.

FIGURE 2–15

Approximation of a Histogram with a Continuous Curve

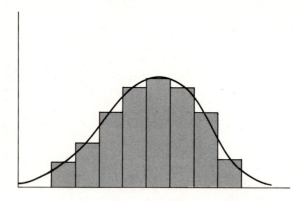

Histograms and frequency polygons are sometimes *smoothed*. The simplest method of smoothing consists of drawing freehand a smooth-curved graph that comes as close as possible to passing all the points used in plotting the histogram or the polygon (Figure 2–15). The outline resembles the curve for a very large number of observations with many class intervals of tiny widths. The smoothed curve tends to remove irregularities, providing a more generalized picture.

Characteristics of Distributions

Once a frequency distribution has been graphed, we may ask ourselves how to characterize the distribution of cases. Two forms are common.

Symmetrical Distribution.   If the histogram or polygon can be folded along a vertical line so that the two halves coincide, the distribution is symmetrical. Two possibilities are shown in Figure 2–16. Curve 1 has one prominent peak and is called *unimodal*. This particular curve is of a "normal" distribution. When some characteristic occurring at random in nature, such as intelligence or weight, is measured in a sufficiently large group, the smoothed frequency curve often looks like this. The frequencies are largest in the center and decrease with increasing distance from the center, with small frequencies occurring at both extremes. Curve 2 has two points of relatively high frequency and is called *bimodal*.

Skewed (A-symmetrical) Distribution.   Here the scores fall more toward one end of the X-axis than the other (Figure 2–17). When the distri-

FIGURE 2–16

Theoretical Curves of Distribution

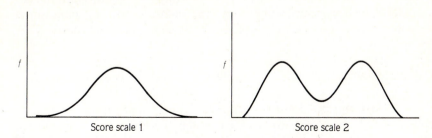

bution is *negatively skewed,* the longer tail points in the direction of the smaller scores, which means that the score values cluster at the upper end of the range. When the distribution is *positively skewed,* the long tail points in the direction of the higher values. The score values now tend to cluster at the lower end of the range.

AVERAGES

When we work with data in frequency distributions, it becomes quickly apparent that most sets of data tend to group themselves about some particular score. This phenomenon is referred to as "central tendency." The implication is that some central value is typical for the entire set and may be used to describe it.

Averages are measures of central tendency or location. They seek to elect some single score or summary value to represent a group of values. They summarize entire distributions by a single numerical value. Averages are brief, concise, economical descriptions of large amounts of date and allow quick comparison between two or more entire distributions. If in

FIGURE 2–17

Skewness

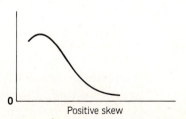

Australia the average number of children born to a woman throughout her entire childbearing span amounts to 2, whereas the figure is 7 for Iraq, we have a quick comparison of fertility levels in the two countries. Averages are widely used in demography; in a later discussion of age composition we will often refer to such concepts as the average age of a population.

Arithmetic Mean

The first and best-known average is the *arithmetic mean*. This is the layman's concept of the average. To obtain the mean of a distribution, add the values of all the cases in a distribution and then divide the total by the number of cases. The mean is commonly written as:

$$\bar{X} = \frac{\Sigma\, X}{N}$$

where $\quad \bar{X} =$ the mean (referred to as "X bar")

$\Sigma =$ "the sum of" (Σ is "sigma," the capital Greek letter, cognate of the letter S)

$\Sigma X =$ the sum of all values of all the cases

$N =$ the number of cases or observations in the set.

To return to our example of Hawaiiana, adding up all the children of the 50 mothers gives us a total of 246 children. The mean number of children per mother is 246/50 = 4.9 children.

Needless to say, no mother really had 4.9 children. Averages describe groups, not individuals. The figure represents the fertility performance of the 50 mothers as a whole. Averages are *not* indicators of individual characteristics.

In spite of advantages like clarity, the mean has its shortcomings. An important one is that a single extreme score can affect the value of the mean so much that it is no longer truly representative of the data. Suppose that six children attend a birthday party. Their ages are 6, 6, 7, 7, 8, 8. The mean age of the children is 7. However, if the 28-year-old mother of the boy whose birthday is being celebrated is also counted in, the mean age of all those attending the party becomes 10. The number 10 is not even near the age of most participants.

Median

Since distributions are often skewed in demography, another measure of central tendency is used. This measure, called the *median,* is less sensitive to a small number of extreme values. The median of a divided high-way is the strip down in the middle that divides it in half. Similarly, in data evaluation, the median is the value that divides the top half of the cases in the distribution from the bottom half, so that half the cases have higher values than the median and the other half has lower values. Assuming that the data are arranged according to size, the median is the value of the middle item. If we have an odd number of items, there is always a middle term whose value is the median. If there is an even number of values—for instance 40, 45, 50, 60, 70, 80—the median is the mean of the two middle values:

$$\frac{50+60}{2}=55.$$

In our example of Hawaiiana we also had an even number of cases—50. So we add case 25 to case 26 and divide it by 2:

$$\frac{4+4}{2}=4.$$

The formula

$$\frac{n+1}{2}$$

gives us the *position* of the median, but it is not a formula for the median itself. It indicates the number of items we have to count, until we reach the item whose value is the median. When we have an even number of cases, it indicates the two numbers that have to be averaged in order to obtain the median, namely, the two whole numbers on either side of the computed number. Suppose we have 7 values: 40, 45, 50, 60, 70, 80, 85. The formula

$$\frac{n+1}{2}$$

tells us that the median is

$$\frac{7+1}{2}=4,$$

or the fourth number in the set: 60. The median for the 50 observations in Hawaiiana is the 25.5th largest number, for which we use the mean of the twenty-fifth and twenty-sixth numbers. Thus the median is 4.

Mode

The last average, seldom used in demography, is the *mode*. This is the value that appears most often in the distribution. If in a classroom of 50 students there are more students of age 20 than of any other age, we say that age 20 is the modal age. In Hawaiiana there were 9 mothers with 4 children. The number 4 was the mode because it was the value with the greatest frequency of occurrence. An advantage of the mode is that it requires no calculation.

ABSOLUTE AND RELATIVE NUMBERS

Statements of frequency of a given trait or process in different populations are basic in demographic work. Such accounts facilitate comparisons between populations and subgroups of a given population with respect to the characteristic or process in question. The simplest form of a frequency statement is in *absolute numbers*.

Much of the demographic material published in yearbooks, census reports, and the like is presented in terms of absolute numbers. We encounter such absolute statements as this: "Two years ago 100,000 immigrants entered the country, but by last year the figure had risen to 300,000." An absolute comparison states that the difference between the two immigrant populations is 200,000 people. If we state, however, that the second wave of immigrants was three times as large as the first, we have made a relative comparison. Alternatively, we could say that the first immigrant population was one-third of the second.

Relative numbers like ratios and rates are different from absolutes in that they usually represent internal comparisons within the distribution, whereby the frequency of one category (such as males) is compared with the frequency of another category (such as females). The comparison between the two data sets takes the form of a fraction.

Relative numbers are abundantly utilized in demographic analysis. Most of the time these relative numbers represent comparisons of particular groups within a population or a comparison of a specific group with the population of which it forms a part. The relative numbers are derived from the absolute ones, which remain the most basic raw material. Relative numbers are especially useful in comparing the behavior of a population at different points of time or in making international comparisons. If, for instance, we wanted to make a comparison between mortality in Canada and mortality in the United States (the latter having a population about ten times greater), we could do so by setting side by side the total number of deaths in each nation. Yet such a comparison in absolute numbers would not make much sense. If, however, we somehow relate the number of deaths for both countries to the population that produces them, the comparison becomes more meaningful.

Ratios

Ratios are a widely used category of relative numbers. If in a classroom there are 32 males and 8 females, we say that there are four times as many males as females. The figure four is obtained by dividing the number of males by the number of females. The quantity 32/8 or 32:8 is called a ratio and is here expressed as a pair of numbers. If the division is completed, the resulting single number, 4, is still an implicit pair of numbers. Thus $32/8 = 4/1$. All single-number ratios are ratios to one. The general formula for any ratio is

$$\frac{fa}{fb}$$

where fa = frequency in one class
               fb = frequency in another class

A ratio, then, is the relation between two frequencies or quantities expressed as a quotient. As stated earlier, the purpose of a ratio is to facilitate comparison between two data sets. If we take the ratio of X to Y we can write it as X/Y, which also means so many X per unit of Y. The two quantities making up a ratio are called the *terms* of the ratio. The term that precedes the word "to" becomes the numerator, and the term that follows "to" becomes the denominator. The quantities of a ratio must be expressed in terms of the same universe. If the numerator population is restricted to a subgroup (say, males) of a given population—for example, that of the United States—the denominator (say, females) should be limited to the same population. A well-known example of a demographic ratio is the *sex ratio,* which summarizes the sex composition of a population in the shortest possible way. It is given by the quotient

$$\frac{\text{Number of males in an area in a given year}}{\text{Number of females in the same area in the same year}}$$

The calculation for the sex ratio in the United States in 1930 is as follows:

$$\frac{62,137,080 \text{ males}}{60,637,966 \text{ females}} = 1.02$$

males per female. Obviously, 1.02 is an awkward number. To avoid such figures, the quotient of the fraction form of the ratio is multiplied by a convenient number such as 100 or 1,000. Multiplied by 100, the above sex ratio becomes 102 males per 100 females. If we let k designate 100 or 1,000, and write a ratio in the form

$$\frac{X}{Y} \times k$$

we express the ratio as X per 100 or 1,000 units of Y. This minor change does not modify the significance of the ratio but merely the way it is expressed.

Rates

A *rate* is a time-based measure, computed as a ratio. With rates we express a relative incidence of events in a given period of time, usually a year. Stated differently, a rate is a measure of the relative frequency of occurrence of an event in a stated time interval. Taking births as an example, we can say that the birth rate expresses the number of births during a year per 1,000 inhabitants of a given country. Birth rates, like death rates, are usually computed per 1,000 persons (indicated by the symbol ‰). The calculation for the Crude Birth Rate in the United States in 1970 is as follows:

$$\frac{3,731,000 \text{ births}}{204,879,000 \text{ population}} \times 1,000$$

$$= 18.2 \text{ per 1,000 persons living}$$
$$= 18.2 ‰$$

Proportions

In demography, a *proportion* is a special type of ratio. It can be defined as the frequency of a given class to the total number of scores:

$$\frac{fa}{N}$$

where fa = frequency of a class
N = the sum of all frequencies in all classes

Proportions are normally used to compare the size of a particular group with that of a larger group of which it forms a part. In other words, the numerator is included in the denominator. One example would be the proportion of blacks in the American population. The computation for 1970 is as follows:

Proportion blacks (U.S. 1970)=

$$\frac{22{,}787{,}000 \text{ blacks}}{204{,}879{,}000 \text{ American population}} \times 100 = 11.1\%$$

The proportion of Caucasians in the 1970 Hawaiian population is calculated as follows:

$$\frac{301{,}429 \text{ Caucasians}}{768{,}559 \text{ Hawaiian population}} \times 100 = 39.2\%$$

By multiplying the proportion by 100, or by moving the decimal point two places to the right, proportions are changed to percentage figures.

Percent

Percent is yet another relative number. The term "percent" is derived from the Latin "per centum" and means literally "by the hundred." Rate percent can be defined as the ratio of two quantities expressed in hundredths. For example, 5% means "5 per hundred" or 5/100 or 0.05. The symbol % can be thought of as replacing the denominator 100. A percent, then, is a particular ratio in which one number is stated as the number of hundredth parts of another. Percentages allow us to make comparisons between groups even when those groups differ greatly in size.

The concept of the percent and its computation may be clarified by considering the following example. Table 2–3 gives us the population of the United States between 1940 and 1945 in absolute numbers and as percentages of the 1940 base figure. How did we express the population

TABLE 2–3

Population of the United States, 1940–45

Year	*Midyear Population (in thousands)*	*Percent Relative (1940 = 100)*
1940	132,054	100
1941	133,275	101
1942	134,675	102
1943	136,371	103
1944	138,170	105
1945	139,767	106

figures of 1941, 1942, and so on, as percents of the 1940 base figure? We divided each number in the table by 132,054 and multiplied the resulting quotient by 100. The formula is

$$P\% = \frac{\text{Value in later period}}{\text{Value in earlier (base) period}} \times 100$$

or more precisely:

$$P\% = \frac{b_1}{b_0} \times 100$$

where $P\%$ = the percent figure
b_0 = the base used for comparison
b_1 = the given data to be compared with the base

Any two numbers can be compared through use of a percent figure, whether over time or instantly. Suppose we want to compare the populations of Canada and the United States 1980.[7] Canadian population: 24,000,000 (value to be compared with base) American population: 226,000,000 (base) The Canadian population as a percent of the American population would be computed as follows:

$$\frac{b_1}{b_0} \times 100 = \frac{\text{Canadian population}}{\text{American population}} \times 100 = \frac{24,000,000}{226,000,000} \times 100 = 10.6\%$$

To express the Canadian population in terms of the population of the United States, we make the American population our base of comparison, or 100 percent. The population of Canada is 10.6% of the American population. If we make the Canadian population the base of our comparison by letting 24,000,000 correspond to 100 percent, we obtain

$$\frac{b_1}{b_0} \times 100 = \frac{\text{American population}}{\text{Canadian population}} \times 100 = \frac{226,000,000}{24,000,000} \times 100 = 942\%$$

The American population is 942% of the Canadian population.

Suppose we want to use percentages to compare change between two points of time. We want, for example, to indicate in percentage the growth of the Hawaiian population between 1970 and 1979. The formula looks like this:

$$\frac{\text{New value-old value}}{\text{Base value}} \times 100 = \frac{b_1 - b_0}{b_0} \times 100$$

[7] The figures for 1980 are estimates.

The base value is normally taken to be the same as the old value. The new value is the value in the later period, and the old value is the value in the earlier period. We obtain

$$\frac{\text{Population 1979} - \text{Population 1970}}{\text{Population 1970}} \times 100 =$$

$$\frac{914,800 - 769,913}{769,913} \times 100 = 18.8\%$$

Thus the 1979 population exceeded that of 1970 by 18.8%.

CONCEPTS FOR REVIEW

Descriptive statistics	Model
Inferential statistics	Frequency distribution
Variable	Bar graphs
Data	Skewed distribution
Ratio scale	Averages
Function	Median
Negative relationship	Ratio
Curvilinear relationship	Proportion
Time series	Percent

QUESTIONS FOR DISCUSSION

1. Nominal scales of measurement are different from ordinal scales. Contrast the two.
2. Compare discrete with continuous variables.
3. Why is the distinction between the independent and the dependent variable vitally important?
4. Give an example of a time series other than one in the text.
5. Why are models used in the social sciences?
6. What are averages? Why is it that in demography we use the median rather than the mean to summarize large amounts of data?
7. Compare a ratio with a rate. How important is the distinction between the two?

BIBLIOGRAPHY

Barcley, G. W. *Techniques of Population Analysis.* New York: Wiley, 1958.
Blalock, H. M. *Social Statistics.* 2nd ed. New York: McGraw-Hill, 1972.

Cohen, L. *Statistical Methods for Social Scientists.* Englewood Cliff, N.J.: Prentice-Hall, 1954.

Lave, C. A., and J. G. March. *An Introduction to Models in the Social Sciences.* New York: Harper & Row, 1975.

Loether, H. J., and D. G. McTavish. *Descriptive and Inferential Statistics.* Boston: Allyn & Bacon, 1976.

Meadows, D. H., et al. *The Limits of Growth.* New York: Universe Books, 1972.

Pressat, R. *Demographic Analysis.* Chicago: Aldine-Atherton, 1972.

Schmid, C. F., and S. E. Schmid. *Handbook of Graphic Presentation.* 2nd ed. New York: Wiley, 1979.

Wright, R. L. D. *Understanding Statistics.* New York: Harcourt Brace, Jovanovich, 1976.

Zeisel, H. *Say It with Figures.* 5th ed. New York: Harper & Row, 1968.

3

Sources of Information
for Demographers

POPULATION REGISTERS

Demographers need statistical information, and its collection is an essential component of the study of population. Statistical information is gathered in a number of ways. Some countries maintain continuous population registers of full information on the sex, age, marital status, religion, occupation, and location of each person in the country. Local registration offices maintain a separate card for each individual on which every change in status (marriage, migration, and so on) is recorded. The system has the advantage of furnishing complete information about the population, but it is onerous and time-consuming. Only certain small developed countries such as Finland, the Netherlands, and the Scandinavian countries maintain population registers. The system is not used in the United States and Canada.

CENSUS

The census is an extremely important piece of information for the student of population. Censuses are inventories or statistical snapshots of the entire population at a given time and include the entire process of collecting, compiling, and publishing demographic and socioeconomic data of a defined population living in a specific area at a specific time. Censuses have been carried out from the earliest civilized times. They were usually implemented for such limited objectives as military conscription and taxation. Rome instituted a district census for these purposes about 550 B.C. In 5 B.C. the emperor Augustus extended them to include the entire Roman Empire.

A typical feature of the modern census is its regularity. In many developed and developing nations the inhabitants are counted every ten years. The first modern census was taken in Sweden in 1749; this country still has the best historical statistics in the world. In the United States the first census was taken in 1790. A provision of the American Constitution specified that a decennial census was to be instituted for the purpose of apportioning both representation and taxes among the states. The 1790 census contained only a few simple questions.

The numbering of the population has many important uses in the United States. First, the census statistics determine the number of seats each state will have in the House of Representatives. Second, revenue sharing takes place on the basis of census. Numerous federal grants for highways, public health, welfare, and other assistance are tied to regional levels of per capita income and population.

The first twelve censuses were taken by temporary organizations created specifically for the purpose. However, assembling and dismantling a complete statistical organization every ten years was inefficient, and in 1902 a permanent Bureau of the Census was established. In 1913 the bureau was assigned to the Department of Commerce. Once established, the bureau possessed the skills and equipment for a complete count of the population and was also assigned additional tasks. Currently the Census Bureau, which calls itself the "Fact Finder for the Nation," publishes more statistics and covers a wider range of subjects than any other agency of the federal government. The *Statistical Abstract of the United States,* which has been published every year since 1879, is one of its best-known publications. The centennial edition of this yearbook, made available in 1980, has become the standard summary of all social, economic, and political statistics of the United States.

Census law requires the decennial count to be made on the first of April in the years terminating in "0." The collection and processing of the demographic information must be completed within eight months, after which the results are reported to the President by the Secretary of Commerce. In conducting the census, the United States has always practiced the *de jure* approach, whereby persons are enumerated at their usual place of residence. In the *de facto* approach each person is recorded wherever he or she happens to be at the time the census is taken. The latter system prevails in the United Kingdom.

Since the 1960 census the United States has made extensive use of self-enumeration. Mail-out/mail-back forms were used in 1970 to enumerate the majority of Americans. By then the census staff had become convinced that average Americans could do a better job of filling out their census schedule than a temporary enumerator could. In the case of incomplete or unreturned questionnaires, however, follow-ups were made either by telephone or by a personal visit from a local enumerator. This new method of census-taking, possible only in a highly literate population, has the advantages of speed, accuracy, and low cost.

In 1980 the Census Bureau tried to reach every one of the nation's estimated 80 million households by asking them to fill out a questionnaire. Seventy-eight percent of the households were asked to fill out a relatively short form; a more extensive form was used for the remaining 22 percent. The census forms were distributed by and returned through the post office. Some ninety percent of the population was counted this way. Census enumerators then collected the remaining ten percent of the completed forms.

Given the mobility of Americans, the goal of reaching the entire population cannot be attained. However, special procedures have been devised to find people without fixed addresses. For instance, on the evening before census day (the first day of enumeration) there was a special count of people in hotels charging more than four dollars a night. For the twentieth decennial census the Census Bureau hired more than 250 thousand enumerators, spending one billion dollars to count an anticipated 222 million Americans. Unexpectedly, there turned out to be some 226 million people.

Like all large-scale enumerations, censuses inevitably contain certain errors. Some errors result from the periodic character of the census, especially from problems of staffing. Mobilization of a large staff of enumerators for short-term employment involves problems of selection, incentive, and field supervision. Mistakes in the collection and analysis of data are unavoidable. However, with existing quality-control techniques, the results in a country like the United States are satisfactory. In 1970 an estimated 97.5 percent of the population was counted. The 2.5 percent missed is called an "undercount." A 2.5 percent undercount still means 97.5 percent completeness. In censuses in third world nations, errors are of course far greater.

SAMPLE SURVEYS

Sample surveys can be thought of as partial censuses. The same kind of information is collected. A small, skilled staff can obtain, relatively cheaply and quickly, vital information from a survey population that is only a fraction of the entire population, but is related to it in a known and regular manner. Partial enumerations are used more and more especially for data needed in intercensal intervals, but also as adjuncts to complete census enumerations. The Bureau of the Census carries out sample surveys on a weekly, monthly, or annual basis on subjects like unemployment and health.

Low-income countries sometimes cannot afford censuses because of a lack of qualified interviewers. Surveys then provide a solution because only a small staff is needed, and experienced personnel can even be borrowed from other countries. Surveys used in the social sciences commonly seek information about people's attitudes. As an example, an appropriate sample of women or couples could be asked how many children they expect to have, and when. Such surveys on fertility expectations are common in a number of countries. In 1972 the International Statistical Institute, in cooperation with the United Nations and the International Union for the Scientific Study of Population, began the World Fertility Survey. The main purpose was to carry out nationally representative and internationally comparable surveys of human fertility in a large number of nations.

VITAL STATISTICS

Vital statistics record the incidence of events at or near the time of occurrence. They pertain largely to birth, marriage, divorce, and death. The origins of civil registration were ecclesiastical. In some parts of Western Europe Church authorities have kept lists of baptisms, weddings, and burials since the eleventh century. In Western Europe vital registration is carried out on a national scale, but in the United States it is a regional responsibility. The states collect this kind of information on a separate basis, while a federal agency—the National Center for Health Statistics, a part of the Department of Health, Education and Welfare—organizes and publishes the information on a nation-wide basis.

INTERNATIONAL MIGRATION STATISTICS

A migrant is a person who moves from one political or administrative area to another. A migrant may move within the nation or cross the national boundary. Recording of United States immigrants began in 1819 under an act that required the captain or master of a vessel arriving from abroad to deliver a list of passengers to a customs officer. Since 1892 a separate Bureau of Immigration compiles immigration statistics. This office is part of the Immigration and Naturalization Service, itself a unit of the Department of Justice. The United States and Canada do not collect information on emigrants.

CONCEPTS FOR REVIEW

Population registers	Undercount
Census	Sample survey
De jure and *de facto* census taking	Vital statistics

QUESTIONS FOR DISCUSSION

1. What innovations have been introduced in recent decades to reduce the cost of census-taking?
2. Discuss some of the advantages of a sample survey as compared with a census.
3. Why is it that only a small number of nations maintain continuous population registers?

BIBLIOGRAPHY

Francese, P. K. *The 1980 Census: The Counting of America.* Washington: Population Reference Bureau, 1979.

Kammeyer, K. C. W. *An Introduction to Population.* San Francisco: Chandler, 1971.

Sauvy, A. *La Population.* Paris: Presses Universitaires de France, 1970.

Spiegelman, M. *Introduction to Demography.* Rev. ed. Cambridge, Mass.: Harvard University Press, 1968.

Thompson, W. S. and D. T. Lewis. *Population Problems.* 5th ed. New York: McGraw-Hill, 1965.

4

The Growth

of Population

A SKETCH OF WORLD POPULATION HISTORY

We have only vague ideas about world population in the distant past, when people lived in small nomadic groups devoted to the basic subsistence activities of hunting, fishing, and food-gathering. Numbers were certainly small, as the primitive hunting and food-gathering technology could sustain only very few people. It has been estimated that a million years ago the world community numbered some 125 thousand inhabitants. The population grew to about five or ten million people at the beginning of the agricultural revolution nearly ten thousand years ago, when humanity began cultivating plants and domesticating animals.

The radical change in agriculture that occurred between the Bronze Age and the Iron Age greatly improved food supplies, while making them at the same time more reliable. As a result, the population ceiling moved upward and population increased. By 3500 B.C. global population had reached about 30 million. At the time of the birth of Christ total numbers

43

had been multiplied by eight. At the death of Emperor Augustus in A.D. 14 the Roman Empire alone counted between 45 and 80 million. In 1800 the world community reached the figure of one billion. By then the rate of increase had risen to 0.5 percent per annum, where it remained until the beginning of the twentieth century.

When the food gatherers and hunters became plowmen and herdsmen, the first acceleration of population growth occurred. The scientific-industrial revolution that began in the sixteenth and seventeenth centuries raised the population ceiling again by increasing food supplies even more, and thus sparked another increase in the rate of population growth. The scientific revolution also resulted in improvements in medicine and public health practices. Longevity increased, and children who in earlier times might have died before reaching the age of procreation, now survived to become parents themselves, contributing to further population expansion.

While the first billion mark was not reached until 1800, it took only 130 years to reach the second billion figure in 1930. In 1960 world population was three billion and by early 1976, four billion. Current estimates indicate that in 1985 or 1986 the five billion figure will be reached. Tables 4–1, 4–2, and 4–3 summarize world population growth and the relevant rates of increase.

TABLE 4–1

Estimated World Population

Years Ago	Population (in millions)	Cultural Stage
1,000,000	.125	Lower Paleolithic
300,000	1.00	Middle Paleolithic
25,000	3.34	Upper Paleolithic
10,000	5.32	Mesolithic (Bronze Age)
6,000	86.5	Neolithic (Iron Age)

Year	Population (in millions)	Cultural Stage
A.D. 1	250	Early Farming & Handicraft
1650	545	Early Industrial & Scientific Revolution
1750	728	Industrial & Commercial Stage
1800	906	Second Industrial Revolution
1850	1,171	Contemporary Period
1900	1,608	Idem

Source: E. S. Deevey, "The Human Population," *Scientific American,* 203 (September 1960) 196.

TABLE 4–2

Estimates of World Population by Region, 1900–2000

Area	Population (in millions)			
	1900	1950	1975	2000 (medium projection)
World Total	1,608	2,501	3,968	6,254
More developed regions	n.f.	875	1,132	1,360
Less developed regions	n.f.	1,644	2,836	4,894
Europe	401	392*	473	540
North America	81	166	237	296
Latin America	63	164	324	620
Soviet Union	n.f.	180	255	315
Asia	937	1,368	2,256	3,637
Africa	120	219	401	814
Oceania	6	13	21	33

Sources: A. M. Carr-Saunders, *World Population, Past Growth and Present Trends* (Oxford: Clarendon Press, 1936), p. 42. United Nations, Department of Economic and Social Affairs, *Concise Report on the World Population Situation in 1977* (ST/ESA/ser. A/63) (New York, 1979), p. 8.

* Until 1950 the figures for Europe include the population of the European part of the Soviet Union. Thereafter, European figures exclude the Soviet population.

TABLE 4–3

Annual Population Increase in the World

Year	Percentage of Average Rate of Increase
0–1499	0.02–0.04
1500–1779	0.2
1800–1849	0.5
1850–1899	0.5
1900–1949	0.8
1950–1964	1.8
1965–1970	1.9
1970–1975	1.9
1975–2000	1.8 (medium projection)

Sources: K. Davis, "The World Demographic Transition," *Annals of Political and Social Science,* 273 (January 1945) 3. United Nations, Department of Economic and Social Affairs, *Concise Report on the World Population Situation in 1977* (ST/ESA/ser. A/63) (New York, 1979), p. 9. United Nations, Department of International Economic and Social Affairs, *Demographic Yearbook, 1977* (St/ESA/STAT/ser. R/6) (New York, 1978), p. 137.

As Table 4–3 shows, the present rate of increase for the world as a whole is close to an estimated 1.8 percent, which implies a doubling time of about 39 years.[1] The demographic rate of increase for the less developed regions, taken together, will be at an estimated 2.2 percent for the 1975–2000 period. The more developed countries will probably grow at a rate of 0.7 percent. As we will see later, the relationship between the level of socioeconomic development and fertility is usually inverse.

THE PRESENT AND FUTURE GROWTH OF WORLD POPULATION

The figures shown above demonstrate that the growth rate has increased while being applied to an ever-expanding base. As a result, the annual increment in the world population has risen constantly. In the early 1970s about 124 million births were recorded each year, while the number of deaths stood at some 51 million. The resulting net increment of approximately 73 million people amounted to about one-third of the entire American population of the same period. In the late 1970s the number of people added each year still stood at about 73 million.

Long-term projections of population trends are difficult to make and are subject to error. We can be certain, however, that the world population will continue to grow for a long time to come. Fertility, however measured, is high in most Asian, Latin American, and African countries. A substantial decline in the number of births per family would imply the deliberate regulation of marital fertility, a custom not as yet prevailing in most developing nations. A quick change in the age-old high fertility pattern is not to be expected. Another reason large increments in the world population are in the offing is that in many populations the younger members outnumber their parents by a large margin. The current generation of parents will therefore be replaced by an even larger one in the near future. Even if the fertility of the next generation of parents fell below present levels, the actual number of births could still be greater. Moreover, further declines in mortality could offset potential decreases in fertility.

One reason for the sharp upturn in world population has been mentioned: the lifting of the population ceiling as a result of increased and improved food supplies. Ever since the early days of pastoral activity and crude agriculture a constant series of inventions, such as the plow and the yoke, has permitted a more intensive use of the land, which could then sustain larger numbers. Under primitive conditions both fertility and mortality are high. When a major check on population growth—in this case,

---

[1] The formula for finding the doubling time is $n = 70/r\%$ where n = doubling time and $r\%$ = the rate of increase.

inadequate subsistence—is gradually removed, death rates fall at least temporarily, and numbers increase.

Another major check on population expansion was the spectrum of diseases that ruthlessly destroyed life. In the face of catastrophic onslaughts of disease, life expectancy at birth was short—usually between twenty-five and thirty years. After the Renaissance, knowledge and experience increased more rapidly, and from the eighteenth century onward the benefits of improved medicine and sanitation became more and more available. The resulting drop in mortality encouraged further population growth, and when such achievements as control of disease-carrying insects, mass vaccinations, new drugs, water purification techniques, and modern garbage collection and disposal systems were transplanted from the Western countries to the developing African, Asian, and Latin American nations, the populations of the latter literally exploded. Hopefully, birth rates in these areas will follow death rates in declining, before catastrophic population densities are attained. For the moment, however, low "artificial" death rates continue to coexist with high "natural" birth rates.

THE GROWTH OF POPULATION IN THE UNITED STATES

The United States numbered about 4 million at the time of its foundation. Two hundred years later the population was more than fifty times as large. During the nation's first century, several factors contributed to population growth. Especially after 1815, immigrants from Europe began to enter in large numbers. American reproductive fertility was also high. As opportunities expanded and transportation improved, the volume of immigration increased. Until about 1850, most immigrants came from the British Isles and Germany. The expansion of the Western frontier, which lasted until about 1890, attracted many foreign settlers, even from neighboring Canada. The rapid settlement of the West coincided with rapid industrialization and urbanization in the East, as southern and eastern Europe now also became large suppliers of immigrants.

Although reproductive fertility in the nation was dropping, increased immigration counterbalanced the trend. After the turn of the century, cheap ocean fares increased the flood of immigrants, and the annual number of entrants regularly exceeded one million. About 40 percent of the population growth of the first ten years of the twentieth century was attributable to immigration. But the First World War and restrictive immigration legislation thereafter stemmed the flow. The epoch of uncontrolled immigration was over. The Great Depression of the 1930s further discouraged immigration. Fertility dropped to historically low levels, and the American population grew at a slight 0.7 percent per year during the period.

After the Second World War, fertility rose sharply again. By the 1960s, however, the "baby boom" had run its course, and in the 1970s birth rates sank below the levels of the 1930s. Meanwhile postwar immigration had been boosted by the entrance of war brides, European refugees, and immigrants from war-torn Europe. At the same time employment conditions in the United States remained attractive, drawing many more foreigners. The Immigration Act of 1965 abolished the quotas based on national origin established by the act of 1924. Under the new act, regional quotas were established and preference was given to persons with specific abilities. As a result of this new legislation, the absolute number of immigrants has increased, while the composition of the flow has changed to the advantage of the developing countries.

During the early years of United States history, annual growth rates were high because fertility was relatively high and mortality relatively low. Although fertility has tended to fall during most of America's history, increased immigration compensated for it at least until 1914. Gibson estimates that of the 1970 population of 203 million, about 105 million or 52 percent was attributable to the 1790 population. The remaining 98 million was attributable to the estimated net immigration of 35.5 million in the 1790–1970 period.[2]

TABLE 4–4

Population Growth (United States, 1790–1980)

Census Year	Population (in thousands)	Census Year	Population (in thousands)
1790	3,929	1890	63,056
1800	5,297	1900	76,094
1810	7,224	1910	92,407
1820	9,618	1920	106,461
1830	12,901	1930	123,188
1840	17,120	1940	132,122
1850	23,261	1950	151,684
1860	31,513	1960*	180,671
1870	39,903	1970	204,879
1880	50,262	1980	226,504

Sources: U.S. Bureau of the Census, *Historical Statistics of the U.S., Colonial Times to 1970.* Bicentennial Edition, pt. 1 (Washington, D.C.: 1975), p. 8. U.S. Bureau of the Census, *Statistical Abstract of the United States: 1977* (98th edition), (Washington: U.S. Government Printing Office, 1977), p. 5.

* Figures prior to 1954 exclude Alaska and Hawaii.

[2] C. Gibson, "The Contribution of Immigration to United States Population 1790–1970," *International Migration Review* (Summer 1975):158.

Between 1941 and 1970 the demographic growth rate of the American population has fluctuated between one and two percent. In the early 1970s it dropped below one percent, yet there was still a net increase of over one million a year. Patterns of marriage and childbearing as well as immigration policies will determine most of the population growth in the years ahead. Table 4–4 and Figure 4–1 show the evolution of the American population between 1790 and 1980.

Figure 4–2 provides information regarding the future growth of the American population. Population projections or extrapolations are estimates of values of a variable beyond the ones we actually know. Because mortality, fertility, and migration are always subject to change, many population projections have proven inaccurate, causing a widespread reluctance to take them too seriously. The following projections assume a mild decline in mortality rates and an annual net immigration of 400 thousand. With regard to future fertility levels, the assumptions are different, ranging

FIGURE 4–1

Population Increase by Decades
(United States, 1790–1980)

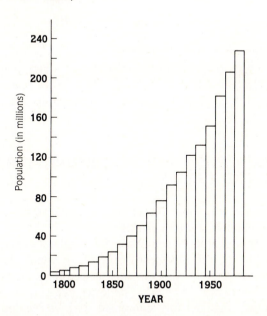

Sources: U.S. Bureau of the Census, *Historical Statistics of the U.S., Colonial Times to 1970*, Bicentennial Ed., Pt. 1 (Washington: U.S. Government Printing Office, 1975), p. 8; U.S. Bureau of the Census, *Statistical Abstract of the United States: 1977* 98th ed. (Washington: U.S. Government Printing Office, 1977), p. 5.

FIGURE 4–2

United States Population Projections to Year 2050

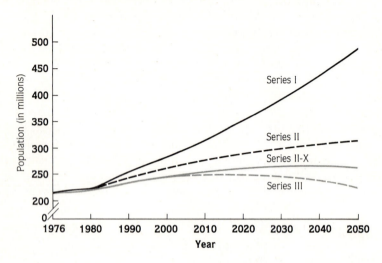

Source: U.S. Bureau of the Census, *Statistical Abstract of the United States:
1979.* 100th ed. (Washington: U.S. Government Printing Office, 1979), p. 4.

from 2.7 lifetime births per woman in Series I to a lower "replacement
level" of 2.1 births per woman in Series II, and a very low 1.7 births per
woman in Series III.[3] Series II–X differs from Series II in that it assumes
no net immigration. The base date for the projections is the year 1976.

THE GROWTH OF POPULATION OUTSIDE THE UNITED STATES,
ENGLAND, CANADA, AND TURKEY

In conclusion, we will show the growth of three more populations; the
English, the Canadian, and the Turkish.

The figures in Table 4–5 indicate that England experienced its most
rapid growth during the nineteenth century, of which the first half was
most conducive to growth. Canada experienced three peaks in its growth:
1851–61, 1901–11, and 1951–61. The latter two periods were characterized by relatively high fertility combined with strong immigration. The
Turkish population began to explode after the Second World War; for the

---

[3] By replacement level of fertility is meant that level at which the population would just
replace itself in the absence of net immigration.

TABLE 4–5

The Population of England and Wales, Canada, and Turkey

		Population (*in thousands*)		
Year	England	Canada	Year	Turkey
1801	8,893	n.d.		
1811	10,164	n.d.		
1821	12,000	n.d.		
1831	13,897	n.d.		
1841	15,914	n.d.		
1851	17,928	2,436		
1861	20,066	3,330		
1871	22,712	3,689		
1881	25,974	4,325		
1891	29,003	4,833		
1901	32,528	5,371		
1911	36,070	7,200		
1921	37,887	8,788		
1931	39,952	10,377	1930	13,648
1941	41,748	11,507	1940	17,821
1951	43,758	14,009	1950	20,947
1961	46,105	18,238	1960	27,755
1971	48,749	21,568	1970	35,605
1977	49,119	22,993 ('76)	1980 (est.)	40,348

Sources: F. Conway, *Descriptive Statistics,* (Leicester: Leicester University Press, 1963), p. 42. Reference Division, *Britain 1979, An Official Handbook* (London: His Majesty's Stationary Office, 1979), p. 7. Prime Ministry State Institute of Statistics, *Statistical Yearbook of Turkey, 1977,* (Ankara: State Institute of Statistics, 1977), p. 29. J. Overbeek, *Population and Canadian Society,* (Toronto: Butterworths, 1980), p. 12.

entire period indicated, annual rates of increase have fluctuated between two and three percent. In this respect, Turkey is a typical developing nation.

CONCEPTS FOR REVIEW

Doubling time of population   Immigration Act of 1965
Checks on population growth   Population projection
"Artificial" death rate   Replacement level of fertility

QUESTIONS FOR DISCUSSION

1. Delineate important factors in raising the population ceiling.
2. Suppose that fertility dropped sharply in less developed nations. Would population growth be brought to a halt automatically?
3. Briefly discuss population growth in the United States from the time of its foundation.
4. Why is it that population projects are not always taken seriously?

BIBLIOGRAPHY

Commission on Population Growth and the American Future. *Population and the American Future.* Washington: Government Printing Office, 1972.

Gibson, C. "The Contribution of Immigration to United States Population 1790–1970." *International Migration Review* 9 (Summer 1975).

Glick, P. C., ed. *The Population of the United States of America.* CICRED Series. Paris: CICRED, 1974.

Reinhard, M. R., and A. Armengaud. *Histoire générale de la population mondiale.* Paris: Montcrestien, 1961.

Wrigley, E. A. *Population and History.* New York: McGraw-Hill, 1969.

5

The Distribution
of Population

A NOTE ON DENSITY

The density of population, or the number of inhabitants per square kilometer or square mile, is usually calculated on a national basis. This density is a ratio—the ratio of people to land—and is sometimes called the "man/land ratio." In the United States the total land area amounts to 9.4 million square kilometers or 3.6 million square miles. The 1977 population was estimated at 216,820,000. For the year 1977, we obtain a density of 216,820,000/9,400,000 = 23 habitants per square kilometer. This *crude* or *gross density of population* (CDP) is a simple but somewhat misleading ratio, because countries are seldom if ever uniformly inhabited. One might say that the usefulness of this index is inversely related to the size of the country considered. The concept also has more significance for predominantly agricultural societies than for industrial and urbanized nations, since the latter are often characterized by heavy concentrations of population in some areas and almost empty spaces in others.

Because in many countries (including the United States) a certain amount of land is useless (desert or tundra, and so on) the number of people per unit area is sometimes expressed on the basis of arable land. With a cultivable 1.8 million square kilometers, the 1977 density per square kilometer of arable land in the United States is 120.

THE UNEVEN DISTRIBUTION OF WORLD POPULATION

In the previous chapter we looked at the question "how many." In this chapter we will ask "where do they live." Earth's total area amounts to approximately 516 million square kilometers, of which some 374 million are covered by oceans. If in 1970 the remaining 142 million square kilometers had been divided equally among the inhabitants of the earth, each person would have been entitled to 3.76 hectares or some 10 acres. With each doubling of the world population this per capita amount of available land is cut in half. Furthermore, the quality of the existing land mass varies greatly. About 60 percent is ill-suited for human settlement and consists of desert regions (17 percent of the world land area), ice caps and tundras (29 percent), and mountains (12 percent). The remaining 40 percent differs widely in quality.

Humankind is unevenly distributed over the globe. Some 50 percent of the earth's population lives on 5 percent of the land, while two-thirds of all inhabitants live on one-seventh of it. Just as the spatial distribution of the world population is highly irregular, so is the regional allocation of people. In the early 1970s the United States had a population of some 210 million people living on a territory of 9.6 million square kilometers, which gives us an average density of about 22 persons per square kilometer. This figure had risen to 24 by 1980. The American population is heavily concentrated in the northeastern and the north central states. The same phenomenon can be observed in other countries. The Canadian population, is heavily concentrated in southern Quebec, southern Ontario, and southern British Columbia, and generally lives close to the American border, leaving the larger spaces of the North virtually uninhabited. In Australia the population is heavily concentrated on the eastern and western coasts, leaving the interior nearly empty.

Causes of Uneven Distribution

Material factors are the foremost reasons for the irregular distribution of the world's population. Physical features like accessibility, climate, availability of water, raw materials, and cultivable soil encourage settlement. Coastal zones attract people, while high altitudes and remoteness repel them. About 75 percent of the world's population lives within 1,000 kilometers (635 miles) of the sea. Coastal areas and islands enjoy easy access to markets and resource areas, while landlocked regions face high transport costs because of their relative inaccessibility. New York, Amsterdam, and Hong Kong easily come to mind as areas extremely conducive to settlement. High altitudes tend to have a low density of population, reflecting the increased material and psychological costs of living in such areas. Exceptions to the rule exist where important minerals are found.

The world's plains and river valleys are among the most favored sites for human settlement. The fertile plains of North America and Europe support dense populations, while the Ganges valley is one of the most congested regions in the world. In river valleys like the Ganges, the Mekong, and the Nile, the abundance of water for farming purposes explains the high density of settlement.

The relationship between climate and settlement is equally obvious. The vast majority of the earth's empty land consists of dry desert areas and hot wetlands. The impact of climate on human settlement is both direct and indirect. In spite of technical progress and human ingenuity, excessively high or low temperatures tend to discourage settlement. Extreme temperatures, short seasons, and the absence of water make agricultural activities and the raising of livestock difficult, which greatly increases the costs of living in those areas. In North America, Europe, and Asia the area above the latitude 60 degrees north is sparsely settled. Only if protected by a costly apparatus of housing, heating, and clothing can people survive there.

A lack of water—the main characteristic of desert areas—also inhibits settlement. Africa's vast Sahara is virtually uninhabited; settlements, in so far as they exist, are near oases. The region's intense heat and lack of water make it one of the earth's most rigorous natural environments. In Iran, too, the deserts of the east are virtually unoccupied. The dryness of the climate is a major factor in Iranian life, and people live near the major water supplies. Densely settled areas are mainly found in the northern and northwestern part of the country. In the Caspian Sea area of the north, humidity is high, and the Zagros Mountains water the western part of the country. Closer to home, in the mountain states of this country—Montana, Idaho, Wyoming, Colorado, New Mexico, Arizona, Utah, and Nevada—the annual rainfall is typically less than 20 inches. Settlement usually clings to oases, and agriculture is possible only with irrigation. This part of the nation has always been and is still sparsely populated, in spite of a considerable influx of people from other areas.

An area's resource base may in certain cases attract population. The discovery of new reserves of raw materials—especially if they can be sold on world markets—has often led to settlement. The discovery of minerals in the western United States attracted people in earlier times, much as oil findings in Canada's Alberta do today. Similarly soil conditions, although difficult to dissociate from other factors, are another consideration; the most fertile soils are obviously the most conducive to human colonization.

Next in importance to the physical features are the economic ones. As long as food-gathering technology is primitive, relatively large territories are needed to support small populations. With the development of agricultural technology and livestock raising, food supplies increase and higher densities are possible. The development of modern economies based on industry and trade usually involve high urban concentrations, sometimes with densities of several thousand inhabitants per square mile. Manhattan is unthinkable without its vital links to the rest of the American economy. Places such as Hong Kong or Singapore are likewise tied to a complex international network of trade and industry. The development of transport on a national and international scale has intensified human concentration, because densely populated places can now acquire raw materials and food cheaply, while their industrial products can be exported at lower costs.

Historical developments like colonization and conquest have also determined the distribution of population. The northeastern region of the United States (eleven states and the District of Columbia) is still the most densely populated area of the nation. It was to this region that the first settlers came, and it was here that the majority of the earlier immigrants from Europe settled. The original French colonization of Quebec, plus the persistent high fertility of the French there, are responsible for the 6 million French Canadians living in Quebec today. In addition, political and social influences may provide clues to population distribution. Wars, invasions, poor government, social or economic backwardness, a lag in technological development—all may help explain concentrations, or absence, of people.

Presently some 63 percent of the world's population lives in four great clusters. In both North America and Europe the heaviest population concentrations are found near the Atlantic Ocean. The populations of these areas are mainly urban and industrialized, and enjoy a high standard of living. Asia has two major clusters, one in East Asia (Japan, Taiwan, China, and Korea) and another in tropical southern Asia (India, Pakistan, Ceylon). The first Asian cluster borders on the Pacific Ocean, while the second adjoins the Indian Ocean.

WORLD URBANIZATION

The phenonomenon of urbanization is closely related to the spatial distribution of people. *Urbanization* is the rise in the urban proportion of the total population; in other words, the urban population rises at a faster rate than the total population of the nation. Urbanization implies a redistribution of people resulting in heavy concentrations in certain areas, such as in and around New York, Chicago, and Los Angeles, leaving other regions virtually uninhabited.

One problem for demographers is that each nation uses a different yardstick in its definitions of urban and rural population. Some countries have set the limit at communities of 5,000 people. In the United States the urban population lives in communities of at least 2,500 persons.[1] The criterion of 2,500 was employed in the 1910 census and continues to be the basis of more recent distinctions. According to the 1970 and 1980 censuses, the urban population in the United States lives in one of the following areas: (1) cities of 50,000 inhabitants or more; (2) urban fringes adjacent to a central city, if these fringes have a population density of 1,000 people or more per square mile; (3) incorporated or unincorporated communities of 2,500 or more; (4) additional densely populated territories not legally constituting a community.

Urbanization has been closely related to socioeconomic development. Each substantial increase in per capita income and production seems to enhance the economies of agglomeration, often resulting in a migratory stream from rural to urban areas. In the city, firms work in close proximity, sharing the infrastructures of railroads, roadways, and power plants, drawing on a concentrated labor force, and often serving an accessible and growing market. Figure 5–1 pictures the typical evolution of a nation undergoing urbanization.

In advanced industrialized societies the rural population is well below

FIGURE 5–1

A Typical Rural to Urban Transition

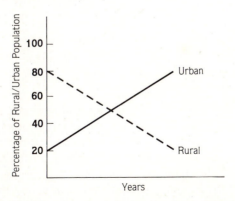

[1] According to the census definition, the American urban population includes individuals residing either in places with 2,500 or more inhabitants, or in the densely settled fringes of those places.

TABLE 5–1

Urban Population in the Major Areas of the World (1950, 1975, and 2000)

Region	*Population (in millions and percentages)*		
	1950	*1975*	*2000 (est.)*
World	719 (28.8%)	1,560 (39.3%)	3,091 (49.4%)
More Developed Countries	460 (53.6%)	790 (69.8%)	1,113 (81.8%)
Less Developed Countries	259 (15.8%)	771 (27.2%)	1,978 (40.4%)

Source: United Nations, Department of International Economic and Social Affairs, *Concise Report on The World Population Situation in 1977* (St/ESA/ser. A/63) (New York, 1979), pp. 62–63.

30 percent. As of 1976, Iran, a transitional nation, had a rural population of 53 percent, while 47 percent of its population was classified as urban. In low income countries with little industry and infrastructure, the rural population will normally exceed 70 percent. As long as agricultural production is characterized by the predominance of small family-size holdings using small amounts of tools and equipment, productivity is bound to be low. In these nations many if not most peasants produce little more than what is needed to cover their own needs. Under such circumstances a large agricultural population produces only a small surplus, barely enough to support a small nonagricultural population.

By the year 2000 about half the world's population will be living in towns and cities; as compared with 39 percent in 1975. As Table 5–1 shows, large numbers of people are involved: between 1950 and 1975 the urban population of the developing countries grew by about 500 million people, and between 1975 and 2000 the increase may exceed one billion.

URBANIZATION EXPLAINED

Urbanization is the result of a combination of circumstances. The revolution in technology brought about a mechanization of agriculture that greatly increased per capita output, producing the food surpluses needed to sustain the cities. At the same time, human energy on the farm was increasingly replaced by mechanical energy, creating pressure on the rural population to leave the land. Improvements in transportation ended the geographical isolation of the rural areas and facilitated the transfer of labor from rural communities to cities.

As incomes rise and nations become wealthier, the demand for city-produced goods and services expands faster than the demand for food items. Beyond a certain threshold, an increased proportion of the rising disposable incomes will be spent on industrial products and urban services, which results in an expansion of those sectors. The latter will then tend to draw labor from the rural areas because of the relatively high wages they can pay.

The clustering of business in urban areas often yields important *agglomeration economies:* the urban area provides the incoming company with potential cost advantages that the rural region lack. An urban-industrial environment, in other words, makes it attractive for new businesses, or for companies located elsewhere, to establish themselves in such surroundings. Among the advantages, for example, is the availability of repair and trucking services. Consulting, banking, marketing, and legal services are likewise more accessible. A pool of skilled labor is at the firm's disposal, which decreases the need for costly training. A business established in a city may be able to reduce its costs by hiring subcontractors to perform part of a production process, thus avoiding investment in specialized tools and equipment. Industries and certain types of service companies tend to cluster in the cities, up to the point where the disadvantages of congestion (increased costs of displacement and transportation and so on) outweigh the advantages of concentration.

Another economic reason for an increasing concentration of people in cities has been the revolution in energy and transport, which liberated industries from such natural sources of power as wind and water. Trains, steamships, and trucks could bring the new fuels and raw materials to the cities, while formerly distant markets were drawn nearer.

Noneconomic considerations are also significant. The level of social and cultural amenities is nearly always higher in cities than in rural areas. The numerous varieties of amenities like schools, hospitals, museums, symphony orchestras, and athletic events attract people to cities.

Especially after the Second World War, the phenomenon of *suburbanization* or metropolitan dispersion was superimposed on the urbanization process. This occurred mainly in the developed countries of the West. The outward expansion of the cities has been made possible by the same forces facilitating urbanization: the widespread availability of cheap electrical energy, improvements in motor vehicles, highway systems, communications, and the like. With electricity available and rapid, cheap, efficient transport possible, many commercial and industrial activities become less location-bound. Once the city has reached a certain density, people and industries tend to move to the suburbs, where land is cheaper, taxes lower, and the environment less congested and polluted. With the growth of the areas adjacent to the cities and towns, agglomerations keep growing without the inconveniences of greater density per square mile.

Historically, the rural-urban transition occurred in the advanced nations when more efficient production techniques were applied in agriculture, while at the same time alternative urban employment opportunities were created by the growing industrial and service sector. In the nineteenth century, medical and hygienic conditions were such that in many instances urban mortality exceeded rural mortality. This helped to balance the amount of available urban employment with the number of job seekers. During that period, millions of rural Europeans migrated directly to the cities of the New World, bypassing their own. The unskilled rural immigrants often occupied the poorer sections of the city and took the least desirable jobs, allowing the older residents to move up and out. By and large, the cities of the developed countries have been able to accommodate the influx. This assimilation of immigrants was facilitated by the fact that, at the very moment when the Western cities began to control their own mortality levels through better drainage systems, the purification of drinking water, and improved health care, the number of children per family began to fall.

AMERICAN URBANIZATION

The first era in American urban history stretches from the early seventeenth to about the middle of the nineteenth century. The cities of that period were merchant cities. Places like New York and Boston were commercially oriented centers restricted in physical area, but providing in leadership and vitality to the rapidly developing regions around them. Throughout the period, the total urban population remained small.

Between 1850 and 1910 a new era began, as the full force of the Industrial Revolution reached the United States. British innovations crossed the Atlantic, and the immigration of British craftsmen and entrepreneurs as well as a flow of financial capital helped to disseminate the new technologies. As the American cities turned to manufacturing, they began to expand physically, pulling in ever-larger numbers of migrants from the American countryside and immigrants from abroad. It was in these decades that the urban-industrial heartland of the Northeast took shape. Between 1890 and 1910 the urban proportion of the total population rose from about 11 percent to just over 45 percent. The rural-urban migration was set in motion by the mechanization of agriculture. Improved plows and the McCormick reaper made many farm laborers superfluous, while expansion in manufacturing provided those unskilled farm hands with opportunities in employment and income. The building of railroads facilitated and cheapened transportation to and from the cities. Many foreign immigrants settled on farms in the developing West, but most established themselves in the growing urban industrial centers. As the railroad network took shape, markets expanded and new towns were planted in the South and West, regional centers that processed agricultural commodities and raw materials for subsequent transfer to the East. By the beginning of the twentieth century, the old frontier and merchant cities of the East had undergone a dramatic transformation. A relatively uncomplicated community of 30,000 inhabitants in 1850, Chicago had mushroomed to over a million by 1890; by 1930 its population had grown to 3.3 million, and the city itself sprawled over more than 100 square miles. Indeed, between 1910 and 1930 the majority of Americans had become urban, and many cities had become metropolises.[2]

The third period, from 1910 to recent times, has been characterized by "metropolitan sprawl." Even before the First World War the construction of interurban railways made it possible for the wealthier to live outside the formal city boundaries. But it was the rapidly expanding production of cheap motor vehicles, as well as intensive highway construction and improvement, that really got decentralization started. This process was characterized by a large-scale migration toward the suburbs. Since highway construction was publicly financed, motor transport of people and commodities was subsidized by government funds.

Especially after the Second World War the best economic opportunities seemed to occur in the outlying fringe of the city. As the residential population of the suburbs increased, so did the retail and service establishments to serve them. The availability of cheap electricity, good roads often connected to urban thoroughfares, and the development of communication facilities encouraged manufacturers to locate at the periphery of the city. Rapid communication between suburb and city center had become a reality, freeing manufacturers from the necessity to locate near sources of supply and markets. Tertiary activities (the provision of education and other services) and administrative functions also became increasingly free to locate in the suburbs. From the late 1940s onward not only the central cities but also their larger satellites began to decentralize, thus accelerating the urban sprawl (Figure 5–2).

In the 1960s, as the metropolitan areas continued to accumulate an ever larger proportion of the nation's population, a sense of urban crisis developed. It had by then become clear that the suburbanization process had sharpened the gulf of social and economic disparity. A radical split

[2] According to the Census Bureau, a metropolitan area, briefly defined, is a Standard Metropolitan Statistical Area (SMSA) that consists of a county or a group of contiguous counties containing at least one city of 50,000 or more residents or two contiguous cities with a combined population of at least 50,000. Contiguous counties are included in an SMSA if they are economically and socially integrated with the base county. In simpler terms, a metropolis can be described as a core city and the surrounding commercial, industrial, and residential orbit that is economically and socially interdependent with it.

FIGURE 5–2

Percentage of Urban/Rural Population
(United States, 1790–1980)

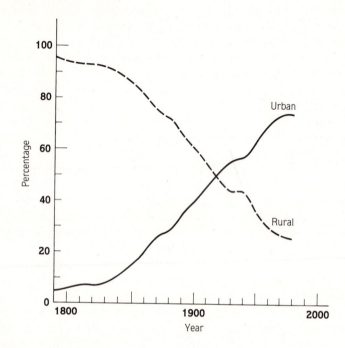

had emerged between the center of the metropolis and the periphery. It was primarily the wealthy and the middle classes who had moved out to the suburbs. Following the Second World War, only the fortunate equipped with specialized skills had been able to take full advantage of the new industries and service activities in the periphery. The unskilled and un-educated—which often meant the blacks, the Chicanos, and the Puerto Ricans—had been left behind in the inner city. The dividing line between city and suburb increasingly coincided with the division between skilled and unskilled, middle class and poor, whites and blacks. The central cities found themselves with a growing proportion of the disadvantaged and increasingly deprived of adequate tax resources.

URBANIZATION IN LESS DEVELOPED COUNTRIES

As shown in Table 5–1, rapid urbanization now occurs in low-income nations. Unfortunately, the flood of rural-urban migrants to larger towns

TABLE 5–2

Urban and Rural Population (United States, 1790–1980)

	Year	Urban Population	Rural Population	Percentage of Total Urban	Rural
	1790	201,655	3,727,559	5.1	94.9
	1800	322,371	4,986,112	6.1	93.9
	1810	525,459	6,714,422	7.3	92.7
	1820	693,255	8,945,198	7.2	92.8
	1830	1,127,247	11,738,773	8.8	91.2
	1840	1,845,055	15,224,398	10.8	89.2
	1850	3,543,716	19,648,160	15.3	84.7
	1860	6,216,518	25,226,803	19.8	80.2
	1870	9,902,361	28,656,010	25.7	74.3
	1880	14,129,735	36,059,474	28.2	71.8
	1890	22,106,265	40,873,501	35.1	64.9
	1900	30,214,832	45,997,336	39.7	60.3
	1910	42,064,001	50,164,495	45.6	54.4
Previous	1920	54,253,282	51,768,255	51.2	48.8
urban	1930	69,160,599	54,042,025	56.1	43.9
definition ↑	1940	74,705,338	57,459,231	56.5	43.5
Current ↓	1950	96,846,817	54,478,981	64.0	36.0
urban	1960	125,268,750	54,054,425	69.9	30.1
definition	1970	149,324,930	53,886,996	73.5	26.5
	1980	164,650,000	57,850,000	74.0	26.0 (est.)

Sources: U.S. Bureau of Census, "Census of Population: 1970," Vol. 1, in *Characteristics of Population,* (Washington: U.S. Government Printing Office, 1972) p. 42. *1980 World Population Data Sheet* (Washington: Population Reference Bureau, 1980).

and cities usually exceeds economic progress and the possible provision of jobs, housing, and other amenities. When urban areas are overwhelmed by large numbers, city governments find it impossible to keep up with the expanding needs for water, sewage disposal, housing, education, transportation, health facilities, and fire and police protection. A crisis results, and scenes of great poverty and discomfort emerge.

The rural-urban migrants often trade rural poverty for urban misery. Urban unemployment and/or underemployment increases, large numbers of people live on the brink of starvation, and the inner-city slums become increasingly overcrowded. Squatters establish themselves on the fringe of the city and build dwellings, using local materials that are either free or very cheap. Shantytowns emerge, their inhabitants often deprived of water, sewage facilities, and police protection. They are exposed to the extremes of cold, excessive heat, and humidity. Often garbage is not collected, and rats, flies, and mosquitoes infest the area. The resulting misery, overcrowding, malnutrition, bad health, and delinquency make these squatter communities a health and safety hazard for the neighboring central city. The discontented masses are sometimes tempted to political unrest.

Lagos, the capital of Nigeria, is a case in point. During the 1970s its population tripled to reach 4 million, and it is likely to triple again by 2000. In terms of squalor, overcrowding, noise, stench, and danger, it is now a city looking for a plague. In some slums 900 people are pressed onto an acre of land with no sewers. The narrow drainage ditches are often clogged and become stinking pools. Garbage piles up uncollected. Unfortunately, Lagos is only one of many cities facing collapse in the developing nations. By the year 2000 many other cities, for example, Bombay and Calcutta, may have grown to 20 and 30 million inhabitants.

CONCEPTS FOR REVIEW

Crude density of population
Population clusters
Urbanization
Rural-urban transition

Agglomeration economies
Suburbanization
Metropolis

QUESTIONS FOR DISCUSSION

1. How do you explain the uneven distribution of humanity over the globe?
2. Discuss some causes of sparse settlement.
3. Why is it that, in the course of their socioeconomic development, nations such as the United States have become more urbanized?
4. Discuss briefly the three phases of American urban history.
5. Do you think that the large-scale movement toward the suburbs was desirable? Analyze some pros and cons.
6. In developing countries rural-urban migration often overburdens the city's facilities. What are some of the consequences?

BIBLIOGRAPHY

Beaujeu-Garnier, J., *Trois Milliards d'hommes*. Paris: Librairie Hachette, 1965.
Clarke, J. I. *Population Geography*. Toronto: Pergamon Press, 1972.
Davis, K. "The Origin and Growth of Urbanization in the World." In *Population and Society*, edited by C. B. Nam. Boston: Houghton Mifflin, 1968.
Gaugh, M. E. *A Geography of Population and Settlement*. Dubuque: Bromen, 1970.

Miller, Z. L. *The Urbanization of Modern America: A Brief History.* New York: Harcourt Brace Jovanovich, 1973.

Schnore, L. F. "Metropolitan Growth and Decentralization." *The American Journal of Sociology* 63 (September 1957).

United Nations, Department of Economic and Social Affairs. *Urbanization in the Second United Nations Development Decade* (St/ECA/132) New York, 1970.

Zelinsky, W. *A Prologue to Population Geography.* Englewood, N.J.: Prentice-Hall, 1966.

6

Mortality

BASIC MEASURES OF MORTALITY

Contemporary demographers tend to discuss mortality before analyzing the two other basic demographic processes: fertility and migration. One reason is that mortality requires little explanation. One may quarrel over definitions of migration or fertility, but with mortality there is no problem: it is simply the termination of life. Questions of motivation need not be considered. There are many studies and arguments as to why people migrate or have babies, but regarding mortality there is no motivation except in the case of suicide.

A large number of rules are used to measure and analyze mortality. First, one can measure the *absolute number of deaths* in a country during a given period, usually a year. The total number of deaths in the United States in 1975 amounted to 1,893,000. Such a figure, as we explained in chapter two, has little significance because it does not take the exposed population into account. Since the use of absolute figures does not permit comparisons between different periods of history or analogies between nations, we employ relative figures.

The Crude Death Rate

The *crude death rate* (CDR) is the most frequently used measure of mortality. It records the total number of deaths per thousand persons in any given population. As a formula for computing the CDR we have

$$\frac{\text{Number of deaths per year}}{\text{Population}} \times 1{,}000 \text{ or } \frac{D \cdot k}{P}$$

where D = number of deaths in the year
   P = midyear population
   k = an arbitrary factor of 1,000

The population in the denominator represents the size of the exposed population at midyear (June 30 or July 1). In 1975, the CDR in the United States was 8.9‰. It was computed as follows:

$$\frac{1{,}893{,}000}{213{,}600{,}000} \times 1000 = 8.9‰$$

The CDR has the advantage of showing the level of mortality of the entire population. Its calculation is quick and easy, and its meaning is readily understood. But it also has important limitations. The CDR expresses the frequency of death in a given population without regard for such important characteristics as age and sex. Other things being equal, a population like that of England and Wales, which contains a larer proportion of older people, will have a higher death rate than a "younger" population such as that of the United States. The CDR, in other words, is heavily affected by a population's age composition. The death rate in the United States and Canada is still influenced by the relative youth of their populations. But because of the lengthening of life and the decline in the birth rate that started in the 1960s, the American population is now aging, and the number of deaths in the numerator will eventually rise.[1]

Table 6–1 shows the historical downward trend in mortality in the United States, Canada, the Netherlands, and England and Wales as measured by the CDR. The downward trend in the CDR is visible in all four populations. The rates for England and Wales are relatively high because

---

[1] Chapter 11 will explain in detail how populations grow older or younger.

TABLE 6–1

Crude Death Rates (United States,
Canada, Netherlands, England and Wales, 1900–1977)

Year	United States	Rate (per thousand population) Canada	Netherlands	England & Wales
1900	17.2	16.2	17.9	18.2
1910	14.7	13.1	13.6	13.0
1920	13.0	13.3	12.3	12.4
1930	11.3	10.7	9.1	11.4
1940	10.8	9.8	9.9	14.4
1950	9.6	8.5	7.5	11.6
1960	9.5	8.0	7.6	11.5
1970	9.5	7.3	8.4	11.7
1975	8.9	7.3	8.3	11.8
1976	8.9	7.3	8.3	12.2
1977	8.8	7.3	7.9	11.7

Sources: O. J. Firestone, *Canada's Economic Development 1867–1953* (London: Bowes & Bowes, 1958), p. 44. U.S. Bureau of the Census, *Historical Statistics of the United States, Colonial Times to 1970,* Bicentennial Edition, Part 1 (Washington: U.S. Government Printing Office, 1975), p. 58. U.S. Bureau of the Census, *Statistical Abstract of the United States, 1980* (Washington: U.S. Government Printing Office, 1980), p. 74. Ministry of Industry, Trade and Commerce, *Canada Yearbook 1978–1979* (Ottawa: Information Division, Statistics Canada, 1979), p. 167.

of the comparatively large proportion of older, high-mortality-risk people in their population.

The Age-Specific Death Rate

Because of the limitations inherent in the CDR, demographers have developed category-specific death rates that remove the effect of population composition. The best-known rate in this class is the *age-specific death rate* (ASDR), which expresses the number of deaths at age i or age interval i in a given year to the total population of age i.[2] The ASDR, which provides death rates computed separately by age group, gives us a reliable picture of mortality as dissociated from the age structure of the population. For reasons of precision and comparison, the age-specific death rates are often computed separately by sex. The general formula is

[2] As Barclay explains: "Small letters designate a portion of the total instead of the total and the letter i designates the i th category" in the population (that is, any category we may specify). See G. W. Barclay, *Techniques of Population Analysis* (New York: Wiley, 1958), p. 22.

$$\frac{\text{Number of deaths of persons of age } i}{\text{Midyear population of people aged } i} \times 1,000$$

or

$$\frac{D_i}{P_i} \times 1,000$$

where D_i = number of deaths of age group i
              P_i = midyear population of that age group
              k = 1,000

To cite an American example, we can compute the average age-specific death rate in 1970 for the age group 20–24. Applying our formula, we obtain

$$\frac{24,232}{16,371,021} \times 1,000 = 1.48\%o = 1.5\%o$$

This figure fell to 1.34‰ in 1977. Age-specific mortality rates in the United States tend to be lower for whites than for nonwhites. In 1977 the figure (both sexes combined) in age group 20–24 was 1.25‰ for whites and 1.84‰ for nonwhites. The rates also tend to be lower for females than for males. We notice that in 1977 the ASDR for age group 20–24 had fallen to 1.34‰ for all races and both sexes. For all males the figure stood at 2.02‰; for all females, at 0.65‰.

For all nations, the ASDR's roughly conform to a U-shaped distribution. This similarity of curves results from the fact that the earliest period in life is one of high susceptibility to lethal diseases, while physical deterioration is an effect of old age. The curve hits its lowest point between age 10 and 14, after which it begins to rise. The upturn becomes steep especially after age 50 (see Figure 6–1).

Distributions of age-specific rates are a kind of frequency distribution, yet differ in some respects. With simple frequency distributions the Y-axis merely records the number of cases. With distributions of age-specific rates, relative numbers are plotted on the Y-axis.

As seen from the curves in Figure 6–2, the rates are lower for women. In most modern industrial nations women tend to have lower death rates than men at all ages. This is also true for the earliest period in life. In the United States, moreover, the rates are also lower for whites than for nonwhites, except for ages 75 and above. For less developed countries the curves lie typically above those of the more developed countries, which is due to better health conditions in the high-income industrialized nations. In countries like the United States and England the curves have continually

FIGURE 6–1

Age-Specific Death Rates by Sex and Race
(United States, 1976)

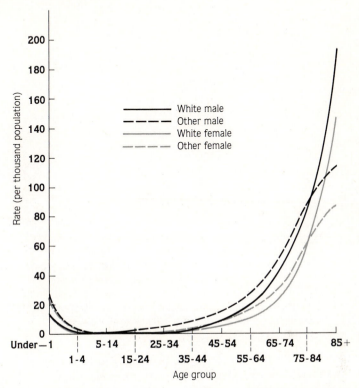

Source: A. Haupt, T. T. Kane, *Population Handbook* (Washington: Population Reference Bureau Inc., 1978), p. 29.

declined over time, this again began due to better health conditions and hygienic improvements (Figure 6–3, p. 73).

Age-specific death rates can be computed for one-year intervals. In practice, however, five- and even ten-year periods are more commonly used. For most purposes such intervals provide sufficient information to get a correct picture of the mortality of the various age groups (Table 6–2, p. 74).

Comparisons between crude death rates that show the actual mortality per 1,000 of population are problematic, in that CDR's do not always provide a true test of mortality conditions. As we observed earlier, crude death rates are affected by the age composition of the population in various communities. Obviously, an "old" high-mortality-risk population will have a higher death rate than a population containing a high proportion

FIGURE 6–2

Age-Specific Death Rates (Canada, 1970)

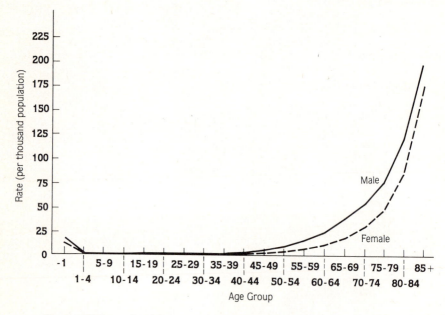

Source: Ministry of Industry, Trade and Commerce, *Canada Yearbook, 1972* (Ottawa: Information Division, Statistics Canada, 1972), p. 259.

of young people. As stated before, the problem can be solved by comparing the age-specific death rates of two or more populations. This implies, however, that relatively large amounts of figures must be set side by side. This process necessitates as many separate comparisons as there are age groups.

Standardization of Death Rates

For obvious reasons, it is desirable to express genuine mortality differences by one single figure. This would imply that the impact of differences in the age compositions of the populations compared had been eliminated. Comparison is one of the main purposes of statistics, but one can only compare like with like. *Standardization* or adjustment is a process that allows us to contrast the death rates of two or more communities, while holding constant the effect of age composition. In other words, the method allows us to compare the mortality of several communities, each

FIGURE 6–3

Age- and Sex-Specific Death Rates
(England and Wales, 1851 and 1951)

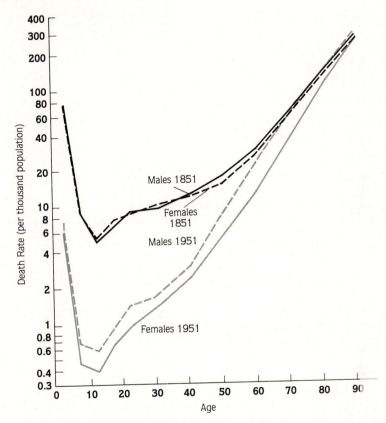

Source: I. Taylor, J. Knowelden, *Principles of Epidemiology* 2nd ed. (Boston: Little, Brown, 1964), p. 22. The chart shown above is an example of a semi-logarithmic or ratio chart, widely used in portraying proportional and percent-age relationships. The vertical axis is ruled logarithmically and the horizontal axis arithmetically. In the arithmetical line chart equal spaces represent equal amounts of change; in the semilog chart, equal spaces represent equal amounts of relative change.

of which retains its own set of age-specific death rates while identical age compositions are simulated.

The method works as follows. (We will discuss only the "direct" standardization technique here.) First, we select a known standard age distribution as our standard population. The choice is arbitrary, but the more

TABLE 6–2

Deaths by Age and Sex (United States, 1977), Five-year Intervals

Male Age Group	Rate (per thousand)	Female Age Group	Rate (per thousand)
Under 1 year	16.59	Under 1 year	13.04
1–4	0.77	1–4	0.61
5–9	0.41	5–9	0.27
10–14	0.44	10–14	0.26
15–19	1.46	15–19	0.56
20–24	2.02	20–24	0.65
25–29	1.94	25–29	0.71
30–34	1.93	30–34	0.90
35–39	2.60	35–39	1.35
40–44	3.93	40–44	2.21
45–49	6.26	45–49	3.46
50–54	9.99	50–54	5.29
55–59	15.24	55–59	7.85
60–64	24.31	60–64	12.17
65–69	34.74	65–69	16.91
70–74	53.20	70–74	27.67
75–79	81.51	75–79	47.40
80–84	113.64	80–84	73.94
85+	172.99	85+	135.42

Source: U.S. Bureau of the Census, *Statistical Abstract of the United States, 1979,* 100th edition (Washington: U.S. Government Printing Office, 1979), p. 73.

realistic the standard population, the more interesting the results. The standard population can be any population or even the sum of two populations. For a long time it was customary to use the 1901 population of England and Wales. Second, we apply to the appropriate age groups in the standard population the age-specific death rates of the population under observation. In other words, each of the age specific death rates in the actual population is multiplied by the number of people in the standard population who are in the corresponding age bracket. For every age group we thus obtain an "imaginary" number of deaths. These are the deaths that would have occurred if the actual population had the age distribution of the standard population. Third, we sum up the "expected" or "imaginary" deaths. Then we divide that total by the number of people in the standard population and multiply the quotient by 1000. The result is the standardized death rate, expressed as a rate per 1000 people.

An example will clarify this procedure. Suppose we want to calculate the age-standardized death rates for Kuwait and Austria for the year 1976, using the Canadian population of 1971 as our standard population or base

TABLE 6–3

Direct-Method Calculation of Age-Adjusted
Death Rates (Austria and Kuwait, 1976)

1	2	3	4	5	6
		Age Specific Death Rate		*Expected Deaths in Standard Population*	
Age Group	*Standard Population Canada, 1971*	*Austria, 1976*	*Kuwait, 1976*	*On Basis of Austria's Rates*	*On Basis of Kuwait's Rates*
	(in thousands)	*(per thousand)*		*(column 2 × 3)*	*(column 2 × 4)*
0–4	1,816	4.1	9.34	7,446	16,961
5–9	2,254	0.3	0.8	676	1,803
10–14	2,310	0.3	0.4	693	924
15–19	2,114	1.0	0.7	2,114	1,480
20–24	1,889	1.2	1.0	2,267	1,889
25–29	1,584	1.1	1.4	1,742	2,218
30–34	1,305	1.5	1.6	1,958	2,088
35–39	1,264	1.7	2.4	2,149	3,034
40–44	1,263	3.2	2.7	4,042	3,410
45–49	1,239	4.6	4.4	5,699	5,452
50–54	1,053	6.9	9.4	7,266	9,898
55–59	955	10.2	11.3	9,741	10,792
60–64	777	16.2	19.0	12,587	14,763
65–59	620	27.6	28.7	17,112	17,794
70–74	457	46.8	46.5	21,388	21,251
75–79	326	77.9	72.0	25,395	23,472
80–84	204	127.3	180.9	25,969	36,904
85+	137	231.7	307.1	31,742	42,073
Total	21,568	12.7(CDR) *(all ages)*	4.4(CDR) *(all ages)*	179,985	216,206

Note: The crude death rates are 12.7‰ for Austria and 4.4‰ for Kuwait. From these figures it would appear that Austria is the more unhealthy place. The more standardized death rates are given by

$$\frac{\Sigma \ (\text{column 5})}{\Sigma \ (\text{column 2})} \times k = \frac{179,985}{21,568,000} \times 1000 = 8.34‰ \ (\text{Austria})$$

and by

$$\frac{\Sigma \ (\text{column 6})}{\Sigma \ (\text{column 2})} \times k = \frac{216,206}{21,568,000} \times 1000 = 10.02‰ \ (\text{Kuwait})$$

It now appears that Austria is the healthier. The difference in the CDR was due to the youthfulness of the population of Kuwait.

(Table 6–3). This procedure allows us to compare mortality conditions of Kuwait and Austria, while the age-structure effect is removed.

In the 1930s and 1940s several countries (Canada was one) commonly published figures on standardized death rates. The standard population selected was the "standard million" based on the age and sex

TABLE 6–4

Age and Sex Distribution of the "Standard Million"

Age Group	Both Sexes	Males	Females
All ages	1,000,000	483,543	516,457
Under 5 years	114,262	57,039	57,223
5–9 years	107,209	53,462	53,747
10–14 years	102,735	51,370	51,365
15–19 years	99,796	49,420	50,376
20–24 years	95,946	45,273	50,673
25–34 years	161,579	76,425	85,154
35–44 years	122,849	59,394	63,455
45–54 years	89,222	42,924	46,298
55–64 years	59,741	27,913	31,828
65–74 years	33,080	14,691	18,389
75 years and over	13,581	5,632	7,949

distribution per million of the population of England and Wales in 1901 (Table 6–4). This standard million, which had the same age distribution as the population of England and Wales of 1901, had been set up for methodological reasons. The structure of that standard million, which comprised a large proportion of young adults, was so different from the age composition of Asian, African, and Latin American populations, which contain a very high proportion of children, that it was abandoned after the Second World War.

As Table 6–4 shows, the English 1901 population and the standard population that reflected it comprised relatively few infants and young children and only a relatively small proportion of aged people; consequently, it constituted a standard inclined to low mortality. This particular age composition of England and Wales was due to the decline in fertility that set in after the 1870s. Before that period fertility had been higher, but the children born in the high-fertility period had already become adults by 1901.

Infant Mortality

The data shown in Table 6–2 and Figures 6–1, 6–2, and 6–3 show the prevalence of a specific pattern of mortality during the first four years of life. The younger the child, the more pronounced the high mortality of that period becomes. Mortality during infancy, the first year of age, is the highest. Mortality during this period is particularly interesting to analyze, first, because it has an important impact on other indices of mortality such as the CDR, and second, because infant mortality is a sensitive index of the socioeconomic development of a nation—its health conditions, the availability of medical care, its food intake, and so forth.

The *infant mortality rate (IMR)* denotes the incidence of death within the first year of age. It is calculated by dividing the number of deaths before the first birthday by the number of births in the year.

$$\frac{\text{Number of deaths below Age 1 per year}}{\text{Number of live births in the same year}} \times 1,000 \text{ or } \frac{Do}{B} \cdot k$$

where Do = number of deaths below age 1 in a given year in a given country

B = number of live births occurring during the same year in the same nation

$k = 1,000$

In 1975, for example, the number of live births in the United States amounted to 3,144,198. The number of deaths of children below age one was 50,525. We find an infant mortality rate of

$$\frac{50,525}{3,144,198} \times 1,000 = 16.1\%_0$$

One can, of course, compute separate rates for male and female infants and for separate ethnic groups.

To get a precise view of infant mortality, it is relevant to distinguish between exogenous and endogenous causes. *Exogenous* causes of death could have been prevented by proper medical treatment or public health measures, whereas *endogenous* causes are related to congenital defects, prematurity, weakness of the fetus, difficult labor and the like. A large proportion of all infants who die during the first year die during the first weeks of life. Such deaths are often the result of antenatal factors that determine whether or not the child has a good chance of establishing an independent existence. Once the first weeks are over, the infant is subject to external factors in the environment to which it is more susceptible than older persons. Hence a distinction is commonly made between *neonatal mortality,* the mortality of live-born children during the first month of life and *post-neonatal mortality,* mortality during the remaining eleven months of the first year. Most neonatal deaths are caused by endogenous causes, while postneonatal deaths are usually associated with infectous and parasitic diseases and other exogenous elements in the baby's environment. In the developed nations mortality has fallen most in the postneonatal category.

Because of their weakness, the ability of new-born babies to survive depends greatly on hygienic conditions and medical care. This explains why in the 1970s infant mortality ranged from between 10 and 30 per 1,000 in the more developed countries to well over 100 in some less developed countries. About 25 years ago infant mortality rates ranged commonly above 200 or 250 per thousand in nearly all third world nations. In 1975, Chad in Africa still scored a high infant mortality rate of 160%o.

Before the eighteenth century, infant mortality was high in Western nations, easily reaching levels of 300 to 400 per 1,000, although 200%o was perhaps a more common rate. In eighteenth-century French Canada, infant mortality has been estimated at 245%o. In the West the secular downward trend in infant mortality started after the 1850s. In France, for example, the IMR amounted to around 200 to 250%o in 1750. In 1850 it stood at about 170%o, whereas by 1950 the figure had been reduced to about one third, or 53%o. By around 1960 the rate had again been cut in half (27.4%o), and by 1973 it had dropped to a low 12.9%o. In Sweden, infant mortality stood at 209 per thousand in 1770, but declined to 132%o by 1870. In 1970 it had fallen to a low of 11%o. To take an American example, the IMR for the white population of Massachusetts stood at 131.1%o for the period 1851–1854, but had been reduced to 11.6%o in 1977.

Under exceptional circumstances the IMR can rise again, as it did in Russia during the Second World War. During the siege of Leningrad in 1942, infant mortality rose to 748%o. Table 6–5 shows the dramatic decline in infant mortality in the United States since 1920. The American

TABLE 6–5

Infant Mortality Rates
(United States, Canada, and the Netherlands, 1920-1977)

Year	IMR, United States White	Nonwhite	IMR, Canada	IMR, Netherlands
1920–21	82.1	131.7	102.0	82.5
1930	60.1	99.9	91.0	51.3
1940	43.2	73.8	58.0	39.4
1950	26.8	44.5	42.0	26.7
1960	22.9	43.2	27.0	17.9
1970	17.8	30.9	18.8	12.7
1975	14.2	24.2	14.3	10.7
1977	12.3	21.7	12.4	9.5

Sources: U.S. Bureau of the Census, *Historical Statistics* (Washington: U.S. Government Printing Office, 1975), p. 57. Buckley Urquhart, *Historical Statistics of Canada* (Toronto: Macmillan, 1965), p. 40. Ministry of Industry, Trade and Commerce, *Canada Yearbook, 1975* (Ottawa: Information Division, Statistics Canada, 1975), p. 182. Centraal Bureau voor de Statistiek, *75 Jaar Statistiek van Nederland* (S'Gravenhage: Staatsuitgeverij, 1975), p. 30.

figures are compared with those of the Netherlands and Canada. Low as the 1977 figure for the United States is, more progress is still possible, as demonstrated by the data for the Netherlands. It should also be noted that the gap between white and nonwhite infant mortality seems to be rapidly narrowing.

The Life Table

Rates do not answer all questions regarding mortality. For example, they cannot answer "What is the average remaining lifetime for persons who have attained a given age?" or "How long can a baby born in the United States in 1975 expect to live?" The answers these questions are given by *life tables* or, as the French call them, mortality tables. The life table technique helps solve problems involving the number of survivors out of an original group. It is indispensable in such investigations as estimates of widowhood or the chances of remarriage.

The life table is not, strictly speaking, a standardization procedure but rather a method of summarizing mortality. Life tables express in compact form the age-sex specific mortality trends of a given period and place. If we were able to observe a cohort (everyone born in the same country during the same year) until all members had died, we could give a detailed mortality account of this group and construct a "longitudinal" or "generation" life table. Since this type of life table can be constructed only after the death of all the members of the cohort, the usefulness of such an endeavor is limited. A second type of life table, which does have practical significance, is called a "cross-sectional," "period," or "time-specific" life table. It traces the mortality experience of a theoretical population from birth to death and is widely used by demographers and planners as well as insurance companies.

Time-specific life tables are produced by starting in a given year with a hypothetical cohort of 100,000 at age zero (just born), called the "radix" of the life table. The age-specific death rates prevailing during that calendar year are applied to the radix. The life table then proceeds to determine how many members of the life table cohort will die in each interval and how many remain at the end of each year. The process continues until all members of the radix have died. In other words, the life table takes a set of age-specific death rates and applies them to the entire lifetime of a hypothetical cohort. A full life table proceeds by single years while an abridged life table may, for example, use five-year age classes. For most purposes abridged life tables are adequate. These tables are usually constructed separately for males and females, because of the difference in the death rates of the two sexes. In the United States different life tables are also drawn up for whites and blacks, for the same reason.

Life tables make it possible to calculate the *expectation of life,* which is the average future duration of life for a person of a specific age, if subject to the death rates of the table. *Life expectancy at birth,* for example, is the expected average number of years to be lived by a newborn child. These tables also facilitate the annual computation of the total number of person–years to be lived by the entire cohort before the last one dies. Dividing this figure by the number of survivors yields the average number of years to be lived by each after exact age x. The symbol x refers to birthday age in years. At birth a person has lived exactly 0 years; at exact age 5, exactly 5 years, and so on.

Normally, abridged life tables have seven columns, as seen in Table 6–6. In the seven-column system, the first column (x to $x+n$) presents the interval between two birthdays or the period of life between two exact ages. This column is labeled "age interval." In it, the designation 1–5 means the five-year interval between the first and the fifth birthdays.

Column 2 ($_nq_x$) discloses the probability of death within one year of a person aged x, if the life table proceeds by single years. Stated differently, this column shows the proportion of those people in the cohort who, having reached age x, will not survive until age $x+n$. The q_x values are a set of mortality probabilities for the cohort as it begins a new year of life; they are calculated per 100,000.[1] For example, according to Table 6–6 the proportion dying between age 10 and age 15 is 0.0020, which means that out of every 100,000 persons living and exactly 10 years old, 20 will die before reaching exact age 15. This 20 per 100,000 is 0.2 per thousand. The rates showing the probability of dying are derived from and very close to the age-specific death rates. The procedures for computing these probabilities are complicated; it is sufficient to remember that they approximate the age-specific death rates but that as a rule they are a little lower.

Column 3 (l_x) is the survivor column; it shows the number of persons out of 100,000 who would survive to exact age x, if subject throughout their lives to the death probabilities of column $_nq_x$. Thus this column reveals the number of survivors at the beginning of each age interval. It starts with the original cohort of 100,000, from which the number of deaths during the time interval under consideration is substracted. The remainder is placed under the 100,000 figure, with the remainders for subsequent time intervals following below.

Column 4 ($_nd_x$), the "number dying during age interval," shows the number of deaths that would occur during any age interval (x to $x+n$). The column ends when the last person of the life-table cohort dies. The sum total of this column must add up to the original life-table cohort of 100,000.

Column 5 ($_nL_x$) is the years-lived column, disclosing the number of

---

[1] The q_x values are sometimes computed per 1,000; they are then called life-table mortality rates.

TABLE 6–6

Abridged Life Table, Total Population (United States, 1973)

Age Interval	Proportion Dying	Of 100,000 Born Alive		Stationary Population		Average Remaining Lifetime
1	2	3	4	5	6	7
x to $x+n$	Proportion of persons alive at beginning of age interval dying during interval	Number living at beginning of age interval	Number dying during age interval	In the age interval	In this and all subsequent age intervals	Average number of years of life remaining at beginning of age interval
	$_nq_x$	l_x	$_nd_x$	$_nL_x$	T_x	e^0_x
Total						
0–1	0.0176	100,000	1,763	98,436	7,134,067	71.3
1–5	.0032	98,237	312	392,201	7,035,631	71.6
5–10	.0021	97,925	203	489,077	6,643,430	67.8
10–15	.0020	97,722	198	488,163	6,154,353	63.0
15–20	.0056	97,524	544	486,372	5,666,190	58.1
20–25	.0073	96,980	710	483,157	5,179,818	53.4
25–30	.0072	96,270	688	479,654	4,696,661	48.8
30–35	.0083	95,582	789	476,029	4,217,007	44.1
35–40	.0117	94,793	1,109	471,376	3,740,978	39.5
40–45	.0176	93,684	1,651	464,587	3,269,602	34.9
45–50	.0278	92,033	2,559	454,233	2,805,015	30.5
50–55	.0408	89,474	3,655	438,772	2,350,782	26.3
55–60	.0638	85,819	5,472	416,170	1,912,010	22.3
60–65	.0929	80,347	7,466	383,968	1,495,840	18.6
65–70	.1314	72,881	9,577	341,370	1,111,872	15.3
70–75	.1948	63,304	12,334	286,576	770,502	12.2
75–80	.2885	50,970	14,707	218,708	483,926	9.5
80–85	.3914	36,263	14,192	145,115	265,218	7.3
85 and over	1.0000	22,071	22,071	120,103	120,103	5.4

Source: U.S. Department of Health, Education and Welfare, *Vital Statistics of the United States 1973*, Vol. II, Section 5, Life Table.

person-years lived by the remainder of the cohort between the ages of x and $x+n$. According to Table 6–6, the residual of the radix of 100,000 would live 489,077 years between ages five and ten. Of the 97,925 persons attaining age five, 97,722 also reach age 10. This category lives five years, which makes a total of 488,610. For the sake of simplicity we assume that the 203 persons who died in the interval lived an average of 2.5 years. This gives us $2.5 \times 203 = 508$. The total thus becomes $488,610 + 508$, or 489,118. That still differs by 41 from the figure in the life table—a discrepancy due to our assumption that those who died in the interval all lived 2.5 years. Column 5, "stationary population in the age interval," and column 6 refer to what is called a stationary population or life-table population. A life table assumes that each year another cohort of 100,000 babies is born and added to the life table population, and the same age-specific mortality rates are applied to them. When the first cohort has died the population is stationary, meaning that its age-composition experiences no further change. Column 6 (Tx) shows the total number of person-years still to be lived by the surviving cohort when it enters age x.

The last column (e_x^0) is the expectation-of-life column. It shows the average number of remaining years to a person entering age x. The figure is found by the fraction Tx/lx (column 6 divided by column 3). For age interval 1–5, then, we obtain the following result: $7,035,631/98,237 = 71.6$.

Life expectancy at birth, is the best recapitulation of mortality conditions in a country. It is used for international comparisons, for contrasting different historical periods, and is not affected by that nation's age composition. The higher that life expectancy, the more effectively a given nation preserves life and combats death. It should be remembered, however, that the life table is an artificial creation: it reveals what would happen to a group of persons if they were subjected to the death rates of one particular calendar year appropriate to their age, as they are followed through life. But reality is different. Persons born in the real-life population to which the life table cohort is compared normally have somewhat higher life expectancies, because during their lifetime preventive and curative medical knowledge continues to advance, and public health measures may still improve. Age-specific mortality rates can therefore be expected to decline somewhat over time.

In all Western nations the life expectancy at birth, both sexes taken together, now surpasses 70 years. For a number of nations, however, it was only about 40 toward the middle of the nineteenth century. In the United States the figure stood at 47.3 in 1900. By 1940 it had risen to 68.2; by 1970, to 70.9. At least since 1900, males live shorter lives than females, while the white population has always lived longer than the blacks. The 1977 average for both sexes was 73.8 for whites, 68.8 for blacks.

Table 6–7 and Figure 6–4 show the evolution of life expectancy at birth by sex for the United States and Canada between the 1930s and the

TABLE 6–7

Average Life Expectancy at Birth by Sex
(United States and Canada, 1930–77)

Year	United States Males	Females	Year	Canada Males	Females
1930	58.1	61.6	1931	60.0	62.1
1940	60.8	65.2	1941	63.0	66.3
1950	65.6	71.1	1951	66.3	70.8
1960	66.6	73.1	1961	68.4	74.2
1970	67.1	74.8	1971	69.3	76.4
1977	69.3	77.1	1977	n.d.	n.d.

Sources: Ministry of Industry, Trade and Commerce, *Canada Yearbook 1978–79*, (Ottawa: Information Division, Statistics Canada, 1978), p. 180. U.S. Bureau of the Census, *Statistical Abstract of the United States, 1979,* 100th edition (Washington: U.S. Government Printing Office, 1979), p. 70.

1970s. A disturbing feature is that the difference between the life expectancies for males and females seems to be growing. This holds true for the United States as well as other Western nations. One could hypothesize that if women are living more and more like men, the gap between male and female longevity should narrow. Yet statistical evidence points in the opposite direction, at least for the moment.

FIGURE 6–4

Life Expectancy at Birth by Sex
(United States, 1900–1977)

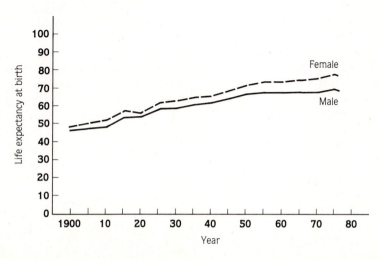

FIGURE 6–5

Age-Specific Life Expectancy (India, 1951 and 1971)

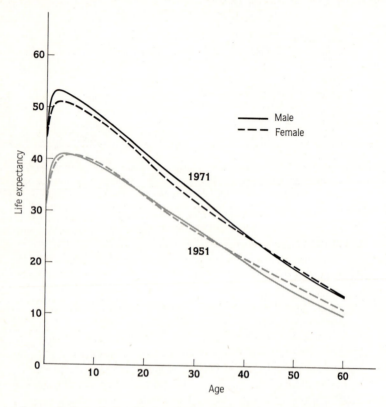

Source: R. Ram, T. W. Schultz, "Life Span, Health, Savings and Productivity," *Economic Development and Cultural Change 27,* no. 3 (April 1979) 401.

The less developed countries have experienced a dramatic increase in life span during recent decades. For 1950–55 we find a life expectancy at birth of 41.6 years for all less developed countries taken together. This number rose to 52.2 for 1975–77 and is expected to reach 62.6 by the year 2000. The case of India is indicative, as seen in Figure 6–5. Table 6–8 presents life expectancies at birth in the world, as a whole, in the more or less developed countries, and in some randomly chosen nations.

TABLE 6–8

Estimated Expectation of Life in 1970–75 for World,
Developed and Developing Regions, and Selected Countries

Area	Life Expectancy at Birth
World	55.2
More Developed Countries	71.1
Less Developed Countries	52.2
Algeria	53.0
Bangladesh	46.0
Brazil	54.0
Denmark	74.0
Soviet Union	70.0

Sources: United Nations, Department of International Economic and Social Affairs, *Concise Report on the World Population Situation in 1977*, (St/ESA/ser. A/63) (New York, 1979), p. 17. U.S. Bureau of the Census, *World Population: 1977. Recent Demographic Estimates for the Countries and Regions of the World* (Washington: U.S. Government Printing Office, 1978), pp. 28, 146, 244, 348, 404.

DIFFERENTIAL MORTALITY

Our discussion of the various measures of mortality was limited to overall mortality. But some fractions of any given population have higher mortality rates than others. Death, the great leveler, operates at different levels in different places and among different groups. The term *differential mortality* is used to indicate such differences in mortality levels between different segments of the population. In Table 6–8 we saw that mortality levels vary within the international community, with about a twenty-year difference in life expectancy at birth between higher and lower income nations. Within nations, however, mortality levels also differ. These differences can be measured by crude death rates, age-specific mortality rates, infant mortality rates, or life expectancies.

The Sex Differential

We have already mentioned that in such countries as the United States, Canada, and the United Kingdom, women have lower age-specific mortality rates than men. Mortality affects both sexes differently. The excess of male over female deaths is manifest even before birth, with the fetal death rate of males running about 10 percent higher. This suggests a biological factor among others. Female superiority in resisting infections and reduced susceptibility to degenerative diseases seems to point in the same direction. Among the socioeconomic and cultural determinants, higher occupational hazards and greater pressure on men to achieve have been noted. Also, women more frequently admit being ill and seem more prepared than men to seek treatment for minor diseases and disorders. It has also been argued that women release and express their emotions more easily than men, which would contribute to greater mental health.

In countries like the United States, death rates have declined more rapidly for women than for men during the twentieth century (Table 6–7). The drop in mortality among women has been accelerated by the fall in maternal mortality and the reduction in the proportion of women who bear a large number of children. In most Western nations the gap between male and female mortality tends to widen during the ages 15–29, because of the higher accident rate of men; at these ages motor vehicle and other accidents are important causes of death. Until the most advanced ages, male deaths exceed those of females. A notable difference between males and females is the higher proportion of male deaths due to ischemic heart disease (in which the heart muscle has its own blood supply restricted), lung cancer, and cirrhosis of the liver. All these illnesses are related to lifestyle factors like stress, smoking, and drinking.

In premodern societies women were often overworked, undernourished, and exposed to the infectious and contagious diseases of other members of the family. Frequent childbearing, and the lack of supervision during pregnancy and immediately following childbirth, contributed to high mortality among females. When the epidemics of infection began to recede and women started having fewer pregnancies, female mortality declined accordingly. Improved medical care and supervision accelerated the process. During the modernization and development process, women commonly switch from a level of mortality as high as or even higher than that of men, to a level well below that of the male population.

The Rural/Urban Differential

Differences in mortality levels also tend to exist between rural and urban areas. Historically, cities have always been characterized by high death rates, since urban congestion facilitates the spread of infectious diseases. Also, in the past garbage was often not collected but thrown in the streets, while streams and brooks were used for sewage as well as drinking purposes.[3] In those times rural areas were looked on as population springs and the cities as population sinks.

---

[3] In some Iranian cities it is still common to see people washing in the dirty water of open conduits.

In the more developed countries, the rural-urban mortality differences have narrowed in the twentieth century and are now close to zero, although there is some evidence of a relatively high male mortality in highly urbanized areas and in areas where mining, heavy industry, or dock yards are concentrated. A number of cities are indeed beset with problems like pollution, violent crime, and traffic accidents. But this disadvantage is compensated by the greater availability of fast, specialized medical care. In so far as rural mortality remains below urban mortality, the variations must be accounted for by differences in age composition between the two populations, or by the exodus of higher income groups from the cities as lower socioeconomic groups move in.

In the developing countries, however, urban mortality is usually below rural mortality, since cities benefit first from the transplantation of public health discoveries from the more to the less developed countries. The drinking water is purified first in the towns, and later in the countryside. Also, there is a greater concentration of medical facilities and personnel in cities and towns. The Central Province in Iran, with Teheran as its main city, contains about one fifth of the population of Iran. Yet in 1975–76, of Iran's 12,000 medical doctors, 5,650 practiced in that area.

The Socioeconomic Differential

Differences in death rates exist also among people belonging to different social classes. Before the eighteenth century, mortality levels were much the same (and always high) for all socioeconomic groups. Since medical care was often ineffectual, the inability to consult a physician did not make much difference. Class-specific mortality increased during the industrialization process, when certain sections of the population were exposed to long working hours in factories and workshops, to low wages, and to crowding in unwholesome dwellings. The middle and upper classes, however, benefited increasingly from improved medical care and facilities. At present, in most countries groups that have achieved the highest socioeconomic status as measured by education, occupation, and especially income have the lowest mortality. Inequalities in the distribution of income and property are thus associated with inequalities in the distribution of life itself. However, in many highly developed nations (in Sweden, for example), where mortality has reached very low levels, class-specific mortality tends to disappear.

The explanations for socioeconomic differentials in mortality are both biological and social. Through a process of competitive selection the stronger and abler individuals tend to reach the higher status occupations, leaving the less desirable activities to others. Conversely, disease may transfer a person to a lower income occupation and class, thereby affecting the higher than average mortality of that class. Furthermore, the less desirable employments sometimes involve dangerous activities—climbing, use of explosives, exposure to high temperatures, or working in a polluted atmosphere where one breathes in chemicals and dust. Since occupation determines to a large extent one's income, the higher income groups can afford good medical care, balanced nutrition, proper clothing, and adequate housing. The lower income groups have less access to these, and therefore a higher mortality incidence.

Ironically, socioeconomic development may initially help widen the disparities in changes of survival. When new health care services are made available to the entire population, programs may give the greatest advantages to the privileged classes who are better prepared to make use of them.

The Educational Differential

Educational attainment is a stable characteristic for nearly all persons 30 years or over, whereas the categories of occupation and income do not apply to women who are not in the labor market. The relationship between mortality and education is inverse: numerous studies have shown that more schooling leads to better health and lower mortality. One possible explanation is that different educational levels result in different attitudes toward health priorities, physical risk-taking, and nutrition. Schooling may also contribute to a more effective use of available medical services, and help one absorb new information about health. Infant mortality conforms to this pattern, being even more sensitive to the level of instruction of the mother than to family income. Ignorance is apparently more deadly than poverty.

Ethnicity and Race

If a nation is inhabited by several ethnic or racial groups, differences in mortality levels between those groups may be encountered. South Africa and the United States are obvious examples. In the United States the white population has had consistently lower mortality and a longer life expectancy than the black population, and the difference has been greater among the young than the old. In 1900 the life expectancy at birth for the white population, both sexes taken together, totaled 47.6 years, and for the blacks, 33.0 years. The figures for 1977 were respectively 73.8 and 68.8 years. Real progress has been achieved as the gap narrowed from 14.6 to 5 in 77 years.

It is unlikely that there is a biological basis for this race-specific mortality. In all probability this situation reflects, at least in part, the socioeconomic differences between the ethnic groups. Whites are usually better educated and therefore enjoy higher incomes than nonwhites. Those higher incomes imply better medical care, housing, nutrition, and the like. The higher education levels of the whites entail a greater willingness to use available medical facilities, and better knowledge of proper diet.

The Marital Status Differential

Another consistent feature of mortality is that death rates from all major causes of death are significantly higher for divorced persons, widowers, and single people than for married persons. For all three categories of nonmarried, the disadvantage of not being married means less for women than for men. Females who are divorced, widowed, or single can cope much better than men without spouses.

The widowed have higher death rates than the unmarried, while the divorced have the highest death rates of all. One major reason is that mating tends to be selective: males and females tend to prefer the healthiest members of the opposite sex as spouses. Good health therefore increases one's marriageability, while those with health problems will tend to remain in the "single" category, contributing to its higher mortality levels. Also, for all the exceptions that confirm the rule, married people—especially men—tend to lead more orderly and harmonious lives than the nonmarried. They eat more regularly, their diet tends to be better balanced, and they get more sleep. They enjoy regular company, sexual or otherwise, and are better taken care of in case of illness. Loneliness can easily lead to depression and sometimes to excessive drinking, poor diet, inadequate exercise, and general neglect of one's body. The widowed suffer the same disadvantages as the single, but in addition they feel the loss of their loved one. It is the divorced, however, who have the highest mortality rates of all. Probably there are among them a disproportionate number of persons who have not been able to adapt themselves to "normal" existence. This may be due to a physical and/or psychological inferiority that exposes them to an above-average casualty rate. Adjustment difficulties after divorce may be another reason.

MAJOR CAUSES OF DEATH

With regard to the causes of all death, an interesting evolution has taken place in the more developed countries. It is probable that at least some developing nations will repeat this pattern. Before 1900, infectious and respiratory diseases as well as illnesses of the digestive tract were the main killers in practically all nations. In the 1650s nearly 75 percent of all deaths in Great Britain were attributable to infectious diseases, malnutrition, and maternity complications. Epidemics of infection including plague itself typically victimized more children and older persons than those in between.

Around 1900, when life expectancy at birth was still only about 50 years in most Western countries, some 30 percent of all deaths were due to infectious, respiratory, and parasitic diseases. Since then the gradual disappearance of these illnesses reflects a better understanding of their nature and transmission, as well as the development of powerful drugs and vaccines. At the same time the general environment had been improving a great deal since the 1880s. From almost every point of view, the environment in countries like the United States, Canada, and Great Britain is now safer and cleaner than a hundred years ago. In addition, houses are now built of better materials; coal and then oil have facilitated heating; personal and public hygiene has made progress; and better means of transport have brought wide varieties of food to the markets of the industrialized countries. Diet has improved in quality and resistance to infectious diseases has grown. After 1950, when in the West life expectancy at birth had approached 70 years, less than 10 percent of all deaths were attributable to infectious, parasitic, and respiratory ailments.

Now that most of the infectious and communicable illnesses have been either eradicated or brought under control, most reported deaths result from the illnesses of middle and old age: degenerative diseases, disorders of the circulatory system, cancer, and external causes such as accidents, violence, suicide, and poisoning. This shift from the age of epidemics of infection to an age of degenerative and man-made illnesses has been called the *epidemiologic transition*. During this transition, yellow fever, cholera, smallpox, typhoid, and other infectious diseases have disappeared as major killers. The same holds for tuberculosis, the bane of the nineteenth century. But as the twentieth century wore on, diseases like heart ailments, cancer, stroke, diabetes, and cirrhosis of the liver took over as the leading causes of death in the United States and have remained such ever since. With an ever rising private automobile ownership, United States mortality from motor vehicle accidents has also risen sharply. At the same time there is a tremendous loss of lives due to homicide and suicide. Among white males of age 15–24, motor accidents and suicide are the leading causes of death, while homicide is the most prominent cause of death among black males of the same age group.

However, two observations are in order. First, the increase in degenerative diseases has been partly exaggerated by the improvement in diagnosis. Second, although the epidemiologic transition has been beneficial to many—especially to the young and to mothers during the reproductive age—it has also created problems. One major difficulty is the accumulation of senior citizens often suffering from chronic ailments like diabe-

FIGURE 6–6

Evolution of Main Causes of Death
(Netherlands, 1966–77)

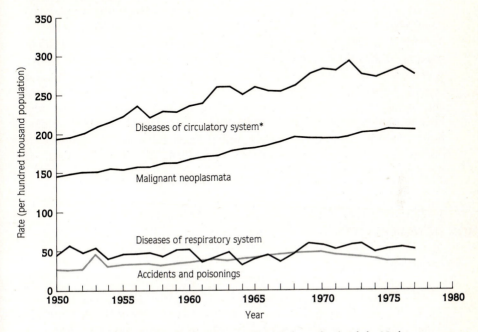

Source: Netherlands Bureau of Statistics, *Statistical Yearbook of the Netherlands 1978* (The Hague: Staatsuitgeverij, 1979), p. 60.

* Cardiovascular diseases excluded.

tes, arthritis, and diseases of the digestive system, which may require
frequent and expensive professional help.

Figure 6–6, picturing the evolution of the main causes of death during
a crucial period of the twentieth century, tells the story. The case of the
Netherlands has been selected because the Dutch classification of the main
causes of death is simpler than the one used in the United States. The rates
indicated are called *cause-specific death rates,* the annual number of persons who die from a particular disease or external cause per 100,000 population. Since in using cause-specific death rates we usually deal with small
numbers, a large constant such as 100,000 is used. The cause-specific death
rate, then, is computed as follows:

$$\frac{\text{Annual number of persons dying from the disease}}{\text{Total (midyear) population at risk}} \times 100{,}000$$

The pattern of mortality in the underprivileged areas of the world is markedly different. The leading causes of death in the developing countries are now much the same as in the technically advanced nations in the last century. They include gastroenteritis, diarrheal diseases, pneumonia, tuberculosis, bronchitis, influenza, tetanus, and typhoid fever. The Iranian demographer Momeni reports that in 1967 there were five leading causes of death in Iran; infectious and parasitic diseases (8.6 percent of all deaths), diseases of the circulatory system (15.4 percent), diseases of the respiratory system (12.1 percent), diseases of the digestive system (13.2 percent), and certain unspecified diseases of early infancy (9.9 percent); together they add up to 59.2 percent.[4] Again, as in the Western countries before the First World War, these diseases particularly affect infants and young adults. But as health conditions improve and the general state of resistance to disease increases, the developing nations are likely to follow the pattern of the Western countries and Japan.

TRENDS IN MORTALITY

Traditional Mortality

Premodern mortality—that is, mortality before 1750—was high and fluctuating in all areas of the world. Life expectancy at birth in Rome 2,000 years ago was perhaps 22–25 years. In Europe around 1750, it was little more than 30. But while it was high, mortality was not uniformly high over this period. Its level was determined by political, economic, and environmental conditions and even by climate. In times of security, order, and favorable weather conditions, mortality could drop to relatively low levels, only to rise sharply in times of war, famine, epidemic, or internal political disturbances. In Europe, food shortages and famines were common well into the nineteenth century, when the dread potato famine decimated the Irish population. Famines also devastated Asia at frequent intervals. Malnutrition and deficient diet were less spectacular but perhaps even more deadly than famine. Until the end of the nineteenth century, diets deficient in protein and vitamins were exceedingly common in Europe and America, and they still are in Asia, Africa, and Latin America. Inadequate diets lead to weakness and reduced resistance against infectious diseases.

Until about 150 years ago and even later, there was hardly any defense against such infectious illnesses as typhus, typhoid fever, and malaria, which took a heavy toll of lives. The same held true for infant and

[4]D. A. Momeni, *The Population of Iran* (Shiraz, Iran: privately published, 1975), p. 169.

children's diseases like enteritis, measles, and whooping cough. Furthermore, when cities began to grow, many infectious diseases became more common, because physical proximity multiplied opportunities for parasitic organisms to pass quickly from one human host to the next. Proper sanitation was also lacking: until the middle of the nineteenth century refuse was commonly thrown in the streets. Small streams sometimes served simultaneously as sewers and sources of water supply. Public water systems and municipal sewage systems became available only toward the end of the last century. Living and working quarters were often clumsily built, damp, and poorly lighted. Plumbing was lacking, dirt and congestion attracted the rodents and lice that spread diseases such as plague. Personal uncleanliness was fearful by our standards, the regular use of soap and water to wash the body being practically unheard of until some hundred years ago. All these factors more than explain the low life expectancy at birth that prevailed until quite recently.

With the Industrial Revolution, all this changed. A steady decline in mortality has manifested itself in the Western world since about 1750. Fluctuations in mortality became less drastic and ultimately disappeared. The drop in mortality was slow at first, but accelerated toward the end of the nineteenth century. Initially, the fall in mortality was conditioned more by economic circumstances than by medical and public health discoveries. In England, for instance, the Industrial Revolution was preceded by an agricultural revolution that promoted commercial farming and a change in the land tenure system. Advances were made in crop rotation; irrigation and drainage were improved; and new implements were invented. Storage facilities were also perfected, and the supply of food increased and became more reliable.

By 1750 the age of massacre by epidemic disease was also over. Most European populations had become disease-experienced. Infectious diseases like diphtheria and measles provoke antibody formation in infected humans, so that one exposure to the disease will create immunity for many years if not a lifetime. In a disease-experienced population, therefore, only children are suitable hosts for these infections.

The subsequent Industrial Revolution increased the quantity and quality of commodities per person. Incomes in such countries as England rose, especially after the 1850s, so that people could afford more and better goods, warmer clothes, and improved houses.

The second part of the nineteenth century witnessed a medical and public health revolution that ultimately helped to curb mortality. The great sanitary awakening began in England during the 1850s, when sewage was still running through the streets, and cholera and typhoid were major problems. The sanitary reform movement resulted in such concrete measures as public refuse removal, sewer systems that helped to combat waterborne diseases, and the provision of purified water supplies that drastically reduced typhoid fever. In most Western cities the filtering and purification of drinking water occurred between 1900 and 1914. New habits of personal hygiene were also adopted. With piped-in water, cheap soap, and a better understanding of the relationship between disease and filth, personal cleanliness improved drastically.

These personal and public health revolutions were accompanied by dramatic improvements in preventive and curative medicine. The eighteenth century had already witnessed the founding of hospitals and the emergence of apothecaries who prescribed and produced medicines. Edward Jenner discovered a preventive serum for smallpox, one of the most deadly diseases, in 1798. Then in the late nineteenth century Pasteur's and Koch's investigations prepared the ground for modern bacteriology and the science of immunization. At the same time antiseptic surgery revolutionized clinical practices, saving countless lives. Diagnostic techniques improved also. Generally, after 1900 medical discoveries began to accelerate. Advances were also made in chemotherapy, especially when sulfa drugs and antibiotics were discovered. Deaths associated with the complications of anesthesia have diminished since the 1950s, when new anesthetics and techniques were introduced, and the number of physician specialists in anesthesia have increased.

The development of insecticides like DDT has permitted a massive attack on insect-borne diseases like malaria. At present, most infectious diseases have virtually disappeared in the more developed countries, and medical science now makes it possible for ever increasing numbers to live out their natural life span.

Contemporary Mortality in Developed Countries

As stated before, the developed nations have now achieved low mortality levels, with stabilized crude death rates of below 15‰ and infant mortality ranging from about 10‰ to 30‰. The drop in mortality has specifically benefited the 0–10 age groups and females in the reproductive ages, because of the susceptibility of these groups to infectious and deficiency diseases. The point is now being reached where most people either die early in life from congenital malformations, specific childbirth problems, and so on, or late in life from degenerative diseases or stoppage of one of the body's components. Stress, the involuntary and nonspecific response of the human body to the intense, highly particularized demands of the twentieth century, has been recognized as a contributor to many modern ailments including heart disease, high blood pressure, and ulcers. Urbanized as we now are, we live in a sedentary age with machines and appliances doing much of the muscular work we used to do ourselves. The hectic pace of urban life causes tension and stress, but we have little chance of working it off through physical exertion. This overirritated and under-exercised existence, which may also suffer from inadequate diet, is prone to a high incidence of cardiovascular and circulatory diseases.

Occasionally, people still die from viral infections, against which modern medicine is still relatively impotent. Furthermore, it seems unlikely that the developed countries will experience further spectacular declines in mortality levels, for our ability to cope with the degenerative causes of death is not apt to change rapidly. The human life span can be increased further only if radical improvements in the understanding of the aging process occur and new biochemical discoveries are made.

Moreover, subtle new killers may be emerging because of the environmental hazards created by the increased production and use of chemical compounds. Health in the more developed nations may now be threatened by the production of industrial chemicals such as PCB's (polychlorinated biphenyls), which float invisibly through air and water. The pesticides, herbicides, and fungicides, which increase productivity on the farm, find their way into the human body; their side-effects will only be known a few decades from now. Thousands of chemicals are added to food to improve appearance, taste, and vitamin content, to extend their shelf life, and so on. Even if each chemical is harmless by itself, what are the effects of all these substances combined? In a country like the United States, each second some 7,000 pills are being swallowed. About the long-term side effects of all these drugs, little is known. It could well be, then, that the future will witness either new diseases or a spread of known diseases (like cancer) that bar a further lengthening of the expectation of life.

Mortality in Transitional Societies

Mortality in the developing nations is a different story. First, the decline in mortality started much later than in the developed countries. The colonizing nations helped reduce mortality in Asian and African colonies by suppressing local wars and quarrels, improving transportation systems, and introducing discoveries in public health and medicine. But it was only after 1945, when most colonized areas gained independence, that an intensive importation of life-saving techniques from the Western nations began, often with the assistance of international agencies such as the World Health Organization. Further, the decline in mortality was much faster than in the West: what took the more developed countries some 200 years to accomplish was sometimes achieved in only 50 years. Finally, in the developing nations the rapid decline in mortality has often resulted not from internally generated socioeconomic and scientific developments, but from a rapid and effective transplantation of public health devices and medical techniques, drug therapies, and pesticides from abroad.[5] All these facilities have made possible a highly successful battle against infectious and parasitic diseases.

Yet much remains to be done. Many diseases still current in developing nations have become curiosities in the West. First, there are illnesses due to a lack of immunization, such as diphtheria, polio, and tetanus. Second, there are infirmities like blindness and rickets that are due to malnutrition. Third, diseases like typhoid fever, enteritis, dysentery, and polio are attributed to a lack of sanitation. Fourth, there are tropical diseases like malaria, yellow fever, and kala-azar, which are by definition absent from the temperate zone. Finally, there are illnesses caused by bad or unsustained medical treatment, as for instance chronic rheumatic heart disease, which tends to occur when repeated strep infections (treated with penicillin in the West) are dealt with insufficiently.

Because the mortality decline in the less developed countries was largely dissociated from endogenous socioeconomic progress, they may now have reached a threshold which will be difficult to cross. With an average life expectancy of about 55 years and an infant mortality of some 110 per thousand, further declines in mortality may well require fresh socioeconomic advances resulting in higher incomes. Further disease control now depends on such factors as more balanced diets, improved housing conditions, adequate waste disposal systems and sewage facilities, purified drinking water, and more hospitals and physicians. Low living standards impede such advances and therefore hold back more rapid progress in mortality control.

CONCEPTS FOR REVIEW

Crude death rate

Age-specific death rate

Standardization

Infant mortality rate

Life tables

Life expectancy at birth

Differential mortality

Epidemiologic transition

Cause-specific death rate

Derived economies

[5] Economist H. C. Wallich has made a pertinent distinction between the economies of the Western nations which developed and grew through internally generated "innovation," and the "derived" economies of the third world nations which attempt development through "assimilation"—i.e., the adoption and transplantation of foreign technology. See H. C. Wallich, "Some Notes toward a Theory of Derived Development," in A. N. Agarwala, S. P. Singh, *The Economics of Underdevelopment,* (New York: Oxford University Press, 1963).

QUESTIONS FOR DISCUSSION

1. Why is the crude death rate in England and Wales higher than in the United States, while health conditions are about the same?
2. Do you agree with the statement that the infant mortality rate is a good indication of a nation's level of socioeconomic development and modernization? Why or why not?
3. What is the difference between exogenous and endogenous causes of infant mortality? Give some examples of endogenous causes.
4. "Because women live more and more like men, the difference between male and female mortality levels becomes smaller and smaller." Comment and evaluate.
5. Why is it that in premodern societies female mortality usually exceeds male mortality levels?
6. "The mortality levels of the middle and upper classes are below those of the lower income groups. This demonstrates that all members of the middle and upper classes are biologically superior." Comment and evaluate.
7. List some major causes of death in the less developed nations.
8. What do you consider the most important causes of the long-term decline in mortality which has taken place in the United States from about 1800 onward?
9. The crude death rate in the United States has declined from 17.2‰ in 1900 to 8.8‰ in 1977. Do you expect this downward trend to continue? Why or why not?

BIBLIOGRAPHY

Brown, H. "Increase in Life Expectancy Due to Modern Medicine." In *Population in Perspective,* edited by L. B. Young. New York: Oxford University Press, 1968.

Carr-Saunders, A. M. *World Population,* London: Cass, 1964.

Goldscheider, C. *Population, Modernization and Social Structure.* Boston: Little, Brown, 1971.

Mitchell, B. R. *European Historical Statistics 1750–1970.* London: Macmillan, 1975.

Momeni, D. A. *The Population of Iran.* Shiraz, Iran: privately published, 1975.

Omran, A. R. "The Epidemiologic Transition." *Milbank Memorial Fund Quarterly* 49, no. 4 (October 1971).

Palmore, J. A. *Measuring Mortality: A Self-Teaching Guide to Elementary Measures.* Honolulu: East-West Population Institute, 1975.

Tranter, N. *Population since the Industrial Revolution.* London: Croom-Helm, 1973.

7

Fertility

A NOTE ON NUPTIALITY

The term *nuptiality* includes marriage, divorce, widowhood, and remarriage. Since most people marry before they reproduce, nuptiality is an important determinant of fertility.

Marriage Rates

The *crude marriage rate* (CMR), a ratio that expresses the frequency with which marriages occur, is determined by the formula[1]

$$\frac{\text{Number of marriages in a given year in a given area}}{\text{Midyear population of the same area}} \times 1{,}000 \text{ or } \frac{M}{P} \cdot k$$

---

[1] A less common method is to compute the marriage rate per 1,000 unmarried women 15–44 years old.

where M = number of marriages in a given area during the year
          P = midyear population of that area
          k = 1,000

The CMR was $2,243,000/218,500,000 \times 1,000 = 10.3\%$ for the United States in 1978.[1] The 1973 CMR for Iraq was 14.7‰.

Several phenomena have an important impact on the CMR: economic conditions, such as employment levels, and demographic factors like the age composition of the population, the latter being a major determinant of the supply of marriageable persons. Religion is also a significant influence. Certain religions emphasize marriage more than others: Christianity—especially Roman Catholicism—has always stressed celibacy and continence among the clergy. Moslem doctrine, by contrast, holds that permanent celibacy is abnormal for men and unthinkable for women. Moslem belief therefore encourages universal marriage and high CMRs.

Compared to other traditional, preindustrial societies, premodern Western Europe had low fertility. Age at marriage was relatively high and often many years beyond the biological minimum age. Also, a fairly high proportion of people did not marry at all, again because of the influence of religion. Another difference between premodern Western Europe and other preindustrial societies was the virtual absence of the extended family system, or kinship-family structure, existing in Africa and Asia. Under the extended family system the burdens of reproduction are often shared by other family members, while the prestige involved in having children is enjoyed by the parents alone. Easy and universal marriage is thus encouraged, and the birth rate is usually high. In Western Europe, where child care was primarily the responsibility of wife and husband, marriage frequently entailed the setting up of a separate household—often an expensive endeavor. In some European societies law supplemented custom by forcing couples to defer marriage until they were able to handle the responsibilities involved. As late as the middle of the nineteenth century there existed a law in Bavaria, dating from 1616, stating that marriage was authorized only to those giving proof of a regular guaranteed income. Perhaps for this reason, Bavaria at that time had one of the lowest marriage rates in Europe. When the law was abolished in 1868, the marriage rate nearly doubled.

While marriage was often deferred or avoided because of an unwillingness to assume the burdens of parenthood, economic circumstances such as harvest conditions, the price of wheat, and employment opportunities also had their impact. In premodern agricultural Europe, in fact, the number of marriages was often inversely correlated to the price of wheat. During the modernization process the link between agricultural production and the number of marriages was broken, but a weak relationship between the economic climate and the number of weddings still persists.

TABLE 7–1

Marriage Rate (United States, Canada, and the Netherlands, 1920–75)

Year	United States	Canada	Netherlands
1920 (1921 for Canada)	12.0	7.9	9.6
1930 (1931 for Canada)	9.2	6.4	8.0
1940 (1941 for Canada)	12.1	10.6	7.6
1950 (1951 for Canada)	11.1	9.2	8.2
1960 (1961 for Canada)	8.5	7.0	7.8
1970 (1971 for Canada)	10.6	8.9	9.5
1975	10.2	8.7	6.5

Sources: U.S. Bureau of the Census, *Statistical Abstract of the United States: 1979* (Washington: U.S. Government Printing Office, 1979), p. 83. Ministry of Industry, Trade and Commerce, *Canada Yearbook 1978–79* (Ottawa: Information Division, Statistics Canada, 1978), p. 182. Netherlands Central Bureau of Statistics, *Statistical Yearbook of the Netherlands, 1976* (The Hague: Staatsuitgeverij, 1977), p. 18.

Table 7–1 gives an overview of the marriage rate, from 1920 onward, in the United States, Canada, and the Netherlands. Marriage rates during the 1920s were relatively high because of good economic conditions and high employment levels. The low figure of 1930 results from the Depression. World War II spurred the creation of jobs, which accounts in part for the relatively high 1940 figure for Canada and the United States. (Holland's low 1940 figure can be explained by the Nazi occupation.) After the end of the hostilities many postponed marriages took place. Favorable postwar employment conditions also boosted the marriage rate. During the 1950s, however, the relatively small cohorts born during the Depression came of age, and by 1960 the marriage rate went down again. The high marriage rate of the early 1970s reflects the arrival at marrying age of a large fraction of the postwar baby boom. The peak in the marriage rate for the United States was apparently reached in 1972, when it was 11‰.

Figure 7.1 shows the relationship in the United States between the marriage boom and the earlier baby boom, with a lag of some eighteen to twenty years (from about 1950 to about 1970) plainly visible. Compared

FIGURE 7–1

Marriage and Birth Rates (United States, 1925–73)

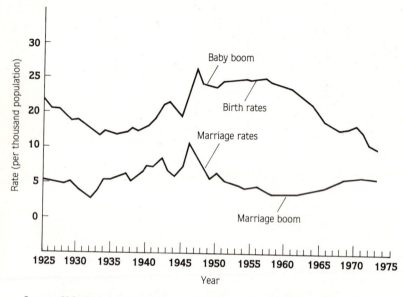

Source: U.S. Bureau of the Census, *Statistical Abstract of the United States: 1974* (Washington: U.S. Government Printing Office, 1974), p. 52.

to other Western nations, the U.S. marriage rates appear high. This is in part due to the fact that the American divorce rates are high as well: since some 80 percent of the divorced remarry, the total number of marriages in any given year is increased.

The Canadian CMR is also falling again. It too reached its highest postwar level in 1972 with a figure of 9.2‰. In Canada as in the United States, the comparatively high CMR's of the late 1960s and early 1970s were a consequence of the relative increase in young people of prime marrying age.

The Median Age at Marriage

A noteworthy evolution has taken place with regard to the median age at marriage—the age above and below which half the marriages occur.[2] Whereas in the immediate postwar period there was a return to early marriage for women, the *age at first marriage* has risen again since the

[2]See pp. 28–29 for an explanation of the *median*.

TABLE 7–2

Median Age at First Marriage (United States, 1930–77)

Year	Male	Female
1930	24.3	21.3
1940	24.3	21.5
1950	22.8	20.3
1955	22.6	20.0
1960	22.8	20.3
1965	22.5	20.4
1970	22.5	20.6
1975	22.7	20.8
1977	23.0	21.8

Source: U.S. Bureau of the Census, *Statistical Abstract of the United States: 1979* (Washington: U.S. Government Printing Office, 1979), p. 81.

1960s. In 1960 about 29 percent of the women aged 20–24 had never married; by 1978 the proportion had risen to about 48 percent. This situation results in lower fertility levels, because women who begin families at an early age tend to have more children than women who enter marriage somewhat later in life. Table 7–2 shows the evolution of the median age at first marriage, for both men and women, since 1930.

The young women born during the baby boom (1946–61) have tended to delay marriage, whereas their mothers born in the 1920s and 1930s entered marriage and parenthood early. The following explanations are the most widely accepted. First, because of the sharp upturn in the birth rate after 1945, women of marriageable age outnumbered men during the late 1960s and early 1970s. Since women tend to select somewhat older men for marriage, the females born in the early part of the baby boom reached marriageable age while the men of conventional marriageable age came from the smaller cohorts born a few years earlier. This *marriage squeeze,* as the phenomenon is called, implied that the ratio of males age 20–26 to females age 18–24 was less than 1. Second, the encouragement given to young people to pursue an education increased college enrollment and led, in many cases, to the postponement of marriage. Third, more young women entered the labor market; some women put off marriage in favor of establishing a career. Moreover, many young men (and women) found it difficult to obtain a suitable job, as the large numbers born during the baby boom put the job market under severe pressure. Finally, there was a reduction in unplanned marriages following unwanted pregnancies, owing to the development of sophisticated birth control technology (the pill and IUD's in particular). The question arises whether these factors will result in a larger proportion of women remaining single throughout their lives. It is certainly too early to say.

The Divorce Rate

The *divorce rate* defines the frequency with which marriages are legally dissolved. The formula is

$$\frac{\text{Number of divorces in an area in a given year}}{\text{Midyear population in that area}} \times 1,000 \text{ or } \frac{D}{P} \cdot k$$

where D = number of divorces in a given area during the year
          P = midyear population of that area
          k = 1,000

Thus we can compute $1,122,000/218,500,000 \times 1,000 = 5.1\%_{00}$ for the United States in 1978. The divorce rate in America increased from 2.6 per thousand in the 1950s to 3.5 per thousand in 1970. In 1975 the figure $5.0\%_{00}$ was reached, representing over 1 million divorces. In 1910 the rate was only $0.9\%_{00}$.

Although many nations have rising divorce rates, the U.S. divorce rate is comparatively high. (If the American rates are computed according to racial groups, we find that blacks rank above whites, with other racial groups occupying the lowest position.) While after World War II there was a temporary upswing in the divorce rate, the steep rise began after 1963. This phenomenon may be partly explained by the rapid growth in the number of people getting married—the segment of the population exposed to the risk of divorce. Also, the total number of married people now includes a larger portion of young adults, for whom the risk of divorce is always greater. The dramatic increase in the proportion of women in the labor force may be another reason: between 1960 and 1977 that proportion rose from 38 percent to 48 percent. Their reduced economic dependence on men may make it more feasible for women to end an unhappy marriage. Most states, finally, have liberalized divorce laws by accepting new grounds for divorce or have made other changes facilitating divorce. These legal changes mirror society's increased tolerance of divorce.

In Canada the 1975 divorce rate was $2.2\%_{00}$. In the West European nations, rates between $1.4\%_{00}$ and $2.5\%_{00}$ are common. In countries like Iran and Turkey, where social pressures not to divorce are still very strong, we find low rates: $0.64\%_{00}$ and $0.33\%_{00}$ respectively for 1975.

Since the number of marriages and the number of divorces in a society are obviously closely linked, it is useful to measure the relationship. One way is to calculate the divorce rate per 1,000 married women of 15 years and over. Another method is to compare the number of marriages in a

FIGURE 7–2

Age-Specific Divorce Rates for Married Men and Women
(United States, 1970)

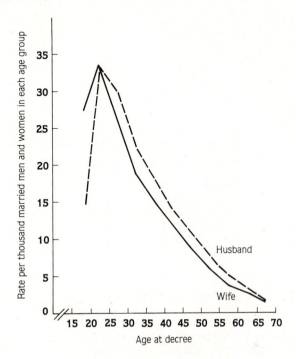

Source: U.S. Department of Health, Education, and Welfare, *Divorces and Divorce Rates, United States* (Hyattsville, 1978), p. 9.

given year with the number of divorces and legal separations in the same year and then obtain the *marriage-divorce ratio*. Finally, we can simply compute the number of divorces per 1,000 married couples. The latter is the method used in the "Annual Abstracts" of statistics published in the United Kingdom.

As mentioned earlier, the risk of divorce is highest among young adults. Available research based on the 1970 United States census and sample data indicates, that the highest divorce rates for both husbands and wives are found in the 20–24 age group. Thereafter the rate falls as age increases. Figure 7–2 reveals the pattern of *age-specific divorce rates*. Note the positive skew in the distribution.

BASIC MEASURES OF FERTILITY

When we analyze fertility, we should first distinguish this concept from *fecundity*. *Fertility* denotes the actual reproductive performance of couples or women, whereas *fecundity* implies the physiological capacity to reproduce. There are a number of measures of fertility, and we will discuss them in this section.

The Child-Woman Ratio

One measure of fertility is the *child-woman ratio* (CWR), which shows the number of children under age 5 per 1,000 women of childbearing age in a given country in a given year. The ratio is computed as follows:

$$\frac{\text{Number of children under 5 years old in a population}}{\text{Number of women in the reproductive period (15–49)}} \times 1,000$$

or

$$\frac{P_{0-4}}{P_f\ 15-49} \cdot k$$

where P_{0-4} = population under 5 years old
$P_f\ 15-49$ = number of women age 15–49
$k = 1,000$

For 1976 the U.S. figures for children under 5 years old per 1,000 women in their reproductive years look like this: $15,339,000/54,090,000 \times 1,000 = 284$.

Some demographers prefer to use the 15 to 44 period instead of the 15 to 49 period, because the number of births occurring during those last 5 years is usually insignificant. In either case, the numerator of the child-woman ratio denotes the number of surviving children born during the five years prior to and including the ratio year, while the denominator comprises those women most likely to be their mothers.

A problem with this ratio is that it actually underestimates current fertility levels, because the deaths of children are not considered. The ratio deals only with the survivors of births during the given five-year period. In some less developed countries infant and childhood mortality is still considerable, and the number of children born may substantially exceed the number of survivors. Also, the ratio is often computed in countries where data for ordinary births are poor. But a sample survey of age and sex composition in a country with inadequate birth registration procedures is all that is needed to compute the ratio. Imperfect as it is, some index is better than none. For a typical developing country like Iran we find, in 1973: $5,583,000/6,679,000 \times 1,000 = 0.836$ children per woman, or 836 children per 1,000 women.

FIGURE 7–3

Child-Woman Ratio
(Canada, 1851–1971 and United States, 1850–1970)

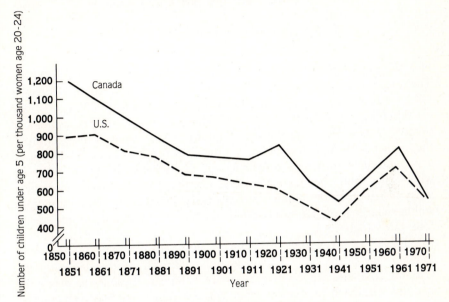

Source: *1971 Census of Canada, Profile Studies, Fertility in Canada*, 5, pt. 1
(Ottawa: Information Division, Statistics Canada, 1976) 5.

For Canada, rates have always been above those of the United States. But the gap is obviously narrowing, as shown by Figure 7–3, which compares the evolution of the Canadian and American child-woman ratios between 1850 and 1971. The particular child-woman ratio used here is the number of children under 5 per 1,000 women between ages 20–44. Although this is not shown in Figure 7–3, the CWR in the United States was higher for black women than for white. For example, in 1850 the adjusted CWR for white women was 892 and for black women, 1,087. In 1970 the two figures were 507 and 689 respectively.

The Crude Birth Rate

A second widely used index of fertility is the *crude birth rate* (CBR), which shows the frequency of births per 1,000 population.[3] It is computed as follows:

[3] The process of calculating standardized birth rates is identical to that of standardizing death rates and will therefore not be discussed here (see pp. 72–76).

$$\frac{\text{Number of recorded live births in an area during the year}}{\text{Midyear population in that area}} \times 1,000 \text{ or } \frac{B}{P} \cdot k$$

where B = number of recorded live births in a given area in a given year

P = midyear population in that area

k = 1,000

In 1977 the United States had an estimated population of 216,900,000. The total number of live births in that year came to 3,329,000. Hence the CBR for that year was $3,329,000/216,900,000 \times 1,000 = 15.3‰$.

Useful as the CBR is, it may easily distort actual fertility measurement because it includes nonproducers of children. As a result, a recognition of the impact of the age distribution on the CBR becomes vital. For example, a population with a high proportion of adults between 18 and 40 years will—other things being equal—show a birth rate well above a more normally distributed population. As of the early 1980s, many Western nations still have large proportions of young adults in their populations and, therefore, fairly high CBR's.

Table 7–3 gives some estimates of birth rates for major world areas. The message of the table is unmistakably clear. The birth rates in the developing countries are, on average, twice as high as those in the developed nations. The birth rate is lowest in Western Europe—12‰—and highest in western Africa: 49‰.

In premodern Northwestern Europe birth rates were considerably lower than in those Asian, African, and Latin American nations now embarking

TABLE 7–3

Estimated Annual Births for Selected Major Areas of the World, 1980 (Per Thousand Population)

World total	28
More developed nations	16
Less developed nations	32
Europe	14
Soviet Union	18
Asia	28
Africa	46
Latin America	34
Oceania	20

Source: *1980 World Population Data Sheet* (Washington D.C.: Population Reference Bureau, 1980).

on the modernization process. In 1750, for example, Norway had a CBR of 30.6‰. Denmark's birth rate was 29.9‰ in 1800, France's 27.7‰ in 1801. In 1850 the birth rate in England and Wales stood at 33.4‰; in Belgium, at 30‰. The rates in other Northwestern European nations were comparable, and, in fact, in all of Northwestern Europe fertility remained far below the biological maximum. Part of the explanation lies in the habit of deferring marriage or avoiding it altogether. This typically European phenomenon, however, never prevailed in old Quebec; as a result, Quebec has, until recently, scored the highest crude birth rates known for Caucasians. Between 1710 and 1775 its CBR remained very close to 54‰, and during 1781–1790 the rate even reached 62.1‰. In 1850 we still find a high 51.9‰, which dropped to 37.6‰ by 1920. Only in 1962 did the CBR in Quebec—25.1‰—fall for the first time below the Canadian average of the same year: 25.3‰.

As seen in Table 7–4, the CBR in the United States, Canada, and several other Western nations has been coming down more or less steadily for about one hundred years. There has been one major but temporary reversal in this long-term downward trend: the baby boom that lasted from 1940–41 until the early 1960s. Figure 7–4 shows the evolution of the white American and the Canadian birth rates between 1921 and 1976. The effect of the postwar baby boom is clearly brought out.

TABLE 7–4

Birth Rate in the United States, Canada, France, the Netherlands, England and Wales (1880–1975)

Year	United States	Canada	France	Netherlands	England and Wales
			Births per 1,000 Population		
1880	39.8	32.5	24.6	35.6	34.2
1890	n.d.	28.6	21.8	32.9	30.2
1900	32.3	27.2	21.3	31.6	28.7
1910	30.1	30.4	19.6	28.6	25.1
1920	27.7	29.2	21.4	28.6	26.5
1930	21.3	23.9	18.0	23.1	16.3
1940	19.4	21.5	13.6	20.8	14.1
1950	24.1	27.1	20.5	22.7	15.8
1960	23.7	26.8	17.9	20.8	17.1
1970	18.4	17.5	16.7	18.3	16.0
1975	14.8	15.7	13.6 ('76)	13.0	12.3

Sources: U.S. Bureau of the Census, *Historical Statistics* (Washington: U.S. Government Printing Office, 1975), p. 49. O. J. Firestone, *Canada's Economic Development 1867–1953* (London: Bowes & Bowes, 1958), p. 44. B. R. Mitchell, *European Historical Statistics 1750–1970* (London: Macmillan, 1975), pp. 104–24.

FIGURE 7–4

Birth Rates for Canada
and the U.S. White Population, 1921 –76

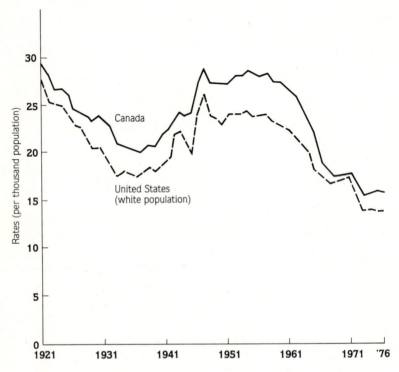

Source: *Canada's Population, Demographic Perspectives* (Ottawa: Information
Division, Statistics Canada, 1979), p. 5.

Table 7–5 indicates that the fertility of blacks and other nonwhites as
measured by the crude birth rate has always been above that of the white
population of the United States. The gap seems to be narrowing, however,
as it is for the crude death rates (see pp. 78–88). Until the 1960s the
CBR of the nonwhite population appears to have approximated the birth
rates in less developed nations.

The Crude Rate of Natural Increase

Now that we have familiarized ourselves with death and birth rates,
we can compute the difference between the two—that is, the *crude rate of
natural increase* (or *decrease*). This rate, the CRNI, is the rate at which a

TABLE 7–5

Crude Birth Rates by Ethnic Groups
(United States, 1920–77)

Year	Whites (in thousands)	Blacks and Others (in thousands)
1920	26.9	35.0
1930	20.6	27.5
1940	18.6	26.7
1950	23.0	33.3
1960	22.7	32.1
1970	17.4	25.1
1977	14.4	21.9

Sources: U.S. Bureau of the Census, *Historical Statistics* (Washington: U.S. Government Printing Office, 1975), p. 49. U.S. Bureau of the Census, *Statistical Abstract of the United States: 1979* (Washington: U.S. Government Printing Office, 1979), p. 60.

population is increasing (or decreasing) in a given year, because of a surplus of births over deaths (or vice versa). The crude rate of natural increase is usually given as a percentage figure. Its computation is as follows:

$$\frac{\text{Number of Births} - \text{Number of Deaths in a Given Year}}{\text{Midyear Population}} \times 100, \text{ or } \frac{B-D}{P} \cdot k$$

where B = number of births in a given year
D = number of deaths in that year
P = midyear population of that area
k = 100

An alternative method is simply to subtract the CDR from the CBR and divide the outcome by 10:

$$\frac{\text{CBR} - \text{CDR}}{10} = \text{CRNI.}$$

The crude rate of natural increase can also be shown graphically as the difference between the CBR and the CDR (Figure 7–5).

The crude rate of natural increase is different from the rate of *population growth* (PG) in that the latter takes net migration (immigration minus emigration) into account. Population growth in *absolute numbers* can be expressed in two ways. The first is in terms of two points of time, say from the beginning to the end of a given calendar year:

FIGURE 7–5

Birth Rate, Death Rate, and Rate of Natural Increase
(United States, 1960–78)

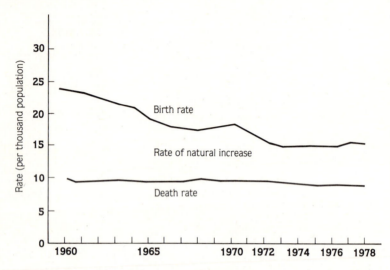

Source: U.S. Bureau of the Census, *Statistical Abstract of the United States:
1979* (Washington: U.S. Government Printing Office, 1979), p. 59.

$$P_2 = P_1 + B - D + I - E$$

where P_2 = the population at the end of the year (or other interval)
P_1 = the population at the beginning of the year (or other interval)
B = births in the interval between time 1 and time 2
D = deaths in the same interval
I = immigration in the same interval
E = emigration in the same interval

Or we can state population growth in terms of the components of growth
to obtain

$$PG = B - D + I - E$$

To find the annual *population growth rate* (PGR), we simply apply
the formula for percentage growth rates referred to in Chapter 2 (p. 34).
Thus as a formula for *PGR* we have

$$\frac{P_2 - P_1}{P_1} \times 100$$

FIGURE 7–6

Positive and Negative Rate of Increase
and Population Change

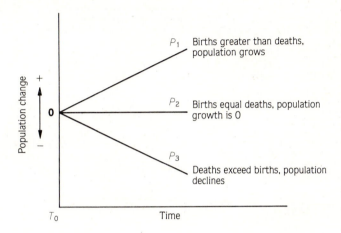

In 1870 the American *rate of increase* of population growth was still relatively high—2 percent. By 1915 it had declined to 1.5 percent. An all-time low of 0.7 percent was reached in 1935. After the Second World War the CBR rose again, while the CDR continued its downward trend, so that the rate of increase rose. For 1956 the figure is 1.4 percent. Once the baby boom was over, the rate of increase fell again, following the trend in the birth rate; in 1975 it stood at a low 0.6 percent. In many less developed countries, rates of increase of over 2 percent can be found. In 1980, for instance, Algeria had a rate of increase of 3.4 percent and Pakistan, 2.8 percent. With a growth rate of 3.4 percent, Algeria's population will double in just under twenty-one years.

Figure 7–6 shows schematically the relationship between population change and the rate of increase. Although the rate of increase correctly expresses the balance of births over deaths, it indicates only the population change in one year and not a trend. This measure should not be used to predict the long-term change in population.

Usually the annual number of births in an area exceeds the number of deaths, but if deaths exceed births the rate of increase becomes negative. In 1980 West Germany was estimated to have a crude birth rate of 9‰ and a crude death rate of 12‰. The negative rate of increase, or *rate of decrease,* stood at −3 percent. Figure 7–7 shows the net increase and decrease of the West German population between the early 1950s and the late 1970s.

TABLE 7–6

Children Ever Born per 1,000 Women
Ever Married of Age 50–59 (United States, 1910–77)

Year	Completed Fertility Index
1910	5,076
1940	3,215
1950	2,822
1960	2,420
1970	2,520
1977	2,944

Sources: U.S. Bureau of the Census, *Statistical Abstract of the United States: 1979* (Washington: U.S. Government Printing Office, 1979), p. 65. U.S. Bureau of the Census, *Historical Statistics* (Washington: U.S. Government Printing Office, 1975), p. 54.

Children Ever Born

Because most of the fertility measures discussed here refer to the current year, a given prior year, or some well-defined span of time, they are appropriately called *current fertility measures.* But the *cumulative fertility index,* which reports trends in family size over time, has come into greater use in the United States as well as in other nations; it is the number of *children ever born* to 1,000 women in a specific age group who were ever married. The index covers all the children born alive to a group of women,

FIGURE 7–7

Population Increase (+) and Population Decrease (−)
(West Germany, 1950–77)

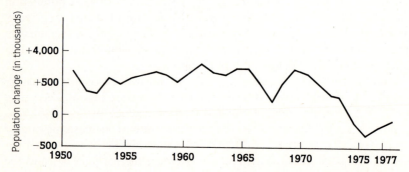

Source: *Statistisches Jahrbuch für die Bundesrepublik Deutschland* (Wiesbaden: Statistisches Bundesamt, 1979), p. 69.

called a cohort, who share a common characteristic—, they were born in the same year or period—and who are passing through the childbearing period or who recently passed out of it. The index enables us to find out how many children, on the average, one woman or 1,000 women of a given age category have borne from the start of childbearing to the time of the census or fertility survey. The result obtained is an age-specific measure: children ever born per 1,000 women of age x. If, on the other hand, we limit ourselves to the women in the age category 49, we obtain a measure, the *completed fertility index,* which shows the number of live births per 1,000 women who have passed through the childbearing period. Census questionnaires in the United States now ask married women how many babies they have ever had (not counting stillbirths). If we confine ourselves to a given census year, say 1980, and to women ever married of age category 49 (hence born in 1931), we can compute the average completed family size as follows:

$$\frac{\text{Number of children ever born to married women age 49}}{\text{Number of women ever married age 49}} \times 1,000$$

This index can be used to report changes over time in the size of completed families, as Table 7–6 illustrates (in this table, the women surveyed were age 50 to 59). In a sense the figures shown in the table are an undercount of cumulative fertility, because some women die before age 50 and some single women also have children. A further problem is that women have a tendency not to report children who were born several years before the census or survey or who died shortly after birth.

The General Fertility Rate

Another important measure of natality is the *general fertility rate,* or *GFR*. It is a more refined measure than the crude birth rate because, instead of relating births to the total population, it attributes all births to the women capable of childbearing: women ages 15–44 or 15–49 (it is rare for a woman outside this age category to bear children). We obtain the GFR by associating all live births in a particular year to the women of reproductive age. The GFR is defined as the number of live births per 1,000 women in the 15–44 childbearing period in any given year. The GFR can be written as follows:

$$\frac{\substack{\text{Number of live births during} \\ \text{a year in a given area}}}{\substack{\text{Midyear population of women} \\ \text{between ages 15–44}}} \times 1,000 \text{ or } \frac{B}{F_{15-44}} \cdot k$$

where $\qquad$ B = number of live births in one year in a given area
$\qquad F_{15-44}$ = females of childbearing age (15–44)
$\qquad k$ = 1,000

As noted, the GFR is a better measure than the CBR, because it restricts the denominator to the population capable of having a baby. However, abnormalities in the age distribution of the childbearing population (age 15–44) are still possible. Fertility tends to decline with age. If two communities have different GFR's, for instance, the discrepancy may not be due to true fertility variations but to the fact that one community has an unusually large number of women age 20–30, while the other has many women age 36–44.

Like the birth rate, the GFR tends to fluctuate from year to year. For the United States in 1978 the GFR was $3,229,000/52,031,000 \times 1,000 = 62.1‰$. Thus in 1978 1,000 women in the childbearing years would have given birth to a total of 62.1 children. For a developing country like Iran, we observe a much higher figure. In 1973: $1,212,000/6,679,000 \times 1,000 = 181.5‰$. The figure for Iraq in the same year was even higher: 198.1‰. Since in countries like Iran many parents fail to register their children at birth, registered births are lower than total births, and the published figures do not give the full picture.

Table 7–7 indicates the behavior of the GFR for two Western nations, the United States and the Netherlands, between 1930 and 1975. Although the actual figures for the two societies differ, the trends indicated are comparable. The "baby boom" that started in the early 1940's and lasted until the early 1960s is readily apparent, as is the "baby bust" that followed it.

TABLE 7–7

General Fertility Rate (United States and the Netherlands, 1930–75)

Year	United States	Netherlands
1930	89.2	99.2
1940	79.9	88.5
1945	85.9	97.6
1950	106.2	103.4
1955	118.3	101.8
1960	118.0	102.4
1965	96.6	95.9
1970	87.9	88.4
1975	66.7	53.9

Sources: U.S. Bureau of the Census, *Historical Statistics* (Washington: U.S. Government Printing Office, 1975), p. 49. U.S. Bureau of the Census, *Statistical Abstract of the United States: 1978* (Washington: U.S. Government Printing Office, 1978), p. 60. Centraal Bureau voor de Statistiek, *75 Jaar Statistiek van* Nederland (S'Gravenhage: Staatsuitgeverij, 1975), p. 13.

The Age-Specific Fertility Rate

A still-more refined analysis of fertility is the *age-specific fertility rate* (ASFR). It is the computation of the number of births per year to 1,000 women *of a particular age*. Such rates can be calculated only in countries in which the age of the mother is recorded at the birth of each child. Usually, five-year age groups are used, although an ASFR can be computed for each single year within the age range 15–49. The ASFR is calculated as follows:

$$\frac{\text{Number of live births to women in age group } i \text{ in an area in a year}}{\text{Midyear female population in age group } i, \text{ same area, same year}} \times 1,000 \text{ or } \frac{B_i}{W_i} \cdot k$$

where B_i = number of births to women of age interval i in a given year in a given area
W_i = number of women in age interval i during the same year
$k = 1,000$

Taking an example from the home population of England and Wales (*home population* means persons actually present in the area), we find 208,084 children born to women age 20–24 for the year 1974 we relate the number of children to the number of women in this age group (1,659,000); thus $208,084/1,659,000 \times 1,000 = 125.4‰$.

Typically, as Table 7–8 shows, the ASFR is low in the 15–19 age

TABLE 7–8

Age-Specific Fertility Rates (United States, 1974)

Age of Mother	Live Births	Female Population	ASFR, or Number of Babies Born to 1,000 Women in Each Age Group
15–19	599,449	10,252,000	58.1
20–24	1,108,051	9,311,000	119.0
25–29	923,318	8,147,000	113.3
30–34	372,907	6,851,000	54.4
35–39	118,115	5,851,000	20.2
40–44	27,878	5,841,000	4.8
45+	1,711	35,460,000	0.5

Sources: United Nations, Department of Social and Economic Affairs, *Demographic Yearbook 1975* (St/ESA/Stat/ser.R/4) (New York, 1976), pp. 200–201. United Nations, Department of Social and Economic Affairs, *Demographic Yearbook 1976* (St/ESA/Stat/ser.R/4) (New York, 1977), pp. 274–75.

FIGURE 7–8

Age-Specific Fertility Rates (United States, 1974)

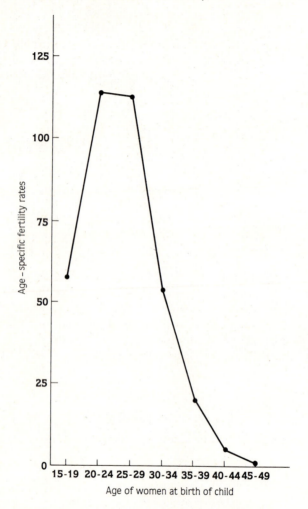

Source: Department of Economic and Social Affairs, *Demographic Yearbook 1976* (St/ESA/Stat/Ser. R4) (New York, 1977), p. 289.

group. Peak fertility is usually reached between 20 and 29. For women in their 30s fertility is normally moderate, while it tends to drop to very low levels in the 45–49 age group.

The typical curve showing the behavior of age-specific fertility first climbs sharply, then declines gently thereafter. It is an obvious example of a positively skewed distribution, with a long tail to the right of the peak (see pp. 26–27). The shape of the curve indicates that in most countries women are most reproductive in their 20s. Figure 7–8 shows the pattern of age-specific fertility in the United States for 1974.

As a rule the pattern is similar in more- and less-developed countries. However, the age-specific fertility rates in the developing nations are usually above those of the developed countries. Another difference is that in developing countries fertility continues to be relatively high among women over 35. Because women in the developed nations are more familiar with contraception, fertility drops sharply after age 30 or so. Hence in the low-income nations the drop in the age-specific fertility curve often occurs later and falls less sharply. These characteristics are evident in the Indonesian age-specific fertility rates shown in Figure 7–9.

FIGURE 7–9

Average Age-Specific Fertility Rates
(Java, Other Islands, and All Indonesia, 1966–70)

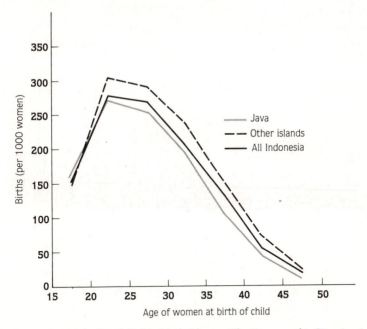

Source: G. McNicoll and Si Gde Made Mamas, *The Demographic Situation in Indonesia* (Honolulu: Papers of the East-West Population Institute, 1973), p. 21.

A Note on Summation

To understand what follows, a short digression is in order. As stated earlier, the letter X is often used to identify a variable. Variables such as fertility or income can have a different score (measured value) in any given frequency distribution. Suppose we study the fertility (measured here as children ever born) of four women of identical age: Nancy, Martha, Doreen, and Wendy. We can assign each of the women an identifying number: Nancy becomes 1, Martha 2, Doreen 3, and Wendy 4. Just as we designated the variable fertility by the letter X, we can represent the score value of each woman by an X to which her number is affixed as a subscript. Thus X_1 represents the fertility score for Nancy, X_2 the score for Martha, and so on. The score X_n represents the score of the last person, while the score X_i designates the score of the ith individual, where i may be any one of the identification numbers 1 to n. Therefore X_i may represent any of the observed scores and is specifically determined when i is replaced by the appropriate number to indicate a particular observation.

Suppose the score values for our four women are as follows:

Name	Number	Symbol	Number of Children Ever Born
Nancy	1	X_1	2
Martha	2	X_2	1
Doreen	3	X_3	4
Wendy	4	X_4	3

Imagine now that we want to total the measured values assumed by our variable (the scores). To symbolize this operation we use the Greek letter Σ (sigma). Sigma, as explained in Chapter 2, instructs us to add up some or all values of whatever variable is listed after the symbol. The symbol Σ (a sign of operation in the same sense as the sign $-$ or $\div$) is thus called the *summation operator*. In our case, $X_1 + X_2 + X_3 + X_4 = 10$ may be written

$$\sum_{i=1}^{4} X_i = 10$$

The Σ notation saves us from having to list all the scores.

The notations below and above sigma are called *limits of summation* and indicate the first and last values to be included in the desired sum. As shown above, $X_1 + X_2 + X_3 + X_4$ can be written as

$$\sum_{i=1}^{4} X_i$$

The limits of summation indicate that index variable i takes on the successive values 1, 2, 3, 4. We are to add the scores from the first through the fourth case. The symbol x_i represents the score for the generalized individual (here, mother). If we write

$$\sum_{i=1}^{n} X_i$$

we mean that we are to go from the first individual ($i = 1$) to the last ($i = n$);

$$\sum_{i=1}^{n} X_i$$

can also be written as $X_1 + X_2 + X_3 \cdots + X_n$. Often the index and limit notations are omitted. The use of the summation symbol without further notation implies that the summation is to be made for all values of the variable. That is, ΣX is shorthand for

$$\sum_{i=1}^{n} X_i$$

or the sum of all the values of a given collection ($i = 1, 2, 3, \ldots, n$).

The Total Fertility Rate

Once we find the age-specific fertility rates we can compute the *total fertility rate* (TFR), which is the *sum* of all age-specific fertility rates of women at each age within the range of 15–49 years *multiplied by* the interval (usually five years) into which the ages are grouped. Obviously, there are only seven five-year intervals between 15 and 49. The TFR, or *synthetic fertility index,* has the advantage of being unaffected by variations in age compostions among women in the childbearing period. Total fertility rates may be expressed either as rate per woman or rate per 1,000 women. If it is used as the rate per 1,000 women, the TFR reveals the average number of children a cohort of 1,000 women would have in their lifetime, if throughout their entire reproductive period they experienced the ASFR's occurring in a specific year. The TFR is computed as follows

$$n \sum_{i=1}^{i=7} \left(\frac{B_i}{W_i}\right) k$$

where n = width of the age intervals used (in our case, 5 years)
            Σ = summation
            i = age group (in our case, 7)
            B_i = number of births to women of age interval i in a year
            W_i = number of women in age interval i during the same year
            k = 1,000

TABLE 7–9

Age Specific Fertility Rates
per 1,000 Women (United States and Canada, 1975)

Age Group	United States	Canada
(1) 15–19	56.3	34.8
(2) 20–24	114.7	112.5
(3) 25–29	110.7	133.3
(4) 30–34	53.1	66.2
(5) 35–39	19.4	21.3
(6) 40–44	4.6	4.7
(7) 45–49	0.3	0.3
Sum	359.1	373.1
Total Fertility Rate *(Sum × 5)*	1,796	1,866

Sources: U.S. Bureau of the Census, *Statistical Abstract of the United States: 1979* (Washington: U.S. Government Printing Office, 1979), p. 61. Ministry of Industry, Trade and Commerce, *Canada Yearbook 1978–79* (Ottawa: Information Division, Statistics Canada, 1978), p. 170.

Female mortality is assumed to be zero until the end of the childbearing period. If the TFR is 2, the parents are close to replacing themselves, and the rate of increase should be near zero. Table 7–9 gives the age-specific fertility rates and the total fertility rates of the American and Canadian populations in 1975.

It is clear from Table 7–9 that peak childbearing occurs later in Canada than in the United States. The pattern of the synthetic fertility index in the Western nations has been more or less identical: the rate was low in the interwar period, rose to its highest level in the 1950s, and started to drop around 1960. Table 7–10 and Figure 7–10 show this clearly. Table 7–10 also reveals the differential fertility of the two main ethnic groups in the United States.

The TFR at which the population replaces itself in the United States is not 2.0 but 2.1 children per woman. A bit extra (0.1) is needed, because not all females survive to the end of the reproductive period. Also, slightly more than 50 percent of all babies born are males.

Rates of Reproduction

Total fertility rates cover all children born, both boys and girls. We can refine this fertility measure by making a separate calculation for girls—

TABLE 7–10

Total Fertility per 1,000 Women for
Ethnic Groups (United States) and Canada, Selected Years

| | United States | | | |
| | | | Black and | |
Year	Total	White	Other	Canada
1941	2,399	2,328	2,956	2,832
1951	3,269	3,157	4,091	3,503
1961	3,629	3,502	4,533	3,840
1971	2,275	2,168	2,933	2,187
1975	1,799	1,708	2,322	1,866
1977	1,826	1,735	2,343	n.d.

Sources: U.S. Bureau of the Census, *Statistical Abstract of the United States: 1979* (Washington: U.S. Government Printing Office, 1979), p. 61. U.S. Bureau of the Census, *Historical Statistics* (Washington: U.S. Government Printing Office, 1975), pp. 50–51. Ministry of Industry, Trade and Commerce, *Canada Yearbook 1978–79* (Ottawa: Information Division, Statistics Canada, 1978), p. 170.

FIGURE 7–10

Synthetic Fertility Index (1930–76)

Source: A. Haupt and T. T. Kane, *Population Handbook* (Washington: Population Reference Bureau, 1978), p. 20.

the *gross rate of reproduction* (GRR), which is defined as the average number of female children born to a woman who survives her reproductive period and to whom at each age the age-specific fertility rates prevailing during a specific year apply. The gross rate of reproduction can also be expressed per woman or per 1,000 women. The measurement of only female babies answers the question "How many daughters will a woman produce during her reproductive period if the age-specific fertility rates of one particular year continue indefinitely?" The GRR also has the advantage of summarizing fertility in one figure, while irregularities due to age composition are again eliminated. The computation of the GRR is similar to that of the TFR, except that only daughters are considered. Consequently, the GRR is usually about half the TFR. The formula for GRR is

$$ n \sum_{i=1}^{i=7} \left(\frac{B_i^f}{W_i} \right) k $$

where n = width of the age intervals used
Σ = summation
i = age group
B_i^f = number of *female* births to women of age interval i in a year
W_i = number of women in age interval i during the same year
k = 1,000

The gross reproduction rate, then, is a reproductivity formula: it shows the number of girl babies produced by a cohort of mothers before they pass out of the parental group. A simple way of finding the GRR is the following:

$$ \text{GRR} = \text{Total fertility rate} \times \frac{\text{Female births}}{\text{Total births}} = \text{TFR} \times \frac{B_f}{B_t} $$

The total fertility rate, in other words, is multiplied by the proportion of female births to total births.[4] In the United States, for instance, about 48.7 percent of all children born are females (of 1,000 births, 487 are girls). If we multiply the TFR for 1975—1.80 per woman—by 487, we obtain 877, which is the number of daughters replacing 1,000 women if age-specific fertility rates of that year continued forever. In other words, if a hypothetical cohort of 1,000 female American babies were exposed, throughout their entire reproductive period, to the age-specific fertility rates

---

[4] The proportion of females to the total population is expressed as Females/Total population. The proportion of females at birth is written Female births/Total births. It is common that male births exceed female births by a small margin.

TABLE 7–11

Gross Reproduction and Net Reproduction Rates (United States, 1940–74)

Year	GRR	NRR
1940	1.121	1.027
1950	1.505	1.435
1960	1.783	1.715
1970	1.207	1.168
1974	0.904	0.875

Sources: U.S. Bureau of the Census, *Historical Statistics* (Washington: U.S. Government Printing Office, 1975), p. 53. United Nations, Department of International Economic and Social Affairs, *Demographic Yearbook 1975* (New York: United Nations, 1976) (St/ESA/Stat/ser.R/4), p. 521.

of 1975, they would produce 877 daughters. An important assumption is that no female would die before age 50.

In the United States and some other Western nations, the GRR has fallen below 1. Yet the population of the United States keeps increasing, because the birth rate exceeds the death rate. But since the American population includes a large proportion of young adults—a consequence of the 1944–61 baby boom—the CBR is well above the CDR, even if 1,000 mothers at present age-specific fertility rates produce fewer than 1,000 daughters to replace themselves. Table 7–11 shows the GRR and the net reproduction rate (NRR) in the United States for 1940–74. NRR is discussed below. The long-term implication of the 1974 GRR would be that the American population is doomed to extinction. The developing countries obviously do not have to worry about this particular problem; rates ranging between 2,000 and 3,500 are still common for those areas.

The GRR does not consider the mortality to which the females of a hypothetical cohort would be subjected, but the *net reproduction rate* (*NRR*) takes it into account. The NRR is a measure of the number of daughters who will be born to a female who is now a baby and who, during her lifetime, will be subjected to both the age-specific fertility rates *and* the mortality rates of a given year. Without going into elaborate technical details, we can say that to obtain the NRR we must first multiply each individual age-specific fertility rate (for daughters only) by the probability of a female surviving to the present age of the parent. If, for instance, we consider the usual five-year intervals and take age group 15–19, we first compute the ASFR for that age group, counting girl infants only. We then multiply that number by the probability of a female living to that age, to find the "expected survivors of female birth per woman." We then add up these expected survivors age group by age group and

TABLE 7–12

Computation of Female Net Reproduction Rate (United States, 1973)

Age x	Age Specific Fertility Rates (Per Woman, Boys and Girls)	Age Specific Fertility Rates (Per Woman, Female Births Only) $(2) \times \dfrac{487}{1000}$	Probability of Daughters Surviving from Birth to Age x lx/Lo	Expected Survivors of Female Births (per Woman) $(3) \times (4)$
1	2	3	4	5
15–19*	0.0597	0.0291	0.97877	0.02848
20–24	0.1207	0.0589	0.97578	0.05747
25–29	0.1136	0.0553	0.97226	0.05377
30–34	0.0561	0.0273	0.96833	0.02643
35–39	0.022	0.0107	0.96301	0.01030
49–44	0.005	0.0026	0.95489	0.00248
45–49	0	0	0.94251	0
Total	0.3771	0.1830		0.1789
Multiply by 5	1.886	0.9195		0.8945

Total Fertility Rate (per 1,000 women) = 1,886
Gross Reproduction Rate (per 1,000 women) = 919,5 = 920
Net Reproduction Rate (per 1,000 women) = 894,5 = 895

* Births for women under 15 have been omitted.

multiply the result by 5. The result is the female NNR. The probability of survival from birth to the age of the mother (life-table survival rate) must be computed from the currently applicable life table *for females*—that is, the life table of the same year as that from which the fertility and mortality rates are selected. That life-table survival rate is defined as *lx/Lo, Lo* being the radix of the life table or 100,000. The values for *lx* can be found in column 3 of the abridged life table (see p. 81). An example taken from the year 1973 will clarify this (Table 7–12).

The net reproduction rate tends to fluctuate widely over time, because the age-specific fertility rates on which it is based also fluctuate. This may reflect such factors as genuine changes in fertility or sudden changes in the marriage rate. If that rate suddenly rises, as may happen after a war or an economic upturn, the age-specific fertility rates for women 15–19 and 20–24 will also tend to increase. A reproduction rate calculated from the ASFR's of such an unusually high fertility year would overstate reproductivity, because it assumes that these rates will continue indefinitely. The NNR, therefore, cannot be used to make forecasts about long-term population change. During the interwar period demographers did in fact use the NNR, then a relatively new tool, for such long-term prognoses. One might, for example, have argued in the 1930–35 period that with an NNR of 0.948, the American population was doomed to die out in the long run. During and after World War II, however, birth rates rose and the pessimistic forecasts of the 1930s were completely upset.

Figure 7–11 pictures the substantial fluctuations of reproduction rates in the Netherlands. The narrowing of the gap between the GRR and NNR due to a long-term decline in mortality is also evident. Because of relatively high mortality levels, however, substantial gaps prevail between the GRR and NRR of many developing nations. To cite just one example, for Pak-

FIGURE 7–11

Gross and Net Reproduction Rates (Netherlands, 1930–72)

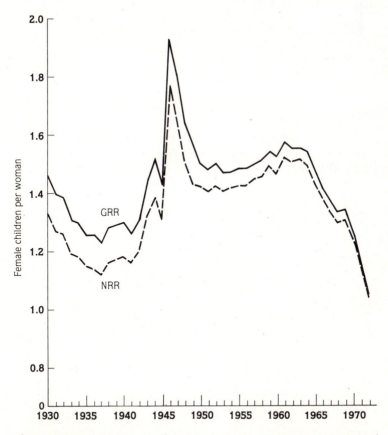

Source: Centraal Bureau voor de Statistiek, *75 Jaar Statistiek van Nederland* (S'Gravenhage: Staatsuitgeverij, 1975), p. 16.

istan in 1973 we find a GRR of 3,500, while the NRR amounted to only 2,530.

DIFFERENTIAL FERTILITY

Fertility varies not only with age but with race, class, religion, education, occupation, income, and residence. As shown in Table 7–10 (p. 123), for example, blacks in the United States have traditionally had a higher fertility level than whites. Some scholars prefer to use current fertility measures, others the cumulative fertility approach, to ascertain the fertility differences of subgroups in the population.

Information about group fertility differentials is important for at least two reasons. First, the study of the fertility of different population groups may provide valuable clues about the determinants of reproductive behavior in general. For instance, if fertility varies inversely with level of education, and if a growing proportion of the population completes high school and college, then overall fertility levels will fall. Second, fertility differentials bring about long-term changes in the population composition of a given geographical area. If the population of the developing countries reproduces faster than the population of the developed nations, the inhabitants of the developing countries will constitute a larger proportion of the world's population a few decades from now. If blacks in the United States have larger families than whites, their proportion of the total American population will eventually increase.

Race

Race is sometimes an important determinant of fertility levels. As mentioned earlier, nonwhites in the United States have traditionally had higher birth rates than whites. First-generation Mexicans in the United States tend to have about twice as many children as the average American-born family. In Canada the fertility of the Indians and Eskimos is well above the national average. Such differences in fertility between racial or ethnic groups are not attributable to innate differences in fecundity, which seems to vary little among racial groups. Socioeconomic and cultural influences are nowadays accepted as the most important determinants of fertility. The willingness to limit fertility depends largely on the motivation of individuals or couples.

Religion

The impact of religion on fertility behavior is twofold. First, a religion can favor large families if it emphasize such pronatalist injunctions as "increase and multiply." Second, a religion may indirectly encourage fertility if it opposes or discourages the use of contraceptives. The long-standing resistance of the Roman Catholic Church may delay the adoption of artificial birth control in some Latin American countries, just as it has already delayed its adoption in certain Western nations. In Western communities fertility differentials between members of the Roman Catholic Church and other Christian denominations have been common. In countries like the United States, Canada, Switzerland, and the Netherlands, where Protestants and Catholics live side by side, Catholics have had larger families than Protestants. During the last decades, however, the differential fertility between Catholics and Protestants has been diminishing rapidly, because the younger Catholics increasingly ignore the tenets of the Church regarding contraception. But for Catholics, commitment to Church doctrine and family size are still positively associated: the stronger the first, the greater the second.

Urban-Rural Residence

Fertility differentials between rural and urban areas have long attracted the attention of scientific observers. For cultural, psychological, and economic reasons, fertility has usually been found to be higher in rural than in urban communities. The grip of traditional social customs is stronger on the rural dweller than on the city resident. The relatively low level of education, combined with geographical isolation, tends to delay acceptance of the small-family ideal. Economic factors are also important: it is easier to raise a child in the countryside than in the city, while children on the farm may have value as producers and often contribute to the family income. And in a number of developing countries, parents still rely on their children, especially their sons, to take care of them when they are old or ill.

Occupation

A comparison of the fertility of different occupational groups in Western nations reveals an imperfect inverse relationship between fertility and occupational status. Generally speaking, farmers and agricultural workers are the most fertile, followed by unskilled and semiskilled workers in manufacturing. The least-fertile groups are the members of the lower-middle class and middle-middle class: clerical workers, shop assistants, semi-professional people, and owners or operators of small businesses. A possible explanation is that the tension between income and perceived needs is the greatest in these social groups. The stronger the desire to improve one's position in society, the lower one's fertility tends to be. In a number of Western nations the fertility of the upper middle class—professionals, managers, and proprietors—although relatively low, tends to be a little higher than that of the lower-middle and middle-middle classes.

Income

The relationship between income and fertility also tends to be inverse. Education, occupation, and income are of course related. Education and training usually open up occupational opportunities that, in turn, lead to high incomes. And in Canada and the United States—as in other Western countries—high income is associated with low fertility whether it is "income of husband" or "income of family."

The inverse correlation between income and fertility holds between nations, regions, and social classes. In the late 1970s the low-fertility, developed countries typically had per capita incomes ranging from $3,000 to $10,000 per year. A larger number of high-fertility developing nations (excluding the oil producers) had per capita incomes of well below $1,000. Some twenty-three nations had a per capita income of less than $200. In the United States, Massachusetts, a relatively rich state, has a lower fertility level than, Alabama, which is relatively poor. In northern Italy, which is relatively prosperous, fertility is low, whereas the south is more fertile but poorer. In Canada, the Atlantic provinces have generally low incomes and above-average fertility levels, but relatively rich Ontario is also relatively sterile.

As we have already noted, the low-fertility levels of the higher-income groups—the urban and the better educated—are related not to differential fecundity but to more effective family planning. The history of the Western nations has shown that family planning started among the educated, urban, upper-middle and middle classes. Family planning requires motivation, communication between spouses, constructive and open attitudes, an understanding of human anatomy, and the ability to obtain contraceptive devices. Among lower-income groups training and the habit of coping with such problems are likely to be less effective. Also, attitudes of passive resignation to fate are more frequent, with higher fertility often the result.

As in the case of mortality, fertility differentials are generally narrowing, perhaps because of such factors as the adoption of various social programs that distribute incomes more evenly among various social groups; changes in attitudes toward human sexuality and reproduction; and the spread of voluntary fertility control. However, this holds mainly for fertility differentials within developed countries.

TRENDS IN FERTILITY

Premodern Fertility

In traditional preindustrial communities, fertility was nearly always high. High fertility can be seen as a logical adjustment to the high uncontrolled death rate then prevailing. The mere survival of the community demanded constant replenishing of the population. Consequently, in many traditional societies the values and institutions tended, and often still tend, to favor early and universal marriage as well as large families. In most societies pressure was put on young people to marry early and procreate.

As noted earlier, in many premodern societies the extended family is a dominant feature. With three generations and two or more married couples living together in a single large household, the individual has obligations toward a much larger number of people than in the nuclear family. The extended family, an institution typical of the subsistence or near-subsistence economy, accommodates high-fertility patterns very well. Wide personal obligations act as a form of insurance for people who have few or no reserves. The parents enjoy all the prestige associated with numerous offspring, while other family members take on part of the burden of raising the children. The social or personal gains from having fewer offspring are limited, to say the least.

Some writers argue that the high fertility of premodern societies stemmed simply from the fact that within marriage avoiding children was hardly an option. Birth control was largely unknown or unthinkable.

Premodern European Fertility

Premodern northwestern Europe differed from many other traditional societies in that marriage often meant the establishment of a separate household, with the full burden of childrearing falling on the parents. The extended family as it existed (and still exists) in many parts of Africa and Asia was unknown. As a result, Western Europeans tended to marry comparatively late, while many avoided marriage altogether. Thus premodern Europe knew "marriage control," which is different from "birth control" but likewise reduces overall fertility levels. In addition, the guilds—of associations of artisans and merchants that arose after A.D. 1000—often restricted entry into a trade; those who were accepted had long periods of apprenticeship, sometimes many years. Marriage could not be contracted until the end of the training period, and, once the apprenticeship was over, the young people often worked as journeymen in other towns to acquire more experience.

The Roman Catholic Church's emphasis on celibacy and chastity, moreover, counteracted social and cultural pressures to get married and procreate. So in northwestern Europe a tradition of relatively late marriage prevailed for centuries, while many people never married at all.

In a society where birth control within marriage is not practiced, marriage patterns are a major determinant of fertility. Marriage control did help to avoid extreme densities of population but could not prevent temporary imbalances between numbers and resources. In premodern Europe, for long periods of time birth rates were above the death rates, with a modest rate of increase the result. In preindustrial England the rate of increase stood at perhaps 0.4 percent toward the end of the seventeenth century. Numbers grew, yet beyond a certain point the environment resisted such growth. Time and again the death rate would rise, because of bad harvests, an epidemic, or the like. More children and adults would die directly or indirectly from hunger, malnutrition, or disease. Fewer women survived their productive years, and more marriages were interrupted by death. Potential marriage partners would defer marriage, and thereby the births these marriages could have produced. Still others would avoid marriage altogether. The incidence of induced abortion and child neglect probably also rose.

Over time, however, the relationship between food and population would improve again and per capita food supplies would increase, partly because disaster had eliminated a portion of the population, and partly because fertility had been reduced for a number of years. Improving agricultural techniques would then ensure an expanding food basis, and the death rates would fall again. Deferred marriages would now be contracted and the mean age of marriage might move downward, in part because those young people who survived the crises could succeed earlier to the agricultural holding, enterprise, or workshop belonging to the family. Because of the demographic depletion during the crisis, employment opportunities and wages would be favorable. Thus the damage done by food scarcity, epidemics, or war would be repaired in time, and population would continue its upward course until the next turn of the tide.

A Simplified Model of Premodern Fertility

The foregoing description of preindustrial fertility can be translated into a simple model which, of course, does not do justice to the complexity of premodern fertility. For instance, fluctuations in mortality have often been produced by events totally unrelated to population density: volcanic eruptions, earthquakes, epidemics, harvest failures, and so on. Yet if we concentrate on the long-term interplay of fertility and mortality in the pre-modern society, Figure 7–12 is a useful point of departure (Figures 7–13 and 7–14 continue the model).

FIGURE 7–12

Fertility and Mortality in a Premodern Community

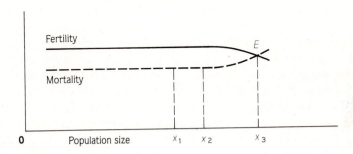

FIGURE 7–13

Technological Progress and Maximum Population

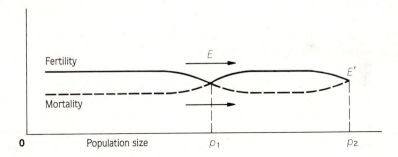

FIGURE 7–14

Fertility and Mortality with Nuptiality Control

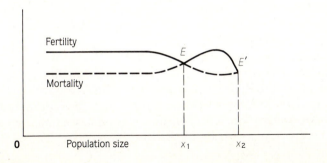

In this hypothetical preindustrial community, with its agricultural economy, there is no change in fertility and mortality as long as the population remains at less than x_2. At x_1, for instance, there is no real pressure of numbers on the environment: food supplies are sufficient. When the population is larger than x_2, however, it begins to approach the carrying capacity of the environment. Density-dependent controls begin to exert an influence, because the population comes closer to the ceiling set by available food supplies. Mortality rises and fertility falls as disease and malnutrition take an increasing toll and as more couples are separated by death. Women may also carry fewer babies to term. Furthermore, new social customs may emerge that affect fertility. For example, more marriages may be deferred and more people remain single permanently. Eventually, fertility and mortality reach equilibrium at E, x_3 being the *maximum population*—the largest number of people the environment can support.

Let us now assume that a technological advance occurs that can alter the pattern. Historically, such changes have included the introduction of the potato in Europe and the development of better storage facilities, new drainage techniques, and improved fertilizers. Now the productivity of the land is enhanced, the food base is enlarged, and health conditions improve. Mortality drops, and fertility may increase because fewer people remain single, people marry earlier, and fewer couples are separated by death. The fertility and mortality schedules probably revert to the levels displayed at x_1 in Figure 7–12.

When the opportunities afforded by the improved state of technology are exhausted, however, the pressure on the resource base increases again, the density-dependent controls reassert themselves, mortality increases, fertility drops, and a new equilibrium with a larger population (p_2) is attained; this equilibrium is represented by E', Figure 7–13. In a premodern population that cannot control mortality and does not control fertility, people inevitably multiply until the maximum population is reached. Innovations may enlarge the stream of food products, but no long-term per capita improvement is possible because the productivity gains are absorbed by new numbers.

If, however, at least a considerable proportion of the population reacts to the innovation by late marriage or lifetime celibacy, the increase in agricultural output will not be entirely absorbed by demographic expansion. An enduring rise in the standard of living now becomes possible. Figure 7–14 shows the evolution of a new fertility schedule permitting a higher living standard. Because E' lies below E, a gain in net social welfare has been achieved.

Classical economists such as Adam Smith (1723–90), Thomas Robert Malthus (1766–1834), and David Ricardo (1772–1823) envisaged a slow but steady flow of improvements in technology, prompting increases in national production. Such increments in production, by increasing the prosperity of the wage-earning class, could easily spur people to marry early and enable more of their children to be well cared for and hence to survive. Adam Smith believed that if the rate of technological change were sufficiently high, production might grow faster than numbers, bringing a semipermanent improvement in living standards. As he saw it, a growing population can lead to an expanding market, which brings an improved division of labor—that is, specialization by skills and occupations, which in turn enhances technological innovation and output. Ricardo argued that if the Corn Laws (high tariffs on foreign grain) could be abolished in the United Kingdom, the real standard of living of the wage earners would be temporarily improved. He hoped that during this spell of prosperity wage earners would acquire such a taste for comforts and conveniences that they would come to regard them as a necessity. In their determination to preserve this better-than-bare-subsistence standard of living they might, Ricardo suggested, acquire the habit of curbing their own fertility by celibacy or postponed marriage. During certain phases of Western history, economic progress did in fact outpace demographic expansion, even though these European nations did not yet control fertility systematically.

A final possibility is that of a premodern population in, say, an African country that experiences no technological innovation and no improvements in productivity, but suddenly imports death-control techniques from other nations. We will assume that the country has some reserves of unused land that are inferior in fertility or location, so that the absolute maximum population has not been attained. When the new death-control technology is introduced, mortality drops, fertility may rise, and numbers increase. The population will move closer to its limit, as the pressure on the resource base increases. As a result there will be a shift in the *causes* of death. Fewer people may die of infectious and bacterial diseases, but more will die of hunger and malnutrition. Overburdened parents may also abandon or neglect their children, such neglect amounting to disguised infanticide. No lasting improvement in social welfare is possible.

The Industrial Revolution and Its Aftermath

Toward the end of the eighteenth century, some countries, including England, witnessed an increase in the rate of population growth; in England the rate peaked between 1780 and 1820. Several factors explain the rise. The agricultural revolution of the eighteenth century improved the quality and quantity of the foods available, while better transportation facilities (canals, roads, etc.) eliminated local food shortages. Mortality dropped somewhat because more and better hospitals were built, while at the same time no major epidemic ravaged Europe. And the Industrial Revolution, which occurred in this period, greatly boosted the demand for labor, both adult and child, in domestic as well as factory industry. The prevalence of child labor reduced the cost of raising children, while employed women became more attractive marriage partners. The mean age of marriage fell and marital fertility increased. Also, rural-urban migration, and the growing accumulation of the population in cities, may have weakened the prudential restraints practiced in the countryside.

Especially after 1850 the downward trend in mortality became firmly established in the Western world. Smallpox was increasingly controlled by vaccination, midwifery improved, more drugs became available, and medical science greatly advanced. Infectious diseases were curbed more easily. Public health also made rapid strides. Water supplies improved in quality; sanitary sewage and garbage disposal became more common; and an understanding of personal hygiene took hold. Food supplies also grew more abundant. The development of the Western Hemisphere added a granary of enormous size and potential to existing food sources; perfected transportation, especially by rail and steamship, quickly brought these rich harvests to other parts of the world, mainly Europe.

While mortality dropped steadily, fertility remained relatively high, at least until the late 1870s. Although this period coincides with the discovery and spread of improved contraceptives (vaginal suppositories and condoms), the decline in fertility was certainly not the result of the development of these devices. Yet effective contraceptive techniques break the link between nuptiality and fertility, since fertility can be reduced without postponement or avoidance of marriage. In fact, after the 1870s married couples increasingly adopted the small-family ideal and consciously limited the number of children they had. Many hypotheses have been offered as to why this occurred. The following explanations are accepted by most population specialists.

First, toward the end of the nineteenth century infant and child mortality had definitely begun to decline. Earlier, a large proportion of all children born never lived long enough to become an economic burden on their parents. With higher survival rates, however, parents had to pay serious attention to the number of children they could support until adolescence. Because more children survived, fewer births were required to produce a given number of surviving children. A second reason for the drop in fertility was that by the end of the nineteenth century child labor in Europe had been abolished and primary education had become compulsory; youngsters therefore were no longer able to contribute to the family income. Furthermore, at that time a growing proportion of the population in England and other Northwestern European countries had become urbanized. Raising children in an urban environment involves relatively high material and psychological costs. The supervision of children is more difficult in the city than on the farm, city children may need more clothing, and so on. These increased costs encouraged smaller families.

The process of modernization, industrialization, and urbanization, creates new occupations and opportunities to move up the social ladder. To take advantage of the possibilities for social advancement often requires an investment, of both time and money, in training or retraining. And sometimes advancement entails migration, if the best opportunities are in another city, region, and so on. Clearly, a large family, because it reduces mobility while making less time available for career-oriented activities, can conflict with the desire to advance.

The emancipation and improved education that accompanied socioeconomic progress, and the widening range of occupations available to them, caused women to question the traditional assumption that marriage and motherhood were the only roles open to them. During and after World War I married women began to join the labor force in large numbers. Since children tie the mother to the home, the increased involvement of women in outside activities tended to reduce the family size desired.

Modernization and industrialization have yet another impact on fertility in that they further the breakdown of traditional family dependence. Many of the functions of the family are taken over by other social institutions. In premodern societies parents often rely on children for financial help in old age: children are a kind of investment requiring initial outlays but yielding a return afterward, so enough of them must be brought into the world to secure at least a few surviving sons. But in the more developed society the family loses the mutual assistance function. Collective private programs and state-controlled welfare systems provide for the aged, and it becomes customary not to turn to one's children for economic help.

Industrialization and socioeconomic progress tend to be accompanied by a spirit of rationalism that replaces custom and tradition, which have nearly always been pronatalist in their implications (see p. 129). The decline of tradition and religion-bound attitudes and values, and the adoption of more rational attitudes in general, prompt a decrease in desired family size.

The greater availability of effective, low-cost contraceptives is a last factor in the decline in fertility to be mentioned. Toward the end of the nineteenth century, better contraceptives became available, while contraceptive information circulated more widely. In 1880 Walter John Rendall, a London pharmacist, experimented successfully with a vaginal suppository containing quinine. The rubber condom was also improved, and higher literacy levels allowed more people to learn about existing contraceptive technology.

France was the first country to experience a decline in fertility. Throughout the second half of the nineteenth century the other Northwestern European nations, the United States, and Canada followed.

Present-Day Fertility in the West

The long-term decline in fertility in the Western world continued unchecked until World War II. In the 1930s birth rates had already reached the low levels to be expected in a modern environment. Rates of reproduction were close to unity and had fallen below that level in some nations, including the United States. A temporary reversal of this long-term trend—the baby boom that started in the 1940s—was a somewhat abnormal phenomenon that petered out in the 1960s. The baby boom has been attributed to a number of causes, of which only a few will be mentioned here.

Because of the economic crisis of the 1930s, a number of couples had postponed either marriage or childbearing. With improved employment opportunities in the 1940s, more marriages took place and some of the deferred births occurred. Moreover, the mean age at first marriage and the mean age at childbearing both declined, while the number of desired children definitely rose. Childlessness among married couples declined considerably. Contraception was still far from perfect, while husband-wife communication on sexual and marital matters sometimes left much to be desired. With a lower mean age at marriage, exposure to both wanted and unwanted pregnancies was obviously lengthened, while continuous medical progress ensured regular improvements in survival.

The "baby bust" of declining fertility started in the early 1960s, by which time the baby boom had obviously run its course. Fertility was reacting to a complex set of social changes. First, contraception has become near-perfect with the introduction of the pill, whose use became widely accepted, while public discussion of sex and family-related matters became more open. Second, a revolution had been taking place with regard to women's position in society. More-equal access to education has opened up opportunities for employment. Increasingly attractive alternatives to housekeeping and motherhood (or, at least, early motherhood) have become available. Growing numbers of wives now stay in the workforce, and more mothers of children under six return to it. In 1960, 35 percent of all wives in the United States were in the labor force; this figure had risen to 44 percent by 1975. Even college enrollment of married women has increased. Perhaps as a consequence of increased opportunities for education and employment, women are again marrying later. Although a later marriage need not prevent a couple from having two or more children, it prolongs the period in which women are involved in nonparental career activities to which they may develop a sense of commitment and involvement.

The divorce rate is also on the rise again. Just under 40 percent of all first marriages end in divorce. Although many divorced people remarry, the remarriage rate has fallen since about 1970. A new pattern seems to be emerging, with a growing proportion of divorced men and women not remarrying. Partly because of this and partly because of the relaxation of social pressures against such behavior, there is now a strong increase in the number of informal unions. In the United States as in other Western nations the number of unmarried couples living together is on the rise. Cohabitation may of course simply be a prelude to marriage, but for a considerable number of people it seems to become a more or less permanent arrangement. Because of the greater instability of cohabitation, and because out-of-wedlock births are still not widely accepted, "living together" greatly reduces fertility.

Western Fertility in the Future

What the future will bring in terms of fertility is difficult to say. Those social scientists who feel that present trends are a response to profound social changes tend to extrapolate them into the future and don't foresee much change in current trends. Still others feel that the future will be more like the past and that important changes are in the making.

One such social scientist is Richard A. Easterlin, professor of economics of the University of Pennsylvania. Easterlin's hypothesis is that many of the things we experience are cohort-specific. (Cohorts are groups of individuals who share the same year or period of birth.) The cohorts born during the 1930s were smaller than those born in previous decades. The 1930s cohorts came of age after World War II, when the economy was growing rapidly and the demand for labor strong. As the cohort was relatively thin, young adults were scarce and incomes rose. This made the "good times" cohorts feel that they could afford to marry early and have large families. A fertility holiday followed and the baby boom was born. But for the baby boom cohorts the situation was exactly the reverse. Their large numbers increased the competition in the labor market once they came of age. In the ten years prior to 1964, the labor force was increasing by about 880,000 per year. When the baby boom cohorts began to enter the job market (1964–74), the annual net growth of the labor force nearly doubled, to about 1,740,000 per year. Job competition became severe and unemployment rose. The young reacted by postponing marriage and reducing fertility. The rising divorce (and suicide) rates can be interpreted as signs of stress. Soaring housing costs further inhibited family formation. This negative relationship between cohort size and fertility leads to the prediction that fertility may rise again when the baby bust cohorts enter the job market in the 1980s. They will discover that competition is no longer so fierce; the economic postion (of young males especially) will have improved, and unemployment rates will be lower. The advantages that the baby bust cohorts will enjoy by virtue of their small numbers will translate into earlier marriage, higher fertility, and a lower divorce rate. Such is

Easterlin's theory. It is provocative and intriguing, but not widely accepted as a valid model to explain the future.

Social demographers like Charles Westoff, Norman Ryder, and Dennis Wrong criticize the concept of a cyclical movement inherent in the Easterlin model. They find it especially difficult to believe that those born after the baby boom will have more children because of the competitive advantage their small number will enable them to enjoy. Westoff, for instance, regards the baby bust of the 1960s as a resumption of the long-term downtrend in fertility prevalent in the United States and other industrial nations since about 1870. The rural-urban transition in those countries has been accompanied by basic social changes, all conducive to lower fertility.

Particularly since the 1960s, Easterlin's critics point out, young people have postponed marriage until their middle or late 20s. This trend could be the beginning of a radical change in traditional family patterns. Also, women's attitudes toward work, marriage, and childbearing have altered dramatically. Women are more educated and eager to devote more years of their life to a career. Finally, improvements in contraceptive techniques have occurred, and information on the subject is now widely available. Unplanned births are becoming a rarity in the United States. In view of all this, the three social demographers mentioned above are unable to anticipate changes reversing the low fertility trends of the present.

Westoff also argues that female participation in the workforce, as explained by the Easterlin model, is somewhat unrealistic. This model views female participation as being adaptive and compensatory: when the economic conditions of young male adults deteriorate, women enter the labor force and have fewer children, but if such conditions improve, the women will return to the home and produce more children. In Westoff's opinion, this theory ignores fundamental modifications in the status and expectations of women.

Fertility in the Developing Countries

The low-income countries have experienced an entirely different demographic pattern. Especially since the 1940s, mortality has dropped sharply because public health improvements and scientific contributions like chemotherapy have been transmitted from the rich to the poor countries. But fertility, buttressed by tradition, culture, religion, and public opinion, has remained high. Modern death-control techniques are often superimposed on traditional peasant societies in which modernization has hardly started and significant declines in fertility are not to be expected soon.

Yet in a number of less developed countries, such as the People's Republic of China, Indonesia, and Mexico, fertility rates have dipped in recent years. The turning point was apparently between 1970 and 1975. Although fertility levels in these nations are still high, the question arises whether or not a long-term fertility decline has started. Family planning efforts may finally be showing some results, while socioeconomic development itself is known to lessen fertility.

THE THEORY OF THE DEMOGRAPHIC TRANSITION

The foregoing historical considerations can be schematically presented by the so-called demographic transition model of which Figure 7.15 is a stylized example. The *demographic transition* (DT) refers to the changeover from the high birth-and-death-rate equilibrium of premodern societies to the low birth-and-death-rate equilibrium of industrialized and urbanized societies. The pioneer in transition theory was the French demographer A. Landry, who in his book *La Révolution démographique* gave an account of three different demographic regimes, or systems, corresponding to different stages of socioeconomic evolution.[5]

In the first demographic regime, corresponding to premodern, traditionalist society, neither fertility nor mortality are controlled. Economic considerations do not interfere, directly or indirectly, with fertility, which in most classes remains uncontrolled. Economic factors do, however, affect mortality, which in turn acts upon population size. As population continues to grow, the standard of living falls and mortality rises to the point at which it equals fertility. As we saw earlier (Figure 7–12), population growth stops at this point.

When basic social, economic, and political transformations begin to take place, a new system emerges. The new demographic regime is characterized by the determination to maintain a certain standard of living. Through late marriage and celibacy, families attempt to prevent their living standard from falling below what they think appropriate to their class. Mortality no longer controls the numbers; nuptiality becomes the regulator.

The contemporary period, with its advanced technology and sharp increases in agricultural and industrial productivity, represents yet another demographic system. Mortality has fallen to low levels and fertility has dropped as well. People in all classes voluntarily limit the size of their families, and the rate of reproduction falls to a level very close to replacement or even below it. People are determined not just to maintain a given

[5] A. Landry, *La Révolution démographique* (Paris: Sirey, 1934), pp. 3–55. See also A. Landry, *Traité de démographie* (Paris: Payot, 1945), pp. 538–47.

standard of living but to raise it. Parents restrict the number of children they have, in order to prevent fragmentation of their land; to be able to send their children to good schools and universities; to allow mothers to continue their own careers; to be able to buy more durable goods and to travel; and so forth. Economic considerations, in other words, have become predominant. Landry calls this state of things a "revolution." The old equilibrium between mortality and fertility has been upset and replaced by a situation of great uncertainty. Numbers themselves are no longer checked by mortality or nuptiality but by fertility—an unstable element.

In more modern versions of this theory, between three and five stages are distinguished (Figure 7–15). Stage 1 corresponds to a society in which both birth and death rates are out of control. Both vital rates are in the 30–50‰ range, but mortality fluctuates more than fertility. The birth rate is usually a little above the death rate. Life expectancy at birth is perhaps as low as 25, and even lower during famines and epidemics.

The second stage might be called the "early expanding interval." Death rates begin to drop, but birth rates remain high and may even rise. Improved health care and nutrition make it more likely that women will survive their reproductive years, that their physical capacity to bear children will be increased, and that they will be able to carry more babies to term.

FIGURE 7–15

The Demographic Transition Model in Four Stages

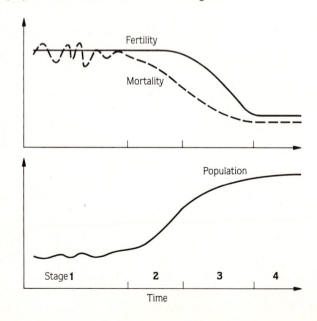

Such conditions make for slightly higher fertility levels. Life expectancy may rise to about 50 years.

The third stage might be called the "late expanding phase." The death rate keeps declining but the birth rate starts dropping as well. This is no longer because of the postponement or avoidance of marriage but because of a fall in marital fertility. Couples plan for smaller families. At the same time, advances in medicine and public health produce a continuous drop in mortality levels. Life expectancy at birth, at least in the Western European experience, keeps rising steadily.

The fourth interval has been termed "low quasi-stationary phase." The death rate falls gradually until it reaches about 8–12‰. The birth rates also decline to between 15 and 20 per thousand. Life expectancy at birth rises to approximately 70 years. Fluctuations in fertility are wider than in mortality. The baby boom in the West occurred during this phase.

In the fifth phase, birth and death rates are about equal, with zero population growth resulting. In many Western nations the death rate is bound to rise somewhat, perhaps to 12–13.5‰, because of the growing proportion of older, high-mortality-risk people in their populations.[6] Life

FIGURE 7–16

Crude Birth and Death Rates (Belgium 1900–1977)[7]

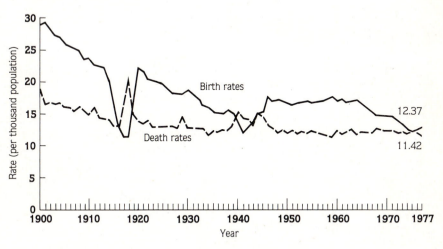

Source: Ministère des Affaires Economiques, *Annuaire Statistique de la Belgique* 98 (Brussels: Institut National de Statistique, 1978), p. 50.

[6]Chapter 11 will explain the aging process of population in greater detail.

[7]The transition model for Belgium shows that this country suffered heavily from both world wars. The influenza epidemic of 1918 produced a sharp upturn of the death rate.

FIGURE 7–17

Trends in Vital Rates (Mexico, 1940–76)

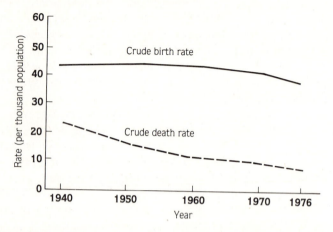

Source: *Mexico, Summary Report* (Columbia, Md.: Westinghouse Health Systems, October 1978), p. 1.

expectancy at birth may rise to approximately 76–77 years. As Figure 7–16 shows, Belgium has come close to zero population growth with both vital rates near 12‰. Several other European nations, including Austria and Germany, are actually experiencing negative population growth. Most economically advanced nations are either in stage 4 or about to enter stage 5.

About two-thirds of the world's population has not yet gone through the transition, and so is experiencing falling death rates in combination with high fertility levels. As a result, the population of the developing countries will increase from about 3.5 billion in 1970 to approximately 6 billion in the year 2000. The only sign of hope is that some of the latecomers in the transitional process—such as Germany, Italy, certain Eastern European countries, and Japan—have moved more rapidly through the demographic transition than countries like France and England, which began the process earlier. There is therefore some hope (but no certainty) that the developing countries will also experience an accelerated transition. As mentioned earlier, some nations like Mexico are experiencing what is hoped will be the start of a long-term fertility transition. This trend can be seen in Figure 7–17.

CONCEPTS FOR REVIEW

Nuptiality
Crude marriage rate
Marriage squeeze
Divorce rate
Child-women ratio
Crude birth rate
Crude rate of natural increase
Rate of Population growth

Children ever born
General fertility rate
Age-specific fertility rate
Total fertility rate
Gross rate of reproduction
Net reproduction rate
Differential fertility
Premodern fertility
Maximum population
Demographic transition

QUESTIONS FOR DISCUSSION

1. Discuss some of the factors which kept the crude marriage rates low in Western European nations.
2. In Western nations such as the United States and Canada there seems to be a link between employment conditions and the crude marriage rate. Discuss the nature of that relationship.
3. Explain why young women born during 1946–61 tend to marry later than their mothers.
4. In less developed countries the drop of the age-specific fertility curve sets in later and falls less sharply than in the wealthier, more-developed nations. Why is this the case?
5. "A gross rate of reproduction of less than 1, meaning that the population is not reproducing itself, can coexist with a positive crude rate of natural increase which indicates that the population is growing." Comment and evaluate.
6. How will the composition of the American population be affected, if for any length of time blacks have higher fertility levels than whites? Assume "other things equal" in your discussion.
7. Explain why, in the past, most societies have evolved institutions and patterns of behavior encouraging high fertility levels.
8. Explain how in a premodern, less developed country the introduction of Western death control technology will merely produce a shift in the causes of death, but not a real reduction in mortality.
9. "During the Industrial Revolution fertility at first stayed high but dropped toward the end of the nineteenth century." Comment and evaluate.
10. Explain the reasons for the 1944–60 baby boom. Do you think another baby boom is possible in the near future? Why or why not?
11. Discuss the demographic transition. Explain at least four different stages.

BIBLIOGRAPHY

Bogue, D. J. and A. O. Tsui. *Declining World Fertility: Trends, Causes, Implications.* Washington: Population Reference Bureau, 1978.

Coale, A. J. "The History of the Human Population." In *The Human Population.* A Scientific American Book. San Francisco: W. H. Freeman, 1974.

Charbonneau, H. *La Population du Québec.* Montreal: Editions Boreal Express, 1973.

Cohen, W. J., and C. F. Westoff. *Demographic Dynamics in America.* New York: Free Press, 1977.

Easterlin, R. A. *Birth and Fortune.* New York: Basic Books, 1980.

Habakkuk, H. J. *Population Growth and Economic Development since 1750.* Bath: Pitman Press, 1972.

Kirk, D. "A New Demographic Transition?" In *Rapid Population Growth,* edited by Study Committee of the Office of the Foreign Secretary, National Academy of Sciences. Baltimore: Johns Hopkins University Press, 1971.

Landry, A. *La Révolution demographique.* Paris: Sirey, 1934.

———. *Traité de démographie.* Paris: Payot, 1945.

Palmore, J. A. *Measuring Fertility and Natural Increase: A Self-Teaching Guide to Elementary Measures.* Honolulu: East-West Population Institute, 1975.

Ryder, N. B. "The Character of Modern Fertility." In *Readings in Population,* edited by W. Petersen. New York: Macmillan, 1972.

Stolnitz, G. J. "The Demographic Transition: From High to Low Birth Rates and Death Rates." In *The Vital Revolution,* edited by R. Freedman. New York: Anchor Books, 1964.

van de Walle, E., and J. Knodel. *Europe's Fertility Transition: New Evidence and Lessons for Today's Developing World.* Washington: Population Reference Bureau, 1980.

Westoff, C. F. "Marriages and Fertility in the Developed Countries." *Scientific American* (December 1978).

Wrigley, E. A. *Population and History.* New York: McGraw-Hill, 1969.

APPENDIX: FERTILITY INHIBITION, OR BIRTH CONTROL

By *fertility inhibition* we mean the prevention of the birth of children who are not wanted. A variety of contraceptive methods can prevent conception, or the union of the male sperm and the female egg. If contraception fails, abortion remains the only means of terminating pregnancy.

Limitation of family size comes about only when couples clearly perceive the advantages of a small family over a large one. At the same time they must have available contraceptive information and safe, inexpensive contraceptive devices. Yet in some parts of Europe birth prevention has been achieved through a method that requires no device—coitus interruptus.

Until the nineteenth century the reproductive process was not well understood. A Dutch biologist and microscopist, Anthony van Leeuwenhoek (1632–1723), discovered the male reproductive cells (sperm). He had earlier discovered methods of grinding single lenses to obtain greater magnification. This enabled him to see "little animals" in seminal fluid. But it was the English physician Martin Barry (1802–55) who in the 1840s discovered that one sperm must penetrate the female egg in order to create new life.

Coitus Interruptus

This method, which consists of withdrawing the stimulated penis prior to ejaculation, is probably the oldest known birth control technique. The Old Testament refers to it, and it has been used with some success in European cultures. This method, of course, requires much disipline on the part of the man. The failure rate is high—probably about 18 pregnancies per hundred women per year.[1]

Post-Coital Douching

The practice of douching after intercourse is at least 2,000 years old. The early Egyptians and Indians apparently used it. Charles Knowlton (1800–50), an early American writer on birth control, discussed this method

---

[1] The failure rate is computed as follows

$$\frac{\text{Annual pregnancies of women using method } x \text{ in a given year}}{\text{Women exposed to method } x \text{ during the same year}} \times 100$$

With no contraception whatever, the pregnancy rate is about 85. With any kind of contraceptive effort, the rate will fall below 40.

in his work *The Fruits of Philosophy* (1832). In the 1930s this method was still widely practiced in Western nations, but its use declined thereafter.

Spermicidal Agents

Spermicidal agents are substances introduced into the vagina before intercourse to immobilize or neutralize the sperm on contact. They too have been in use for a long time, though it has sometimes been thought that they should be introduced after, instead of before, intercourse.

As early as 1850 B.C., Egyptian women were advised to use plugs made of a mixture of crocodile dung and a pastelike substance such as honey. Vaginal suppositories have been made in many areas from local plants like cabbage, crushed herbs, and pulp of figs. In 1880 Walter John Rendell, a London pharmacist, produced the first vaginal suppository that was reasonably safe. It was made from quinine and cocoa butter and soon enjoyed a wide reputation. Since about 1935 an increasing variety of spermicidal agents (creams, jellies, and foams) has been developed.

Barrier Contraceptives for Women

A barrier contraceptive for women prevents fertilization by blocking the cervix so that sperm cannot reach it. The ancient Hebrews used the sponge method, which apparently became popular in France in the eighteenth century and was in use as late as the 1930s. The method is cheap and the sponge can be removed by a thread attached to it.

A German physician named Wilhelm Mensinga improved and popularized the rubber cap. In the United States prior to the advent of the pill, the diaphragm combined with spermicidal jelly or cream was the most widely used contraceptive method. Properly fitted by a physician, the diaphragm provides a mechanical barrier over the cervix, while jelly provides a chemical barrier to migrating sperm. The diaphragm has to be inserted prior to sexual activity and must be left in place for at least six hours after intercourse.

Condom

The condom is worn by the male to prevent sperm from entering the vagina. When used with care and consistency, it offers a high level of protection against conception. It can be used by the man as the need arises, and has the additional advantage of providing protection against venereal disease.

The condom too has a long history. Dr. Condom, physician at the court of Charles II (1660–1685), discovered that the intestines of lambs, if suitably processed, provided an appropriate material for sheaths, which could then be secured at the open end with a ribbon. Worried about his ever-growing number of children, Charles II had asked his doctor for advice in the matter, or so the story goes. Mass production of the condom, however, had to await the development of vulcanized rubber in the nineteenth century.

Oral Contraceptives

Oral Contraceptives are also as old as recorded history. Everything under the sun has been swallowed to prevent pregnancy, including tea made from crushed willow leaves, dead bees, and spider's eggs. In the 1950s Dr. Gregory Pincus, starting from the idea that ovulation can be inhibited by orally ingested estrogens (female hormones), demonstrated that pills containing a combination of estrogen and progesterone are an effective and relatively safe means of birth control. A natural precedent exists for this type of contraception since during pregnancy the combined high levels of estrogen and progesterone prevent ovulation. The pill creates a condition similar to pregnancy and thus stops ovulation. A large variety of oral contraceptives are on the market. They either suppress ovulation, or alter the cervical mucus to make it hostile to sperm. The pill is the most widely used birth control method in the United States.

Intrauterine Devices

Intrauterine devices (IUD's) reduce chances of fertilization or otherwise prevent maturation of the fertilized ovum. For many centuries Arab camel drivers knew the trick of inserting small pebbles into their animal's uteri to prevent pregnancy during the long journey through the desert. Earlier in this century medical researchers extended the practice to women but, instead of pebbles, they used silver rings and devices of silk. In 1928 Dr. Ernest Grafenberg, a German physician, experimented successfully with an intrauterine ring made of silkworm gut and later of silver wire. Prior to the advent of antibiotics, which permit effective treatment of infections, the method had limited popularity, but since the 1960s it has been widely used. The IUD somehow alters the characteristics of sperm cells, so that they loose their ability to fertilize the egg. Today, IUD's are produced in a great variety of shapes. They are mostly made of flexible plastics, noninjurious to body tissues.

Sterilization

Permanent contraception, or sterilization, can be achieved by surgical methods. Female sterilization involves surgical ligation of the fallopian tubes. Tying the fallopian tubes prevents the eggs from reaching the uterus. The contraceptive effect is immediate upon recovery from surgery.

Male sterilization includes surgical tying of the vas deferens and/or the removal of a small portion of it. The vas deferens is the canal along which the sperm travels from the testicles to the penis. Semen is still produced, but it does not contain any sperm. A great deal of research is being done on *reversible* methods of male sterilization. The main idea is to plug the spermatic duct, instead of cutting and tying it; valves, clips, and silicone plugs could be used. Dr. Sherman J. Silber of California has been successful in developing certain surgical techniques which are, however, still in an experimental stage.

The Rhythm Method

The rhythm method, the temporary abstinence from sexual relations during the fertile period, is based upon the knowledge that ovulation takes place about twelve to sixteen days prior to the next menses. When the menstrual cycle lasts twenty-eight days, the first day of the fertile period would be day 10 and the last would be day 17. Sperm survival is estimated at two days, while the ovum may last twenty-four hours after ovulation, which adds three days (two before and one after). The method is very unreliable, however, because many women experience variations in their menstrual pattern. The failure rate is high: about twenty-four pregancies per 100 women per year in the United States.

Abortion

Induced abortion is not actually a contraceptive method, since it involves terminating the embryo's existence once fertilization has taken place. Abortion has played a significant part in the decline of birth rates in industrialized, urbanized societies. Ideally, this procedure should be used only if conventional contraception fails rather than as a substitute for contraception.

Table A–1

Patterns of Contraceptive Use Among Married Couples,
Wife 15–44 Years of Age (United States, 1976)[2]

Contraceptive Method	Percentage Distribution of Users
Pill	22.5
Condom	7.3
IUD	6.3
Rhythm	3.4
Foam	3.0
Diaphragm	2.9
Withdrawal	2.0
Douche, other	1.7

[2]U.S. Department of Health and Human Services, *Contraceptive Utilization United States 1976* (Hyattsville: March 1981), p. 17.

Who Uses What?

It appears that in the United States as well as in most other Western nations the pill, the condom, and the IUD are the most widely used non-surgical methods of contraception. Noteworthy is also the growing popularity of sterilization as a contraceptive technique. In the United States at least 19 percent of all married couples are protected from pregnancy by contraceptive sterilization elected either by the man or the woman.

In 1976, 49.2 percent of all married couples with wives of 15 to 44 years of age were using reversible methods of contraception. The distribution is shown in Table A–1.

Among America's 4.4 million postmarried women (widowed, divorced or separated) of childbearing age, the pill and the IUD are also by far the most popular nonsurgical method of contraception. Contraceptive use among never-married women shows a similar pattern.

Abortion in the United States

In 1978 there were an estimated 1.4 million legal abortions in the United States. In 1979 this number had risen to 1.5 million. Much earlier in 1973 the number of abortions only totalled 744,600. The abortion rate which shows the number of abortions per 1,000 women of reproductive age in a given year, rose from 16.6 per 1,000 in 1973 to 30.2 in 1979. Despite the strong increase in the number of abortions over time in 1979 an estimated 641,000 women were unable to obtain the abortion services they wanted largely because of geographical and financial inaccessibility.

In 1978 about one in three abortions was obtained by teenagers and three in four by unmarried women.

BIBLIOGRAPHY

Hafer, E. S. E., and T. N. Evans, *Human Reproduction.* New York: Harper & Row, 1973.

Overbeek, J. *The Population Challenge.* Westport, Conn.: Greenwood Press, 1976.

8

Migration

BASIC CONCEPTS AND MEASURES OF MIGRATION

Humans are not the only species capable of adopting, either temporarily or permanently, a new country or a new climate. Throughout recorded time, a number of animal species, especially birds, have traveled, seasonally or for good, in search of food and shelter. Migration of people is not new either. Migration over short and long distances has played a continuing role in the adjustment of humans to their environment.

After mortality and fertility, migration constitutes the third population process. And like mortality and fertility, migration has a direct impact upon the size of a population. Fertility and *immigration* increase population, while mortality and *emigration* produce a decline in numbers. Demographically speaking, migration implies a change of residence from one clearly defined geographical unit to another. Sociologically speaking, it entails a significant change in community ties and conditions of life.

Migration, then, refers to the movement of people in space, or geo-

graphical displacement. A *migrant* is someone who changes permanent residence for a long period of time and crosses political or administrative
boundaries in the process—unlike someone who simply moves from one
dwelling to another without crossing administrative or political frontiers.
It is customary to subdivide the field of migration into two areas: *internal*
and *international* migration. Internal migrants move within a nation's
frontiers; international migrants cross national boundaries. Internal migration streams tend to accompany economic and social changes and are usually on a larger scale than their international counterparts.

The terms *in-* and *out-migration,* normally used with reference to internal migration, indicate the arrival at a destination and the departure
from point of origin during a migration *interval.* The interval itself may
last one, five, or ten years. The corresponding terms *immigration* and *emigration* are commonly used with reference to international migration.

Net migration is the number of migrants coming into an area minus
the number of migrants the area loses to other regions; the balance may
be either positive or negative. (For the United States as a nation, the net
international balance is usually positive.) The sum total of people leaving
an area and entering it during a given period of time is called *gross migration* or *population turnover.*

Just as fertility and mortality have their crude rates, so does migration. A *migration rate* is the ratio of migrants, observed or estimated, to
the exposed population during a given period of time. Normally, the exposed population consists of the initial population in the case of out-
migration and of the terminal population in the case of in-migration.

Disregarding for a moment the difference between internal and external movements, we can distinguish four commonly used migration rates:

Crude in-migration or immigration rate: $\dfrac{I}{P} \cdot k$

Crude out-migration or emigration: $\dfrac{O}{P} \cdot k$

Crude net migration rate: $\dfrac{I-O}{P} \cdot k$

Crude gross migration rate: $\dfrac{I+O}{P} \cdot k$

where I = the number of in-migrants to an area
         O = the number of out-migrants from an area
         P = the exposed midyear or average population of an area
         k = a constant—in this case 1,000

Table 8–1 shows some immigration totals and rates between 1890 and
1977 for the United States and Canada. The table shows that, for reasons
to be explained later, immigration in both countries peaked around 1910.

TABLE 8–1

Immigration and Immigration Rates
(United States and Canada, Selected Years 1890–1977)

| | United States | | Canada | |
Year	Number of Immigrants	Crude Immigration Rate	Number of Immigrants	Crude Immigration Rate
1890	455,302	7.2	75,067	15.7
1900	448,572	5.9	41,681	7.9
1910	1,041,570	11.2	286,839	41.0
1920	430,001	4.0	138,824	16.2
1930	241,700	2.0	104,806	10.3
1940	70,756	0.5	11,324	0.1
1950	249,187	1.6	73,912	5.4
1960	265,398	1.5	104,111	5.8
1975	373,326	1.8	187,881	8.2
1977	462,000	2.1	114,914	4.9

Sources: U.S. Bureau of the Census, *Historical Statistics*, pt. 1 (Washington: U.S. Government Printing Office, 1975), pp. 105–06. Buckley Urquhart, *Historical Statistics of Canada* (Toronto: Macmillan, 1965), pp. 14, 23. U.S. Bureau of the Census, *Statistical Abstract of the United States* (Washington: U.S. Government Printing Office, 1978), p. 86. Ministry of Industry, Trade and Commerce, *Canada Yearbook 1978–79* (Ottawa: Information Division, Statistics Canada, 1978), p. 185.

During the Depression of the 1930s, the inflow plummeted, while immigration since World War II has been quite steady at intermediate levels.

SOURCES OF DATA ON IMMIGRATION

There are three primary methods of collecting data on migration. Countries such as the Netherlands and Denmark, which record all vital events, including the migratory movements of individuals, are ideal for studying migration. Countries like the United States, which do not possess such registers, must rely on census counts and surveys—the second method of obtaining data. When a census is taken, inhabitants can be asked where they were residing at a certain time (say, five years ago). It is also possible to compare the place of birth with the current place of residence. In the 1970 census such questions were in fact included. The information, of course, does not reveal how many times the individual moved between birth and the time the census was taken. The third major method of collecting migration data is sample surveys, which involve interviewing or sending questionnaires to representative samples of the population.

Data on international migration streams are sometimes obtained from port statistics. Customs officers are provided with passenger lists that normally distinguish between outward-bound passengers who are emigrants and those who are not. Land frontier statistics and passport statistics are equally important sources of information on migration.

FUNCTIONS OF MIGRATION

Migration obviously plays an important role in modern society. One key function is to redistribute population. In both industrial societies and in societies undergoing development and modernization, constant redistribution of population is a necessity. Areas like the Persian Gulf, where new resources are being discovered or developed, need extra labor. Industrial cities like Detroit need many skilled and unskilled workers—perhaps more than the local residents can supply. Similarly, the local supply of office workers in Washington may be insufficient to staff all government agencies.

Migration also helps maintain an equilibrium between the various regions of a country, whether between states or between rural and urban areas. Fertility and mortality rates differ from area to area, and so do economic opportunities. Without migration, people would concentrate in certain areas while other regions faced acute labor shortages. In the industrial towns of the eighteenth and nineteenth centuries, for instance, age-specific mortality rates were higher than in rural areas. Without constant rural-urban migration, the towns and cities could never have grown.

Migration also permits a better use of specific skills and talents. Specialists of all sorts may be concentrated in one area and be in short supply in another. Normally, income and opportunity differentials reflect relative scarcity and abundance. Migration streams tend to close the gap between localities that have a relative abundance of skilled workers and those in short supply.

On the individual level, migration helps people cope with regional or national problems. Droughts, harvest failures, soil erosion, the exhaustion of raw materials, racial and religious persecution, social oppression—all these problems can be resolved to some extent by voluntary migration to other areas.

SIGNIFICANT TYPES OF MIGRATION

Traditional Versus Modern

The first distinction to be made is between traditional and modern migration. *Modern migration* is migration that occurs once the modernization process hus started; *traditional migration* involves movements that take place in a premodern, traditional society. Traditional migration includes both group movements, by nomads and tribes, and erratic displacements of individuals. Among the most common reasons for traditional migration are changes in season and the availability of food, water, and pasturage; such ecological factors as lasting changes in climate, and the various forms of ecological collapse, such as large scale erosion; political factors like war and the threat of conquest; and social factors such as exogamous rules that force individuals to choose marriage partners outside the community.

In traditional societies the rate of migration is usually low. Because these societies are relatively unchanging and social mobility is often nonexistent, the rewards of migration are usually negative. Migrants are frequently regarded as undependable and untrustworthy by their community of origin, and are hardly welcome in the area of destination.

Continuous Versus Terminal

A similar classification has been made by the writer Dollot, who draws a distinction between continuous and terminal migration.[1] *Continuous migration* is frequently premodern, nomadism being the best example. Nomadism usually implies a close relationship between shepherd and flock, between humans and the grazing animals they raise. A major cause of nomadism is lack of water. In Iran, for instance, a large part of the country is outside the limit of pluvial agriculture; without irrigation most crops cannot be grown. With the exception of the Caspian Sea area and the foothills of the mountains in the north and west, vegetation is sparse. Thus nomadism can be considered a logical adjustment to the barrenness of the land; for centuries it has been a predominant factor in Iranian life and still is today. In the spring the nomads and their animals—mostly goats and sheep—move to the north. In the fall they return to the south, always following exactly the same roads.

Cyclical migration is a particular kind of continuous migration. The seasonal nature of certain types of agriculture can produce significant swings

[1] L. Dollot, *Les Migrations humaines* (Paris: Presses Universitaires de France, 1976), pp. 29, 40.

in the demand for labor. When the demand is low, workers may spend their time in cities or in other rural areas. When planting and harvesting increase the demand for temporary labor, workers flock to the farms. Some of these cyclical migrations involve the crossing of national borders, like the one between Mexico and the southwestern United States.

Terminal migration which involves a definitive move, is the most common type of migration. Migration from rural to urban areas is a prime example.

Internal Versus International

A third classification, basically geographical, is that between internal and international migration. *Internal migration* occurs within the limits of a nation or a given geographical area, and is usually either seasonal or terminal. *International migration* can be analyzed according to motivations that underlie it. The French author P. George differentiates between political and economic causes.[2] *Political migration* occurs mostly because of the breakdown of societal mechanisms that had guaranteed peaceful coexistence between different religions, cultural, social, or ethnic groups. The breakdown may result in war, revolution, and racial or religious persecution. The Christian and Moslem communities in Lebanon had lived together peacefully for many decades, but the status quo broke down in 1976. Other recent examples of social breakdown are Afghanistan and Iran. When the Weimar Republic in Germany collapsed in the early 1930s as the Nazis took over, the Jews suffered racial persecution. Much of this political migration obviously, has been *forced migration.* The refugee movements so characteristic of the twentieth century belong to this category.

Economic migration is a kind of corrective action to individual or collective poverty. The causes of the poverty may be social, economic, demographic, or ecological. For instance, the largest influx of immigrants into the United States are, at present from Cuba, Mexico, and the Philippines; both Mexico and the Philippines have demographic explosions they are unable to cope with. Canada has also received an increasing percentage of immigrants from Asia and Africa. The decision to migrate is usually taken by individuals, primarily to improve their economic position.

Free, Group, and Mass Migration

Most economic migration can also be termed *free migration,* since the migrants move according to their own wishes. In his book *Population,* W.

[2]P. George, *Les Migrations internationales* (Paris: Presses Universitaires de France, 1976), p.23.

Peterson draws a distinction between free, group, and mass migration.[3] Free migration is migration by people who move, with their families or individually, on their own initiative rather than under any kind of pressure. Such individuals are usually in search of new experience, economic improvement, or both. Migration may be free at the start, but as word gets around that the migrants have become successful in their adopted homes, free migration may develop into *group migration,* as it has done in Ireland, Sweden, and Italy. Group migration refers to the movement of people in clusters larger than the family. A clan, tribe, or other social group may move as a unit under the leadership of a religious or social leader. Finally, group migration may evolve into *mass migration,* when people in a certain area are so intensely exposed to migration that each eligible individual must make a conscious decision either to move or to stay.

Stage Migration and Return Migration

Two more migration patterns deserve mention here, stage migration, and return migration. The British social scientist E. G. Ravenstein, in a paper entitled "The Laws of Migration" presented to the Statistical Society in 1885, observed that migration in nineteenth-century England often proceeded by stages, one person filling the gap left by another who had moved earlier.[4] For instance, an individual may move from a large town to a metropolis, his or her place being taken by a former resident of a smaller urban area, and so on, until at the end of the chain a peasant leaves the farm for a neighboring small town. Another possibility is that individuals may reach their final destination only after a sequence of moves. Rural migrants first move into a nearby small town and then after an adaptation period, move on to the larger cities. Both types of migration are examples of *stage migration.*

Ravenstein and others since have noted that each current of migration produces a compensating countercurrent. *Return migration* can be explained by such factors as disillussionment with the new environment or the desire to retire in the place of one's birth. Also, migrants may become aware of possibilities in their native land that they had overlooked when they left or that had developed after they left. Although every migration stream produces its own counterstream, return migration tends to be smaller.

[3] W. Peterson, *Population,* 3rd ed. (New York: Macmillan, 1975), pp. 321–24.
[4] E. G. Ravenstein, *The Laws of Migration* (New York: Arno Press, 1976), p. 199.

DIFFERENTIALS AND SELECTIVITY OF MIGRATION

Some groups are more migratory than others. Like death and birth rates, migratory movements are associated with such characteristics as age, sex, and education. Yet the search for universally valid migration differentials has not been very successful, because migratory streams reflect profound social and economic mutations that vary with time and place. An examination of the personal characteristics of typical migrants is one means of analyzing migration, and this for two reasons. First, it helps us understand what causes migration. Second, migration has a direct impact on both the area of origin and the community of destination, and a profile of typical migrants enables us to study the impact more closely.

Age

The safest generalization that we can make is that the typical migrant is a young adult eligible for work or eager for marriage. The first move is usually made between ages 15 and 30. The age differential has withstood the test of time; in the past as well as the present, in both internal and international migration streams, young adults prevail. They often move in search of a job after completing their education. Not being burdened with family ties, they are free to move alone, and the cost of moving is therefore fairly low. Many young adults want to try their luck in the large cities, either at home or abroad, which is why urban areas receive so many newcomers between 18 and 29. The stream of migrants moving out of the cities and into the suburbs is also young, yet older than the current that is moving to the cities. Dominating the suburban-bound stream are parents between 25 and 35 who are looking for a suitable house, in a more quiet environment, for their growing families.

Another age group has become increasingly mobile: the retired. Growing numbers of the elderly are leaving the cities and towns where they have worked and heading for localities offering milder climates, well-developed services for the aged, and outdoor activities. The Sunbelt states, which extend from Florida to California, are strongly favored in the United States, while British Columbia is the new magnet in Canada.

Sex

Migration can also be selective by sex. Just as migration tends to reflect employment opportunities, so the preponderance of either sex in the migratory stream is heavily influenced by economic variables. There is some evidence that in international migration, when distance are long and when migration has an innovative and/or pioneering character, males dominate. To a certain extent, this also holds for internal migration. In the earlier stages of a region's development—when economic uncertainties are still great—more men than women migrate. Female migration is restricted by traditional attitudes toward women's roles. When the migratory process becomes routine and traditional attitudes are weakened or eliminated, female participation increases. In our time, the large-scale entry of women into the labor force in the United States has made women as ready to migrate as men. In the Philippines, which is more modern than most neighboring Asian countries, women are even more migratory than men. It should be emphasized, however, generalizations regarding sex selectivity of migration do not have the same validity as those regarding age.

Education

What role do education and skills play in determining migration? Many studies suggest that the inclination to migrate increases with formal education. In rural-urban migration, for example, young people may move to the urban areas to continue or complete their education. Once they are trained, though, they may not return, because it is often easier to find skilled employment in urban areas. Educated people may also be more mobile because they have a greater awareness of career opportunities and of the quality of life in other localities. In addition, those with education tend to have national rather than localized markets for their skills. And schooling may weaken the ties of family and tradition, making it more acceptable, and less traumatic, for young people to move away from their parents.

Studies in developing nations have shown that rural schools often tend to make town life seem more attractive than farm life, because the curriculums don't emphasize locally needed agrarian skills.[5] In many less developed countries the education brought to rural areas has in fact been urban in character. Often it alienates young people from their own culture, exposing them to a way of life more often found in towns and cities. No wonder such education has accentuated the flight to the cities. In developed countries, of course, schooling also tends to make people more likely to migrate, for the reasons we noted. College graduates and skilled workers are among the most mobile segments of the population.

[5] J. C. Caldwell, *African Rural-Urban Migration* (New York: Columbia University Press, 1969), pp. 60–61.

MOTIVATIONS FOR MIGRATING

A number of theoretical explanations of migration have been propounded, of which we can survey only a few here.

Economic Factors

Neoclassical economic theory, assuming that labor is homogeneous and that no obstacles exist between countries and regions, sees migration as simply flowing from areas with low earnings to regions with high earnings.[6] The high and low earnings reflect high and low productivity levels. As migration continues, the disparity in wages and productivity between the two regions narrows and eventually disappears. The assumptions of homogeneous labor, lack of geographical and administrative obstacles, and absence of migration costs do not reflect reality faithfully, but the model is a useful point of departure. Yet it also seems that, in spite of migration, local differences in wages and productivity do not always disappear. Wages tend to remain higher in growing areas. But the main weakness of this theory is that it does not take expectations into account. If there is a small real-wage differential between two regions, for instance, migration to the higher-wage region may not take place because people expect the difference to be temporary only.

Push and Pull Factors

Another theory identifies two kinds of pressures, one inducing people to leave the area of origin and another drawing people into the area of destination.[7] The two pressures have been designated "push" and "pull." Among *push factors* we note rural poverty; low wages; declining employment opportunities; decreased demand for locally produced commodities; the absence of educational, cultural, and health facilities; and the like. *Pull factors* include free or cheap farmland; attractive employment opportunities; good salaries; and the availability of schools, hospitals, and entertainment facilities. Obviously, many forms of migration result from some combination of the two. The Irish potato famine of 1846–47 was a powerful push factor: for many peasants, the choice was between moving or death. The so-called brain drain—the flow of scientists and engineers to the United States in the 1950s and 1960s—illustrates a strong pull factor:

[6] See, for example, J. Isaac, *Economics of Migration* (London: Kegan Paul, 1947).
[7] International Labor Office, *Why Labor Leaves the Land,* Studies and Reports, New Series, no. 59 (Geneva: Tribune de Genève, 1960), p. 17.

FIGURE 8–1

Lee's Origin and Destination Factors
and Intervening Obstacles in Migration

Origin   Intervening obstacles   Destination

Source: E. S. Lee, "A Theory of Migration," *Demography* 3, no. 1 (1966) 50.

the salaries of scientists and engineers in the United States were much higher than those offered by other nations.

An interesting amendment to the push-pull theory can be found in an article by the demographer E. S. Lee.[8] According to Lee, the components of the decision to migrate are the following:

1. Positive and negative factors in the place of origin.
2. Positive and negative factors in the area of destination.
3. Intervening obstacles standing between place of origin and destination.
4. Personal factors.[9]

The positive and negative factors in the areas of both origin and destination will either attract or repel the potential migrant. The *intervening obstacles* can be physical, such as distance, or may be restrictive migration laws or simply the costs of moving. The fourth and last factor allows for individual differences in the perception and assessment of the other elements. Figure 8–1 summarizes the theory.

The Cost-Benefit Theory

Another approach to migration can be found in the works of the economists Theodore Schultz and Larry Sjaastad.[10] Their argument is presented within the framework of investment in humans, generally defined

[8] E. S. Lee, "A Theory of Migration," *Demography* 3, no. 1 (1966): 47–59.
[9] Ibid.
[10] T. W. Schultz, "Reflections on Investment in Man," *Journal of Political Economy* 70, Supplement (October 1962): 1–8; and L. A. Sjaastad, "The Costs and Returns of Human Migration," *Journal of Political Economy* 70, Supplement (October 1962): 80–93.

as the human capital approach. Migration is seen as a decision entailing costs as well as benefits. There are disadvantages to relocating, but the move may yield returns as well. Thus the decision to migrate can be compared to the decision to make an investment of any other kind, like education. An individual migrates when the perceived benefits are judged to exceed the costs. The costs can be divided into *direct money costs,* such as the expense of moving, and the *indirect,* or *opportunity, costs*— primarily the earnings forgone while traveling and obtaining a new job. Sjaastad also recognizes the *psychological costs* of migration: the discomfort ("disutility," in economists' jargon) associated with leaving home, family, and friends; adjustment to an unfamiliar environment; the need to set up a new routine, and so on. The costs of migration are incurred as soon as the decision to migrate has been made or shortly thereafter, whereas the benefits are further off and must therefore be discounted.[11]

The model presented by Schultz and Sjaastad has many implications. If, as has been observed, the migratory flow tends to be inversely related to distance, it is because the greater the distance the higher the direct cash costs of traveling and moving. The psychological costs also increase with distance, since the separation from the previous environment becomes more radical. The fact that younger people are more likely to migrate than the old makes sense according to Schultz and Sjaastad's model. The opportunity costs increase with age, while the remaining lifespan over which an increased income might be earned is reduced.

Schultz and Sjaastad do not explain, however, why, in a number of developing countries, people are moving at increasing rates to the urban areas, even though unemployment rates in towns and cities are high. As a way out of this problem, the American economist M. P. Todaro has observed that, along with existing rural-urban income differentials, we must consider the "anticipated income differential."[12] It is reasonable to assume, says Todaro, that migrants think in terms of the long run. They hope to make useful contacts, learn about employment opportunities, and in time find a rewarding job that will compensate for their initial losses. They may disregard the fact that, initially, they will be worse off by moving to the city, as they anticipate ultimately being better off.

Todaro's amendment to the Schultz/Sjaastad model is ingenious. Figure 8–2 summarizes the typical net-income stream of a young man who, upon completion of his education, moves to the city. While he is in school, his net income is zero. At A_1 he begins life in the city. Presumably he is unemployed for a while and his net income is negative, which means that he lives on previous savings or borrowed money. At A_2 he becomes em-

---

[11] A given sum or income due in the future, or "deferred," has a present value of less than that sum; the more distant the deferred sum or income, the lower its present value. The present value of something that is available only in the future is known as a *discounted* value.

[12] M. P Todaro, "Income Expectations, Rural-Urban Migration and Employment in Africa," *International Labour Review* 104, no. 5 (November 1971): 387–413.

FIGURE 8–2

A Typical Net-income Stream

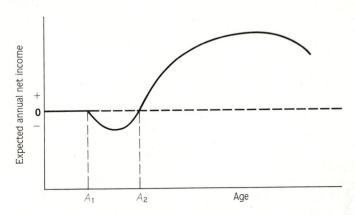

ployed and his net income becomes positive, rising to a peak and then decreasing with age as his productivity begins to drop.

In conclusion we may say that, apart from purely political migrations and Malthusian evacuations that result from a collapse of the environment, or massive overcrowding, the economic factor seems to predominate in the decision to move. Migration frequently occurs because individuals experience a gap between ambition and accomplishment. They fear that the old social system will not meet their aspirations and expect that the migratory move will permit them to improve their economic lot eventually if not immediately. Migration and redistribution of people also occur in response to changing opportunities that emerge in the course of economic development. Areas that offer relatively attractive employment opportunities and high pay usually pull people in, while areas of unemployment or underemployment tend to lose their residents, at least as long as better alternatives are available. For instance, the Sunbelt—the frontier of the 1970s (and 1980s)—is now the most rapidly growing section of the United States. Jobs are more plentiful in the Sunbelt, the warmer climate reduces heating costs, and the greater availability of outdoor leisure activities can be considered a form of psychological income.

CONSEQUENCES OF MIGRATION

Migration has profound demographic, economic and social consequences, yet many of the ideas discussed here are only hypotheses awaiting further empirical testing. And although the consequences of internal and international migration are comparable, the implications of migration between nations have so far received more attention, and therefore we will concentrate on international migration.

Demographic Effects

Migration, first of all, has an impact on total numbers. Immigration increases the population of the countries of destination by a certain number of units, while a corresponding decrease takes place in the countries of origin. Between the founding of the earliest colonies and the mid-1970s, between thirty and forty million people migrated from Europe to the United States. Other nations—such as Canada, Australia, and Argentina—are also the product of immigration. Gibson has estimated that of the 1970 U.S. population of 203 million, about 105 million, or 52 percent, is attributable to the 1790 population. About 98 million, or 48 percent, then, is attributable to the estimated net immigration of 35.5 million individuals in the 1790–1970 period.[13]

Table 8–2 and Figure 8–3 provide information about United States immigration from Europe and the world as a whole for the period 1820–1976/77.

A second demographic effect of migration is that on the growth potential of both the sending and the receiving nations. Because of the sex and age selectivity of migration, a flow of people from one area to the next tends to change the existing sex-age composition in both the home country and the area of destination. As we observed earlier, migrant streams contain high proportions of young adults—that is, individuals of family-formation ages. Birth rates among such populations tend to be high and death rates low.

To the extent that the migratory stream contains married couples, emigration deprives the homeland of births. These births take place, instead, in the country of destination, which, other things being equal, acquires a higher demographic growth rate. To the extent that the migration consists of single persons, there are sex-distribution changes in both area of origin and of destination. If, for example, the migration stream is characterized by a small excess of marriageable males, the women in the country of reception have improved chances of getting married. The marriage rate may rise in the area of destination and drop in the home country. A modification in the marriage rate may, in turn, ultimately change birth rates and growth potentials as well. In such traditional areas of emigration

---

[13]C. Gibson, "The Contribution of Immigration to the United States Population 1790–1970," *International Migration Review* 9 (Summer 1975): 158.

TABLE 8–2

Immigrant Arrivals to the
United States from Europe, 1820–1976

Country of Origin	Number of Immigrants (in thousands)	Country of Origin	Number of Immigrants (in thousands)
Germany	6,960	Spain	248
Italy	5,278	Belgium	201
Great Britain	4,863	Romania	168
Ireland	4,722	Czechoslovakia	137
Austria and Hungary	4,313	Yugoslavia	109
U.S.S.R.	3,362	Bulgaria	68
Sweden	1,270	Finland	33
Norway	856	Lithuania	4
France	744	Luxembourg	3
Greece	638	Latvia	3
Poland	506	Albania	2
Portugal	422	Estonia	1
Denmark	363	Other Europe	55
Netherlands	357		
Switzerland	347	*Total*	36,033

Source: L. Bouvier et al., *International Migration: Yesterday, Today, and Tomorrow,* Population Bulletin 32, no. 4 (Washington: Population Reference Bureau, 1977): 17.

FIGURE 8–3

American Immigration (1820–1977)

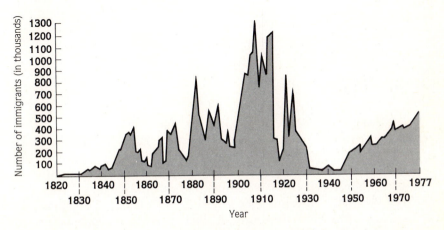

Source: U.S. Bureau of the Census, *Statistical Abstract of the United States: 1978* (Washington: U.S. Government Printing Office, 1978), p. 85.

as Ireland and southern Italy, for instance, the heavy outflow of males has resulted in an unbalanced sex composition. The decline in birth rates that those areas have experienced may be due in part to this phenomenon. The areas of origin that witness an outflow of young people may also experience an increased death rate, since the older, high-mortality-risk people stay behind. The proportion of such people in the total population automatically increases when the younger ones leave, so that the community's overall mortality figure is modified.

The third demographic effect of migration is on the age and sex structure of the population in both the country of destination and the area of origin.[14] Migration streams often consist mainly of young adults, with males dominating when distances are long. The exodus of the younger segment of the native population reduces the number and proportion of people of prime working age. The area of origin may find itself stuck with a relatively greater share of children and of aged and sickly residents. The situation in the area of destination is the reverse. (Migrations of political refugees are the exception to this rule, since the motivation for departure is different.) The usual impact of predominantly economic migrations, therefore, is to raise the median age (see pp. 28–29) in the country of origin and to lower it in the country of destination. In 1977 the median age of immigrants into the United States was 26.5, while that of the total receiving population stood at 29.4.

Migration flows may also alter the sex composition of both area of origin and destination. At present, immigration in such countries as the United States and Canada is slightly female-dominated. In 1977 216,400 male immigrants and 245,900 females entered the United States. The sex ratio (briefly defined on p. 31), which is written as males /females × 100, stood at 88. In Canada in 1976 there were 72,605 male and 76,824 female immigrants, giving a sex ratio of 95 males for every 100 females. The double-barreled effect of current immigration in the United States is to rejuvenate the population while making it more female-dominated.

Economic Effects

The economic effects of migration are linked, in part, to the demographic consequences. This is especially true for the so-called *labor force effect* of migration. Migrants who move for nonpolitical reasons are usually young and economically active—and often move in order to improve their material well-being. Consequently, they often make up a higher percentage of the labor force than the receiving and sending populations as a whole. Normally, about 40 percent of the population is economically ac-

---

[14] The concepts of age and sex structure will be discussed in detail in Chapter 11.

tive or potentially so. Among migrants the percentage may vary from 50 to 100.

The first economic effect of immigration, therefore, is that it tends to increase the ratio of the economically active to the total population in the country of destination. And immigration often produces a greater percentage increase in the labor force than in the total population. The reverse may happen in the area of origin.

The second economic effect of migration is that on incomes and economic growth. The impact of immigration on the country of destination depends a great deal on the conditions prevailing in that nation. The inflow of young workers in nineteenth-century America was almost certainly beneficial. The frontier was expanding, new resources were constantly being discovered, and the supply of capital both from American savings and from abroad (mainly the United Kingdom) was abundant. Technological advances were rapid, but labor was scarce. One can hypothesize that during that period immigration raised incomes and the rate of economic growth. Net out-migration would probably have been harmful.

The effects of immigration—say, of refugees from a neighboring region—on an economy with a chronic oversupply of labor and/or scarcity of landed resources and capital are of course wholly different. Immigrants, if they are willing to work for less pay, tend to drag down wage levels as the competition for scarce jobs is sharpened. When underemployment and unemployment prevail, out-migration is likely to be beneficial. Emigration reduces the excess labor that the agrarian and other sectors cannot absorb. For those who stay behind, the pressure of numbers on employment is relieved. The amount of land and productive equipment per worker increases, which tends to increase productivity and eventually wage levels. A rapid rate of population increase, however, may negate the potential unemployment-reducing effects of out-migration.

Migration and Third Parties

In Chapter 5 we discussed "economies of agglomeration," which induce firms to move to industrialized cities. Economies of agglomeration can be thought of as benefits created by other firms for which incoming firms do not pay. Economists sometimes term such benefits *positive externalities. Negative externalities,* on the other hand, occur when private decisions are made in which the interests of some affected party are *not* considered; usually the decisionmaker imposes an uncompensated cost on others. Certain instances of national or international migration, whether they are rural-urban or urban-urban, can be viewed in the light of this concept.

When a potential migrant is deciding whether to move to a certain city—say, Los Angeles—he or she balances advantages such as the possibility of a better job, improved contacts, or the nearness of ocean and beaches against the costs of living there. A longer commute or higher smog levels may be among such costs. However, our migrant considers only the costs which every inhabitant of the city must bear, and if the migrant feels that the benefits will exceed the perceived costs, he or she will move. But the migrant does not take into account the contribution that he or she is likely to make to the existing pollution, crowding of streets and highways, and noise in the area of destination. As often happens in developing nations, an additional urban resident may help depress local wage levels or drive up housing prices. The migrant's move may create an involuntary cost to others for which he or she will not have to compensate and which therefore plays no part in the decision. Obviously, then, the total costs of the migratory move may exceed the private costs which the migrant considers—the remainder is the burden he or she may impose upon others. As long as this situation is allowed to remain, the migratory stream will be too large and congestion may result. Los Angeles and Honolulu are cases in point. If the migrants had somehow been forced to assume the full costs of their move, including the costs accruing to others, they might have decided to locate in a less-congested region.

Social Effects

Our discussion of the social effects of migration will be limited to the migrant's adjustment in the country of destination. Generally speaking, the international immigrant moves through four stages: *settlement, adaptation, acculturation,* and *assimilation.* The precise terminology used often depends merely on the preferences of the individual social scientist.

There can be little doubt that even prior to departure, migrants experience some anxiety as they are about to leave the familiar and relatively secure environment of their home community. As they move into the host society, with its different customs and perhaps, language, they are likely to experience "culture shock." Being transplanted into a relatively strange environment, they inevitably experience some disorientation and frustration. Their former routines no longer fit in, while their former social position and status have diminished or even vanished. Both number of roles they can play and the number of groups in which they can be active have shrunk. Sometimes they can join an immigrant community, in the area of destination, that serves as a beachhead from which they can move on later and that provides minimal security while they learn the new ways.

Settlement is completed when the migrant has found a place to live and a job permitting him or her to take care of basic needs. The necessity to work and live forces the immigrant quickly into minimal economic cooperation with individuals in the host country. The acquisition of a private dwelling is also a major step. The immigrant becomes anchored: in one's own home, one can eat, drink, sleep, and interact with family members (if any) in the old, familiar ways.

Adaptation is the next stage. The migrant now abandons the trappings of the previous culture and begins to adopt the values, norms, and patterns of behavior of the host society. He or she accepts the new language as the normal means of communication, gets used to the climate, adopts the local style of dress, and learns to enjoy the local food and drink. The migrant may join community groups and clubs and generally follows the example of the local host population. The new setting absorbs the migrant increasingly.

Acculturation follows adaptation. The migrant has now internalized most of the attitudes, beliefs, and behavior of the host community. His or her customary modes of thought and action have now been replaced by new ones.

Assimilation is the last and most difficult step; often it does not occur in the first immigrant generation. An assimilated individual has become fully absorbed by the new setting and is an accepted member of the social groups in the host society. Assimiliation implies that the migrant and the host population have melted into one. In the process of assimilation both the immigrant and the host population undergo changes. One of the reasons why those who immigrate as adults hardly ever reach the final stage is that their minds have been molded to fit the community of departure. The new attitudes, behavior, and beliefs acquired in the area of destination are adopted within the context of a basically different personality structure.

A number of factors facilitate or retard acculturation and assimilation. The ability to earn a living enhances self-esteem and a feeling of belonging. Besides, the need to cooperate with others on a daily basis encourages new habits and behavior. A flexible social structure with political equality and equal opportunity fosters integration. Similarity of language, religion, and cultural traditions speeds up the assimilation process, whereas dissimilar cultural values and behavior patterns retard it.

When people of widely divergent cultures and different racial stocks come together, acculturation and assimilation take place very slowly—or not at all. Members of an ethnic minority wear a "racial uniform" that prevents them from melting into the rest of the population. As the United States, Canada, and some European nations are increasingly faced with immigration by different ethnic stocks, a great deal of social tension must be anticipated. Many migrant cultures may be hostile or apathetic to values of the Western host cultures, which inevitably results in antagonism. The conflict of coexisting cultures may also manifest itself in a social climate of cold indifference.

Thus as the attitudes and customs of the migrants and the host of communities become more divergent, the problem of maintaining a well-integrated social organization becomes more difficult. Individuals wrenched out of their accustomed environment may all too easily encounter severe adjustment problems in their new surroundings. Demoralized if not disoriented, they may fail to perform essential social functions and thus interfere with the effective action of the community as a whole.

The United States and Canada now contain foreign colonies, or enclaves, where English is hardly ever spoken. Because of the divergence of cultural traditions in the sending and receiving countries, often combined with differences in appearance, the adjustment and assimilation of immigrants can become soul-wrenching. The resulting bitterness is often transmitted to the second or third generation.

Even under more favorable circumstances like relative cultural homogeneity, there are always those who fail to integrate themselves into the new society. Stress and symptoms of severe personal disorganization such as delinquency, mental illness, and even suicide result. Others will return to the home country and thus join the return flow which always accompanies any major migratory stream.

CONCEPTS FOR REVIEW

Migration	Push factors
Moving	Pull factors
Crude net-migration rate	Intervening obstacles
Traditional migration	Psychological costs of migration
Modern migration	Deferred income
Continuous migration	Negative externalities
Terminal migration	Adaptation
Stage migration	Acceleration
Return migration	Assimilation

QUESTIONS FOR DISCUSSION

1. What is the difference between political and economic migration?
2. Why is it typically the young adults who migrate? Consider the psychological costs and the opportunity costs of the migratory decision in your answer.
3. List two reasons why educated people are more mobile than people with fewer skills and less training.
4. Migration is often explained in terms of "push" and "pull" factors. List

the push and pull factors you are familiar with. Can you explain your present residence at your college or university in those terms?

5. People often migrate because incomes and job opportunities are better in the area of destination than in the area of origin. In a number of less developed nations, however, people move from rural areas to cities, although the chances of finding a job in the city are slim. Can you explain this paradox?

6. Explain the effects of out-migration on the age composition of the population in the area of origin.

7. In what sense were the economic effects of immigration in early nineteenth-century America beneficial?

8. Suppose that a person ponders moving to a city of 1 million inhabitants. Suppose further that the average congestion costs that every inhabitant of the city must bear are $10. One additional person in the city would raise congestion costs by 1 cent per capita which, multiplied by 1 million, amounts to $10,000. The potential migrant takes the $10 (plus 1 cent) to be the congestion price of moving to the city. But the extra social costs he imposes on others is $10,000, which he is not made to pay. Conclusion: in the absence of government intervention cities will grow too large. Do you agree? Explain.

9. At present most immigrants in the United States come from Latin America and Asia. They come, in other words, from very different cultures and racial stocks. Discuss some social problems involved in this recent trend.

BIBLIOGRAPHY

Caldwell, J. C. *African Rural-Urban Migration*. New York: Columbia University Press, 1969.

Dollot, L. *Les Migrations humaines*. Paris: Presses Universitaires de France, 1976.

Eisenstadt, S. N. *The Absorption of Immigrants*. London: Routledge, 1954.

Ex, J. *Adjustment After Migration*. The Hague: Nÿhoff, 1966.

George, P. *Les Migrations internationales*. Paris: Presses Universitaires de France, 1976.

Gibson, C. "The Contribution of Immigration to the United States Population 1790–1970." *International Migration Review* 9 (Summer 1975).

International Labor Office. *Why Labor Leaves the Land*. Studies and Reports, New Series, no. 59. Geneva: Tribune de Genève, 1960.

Isaac, J. *Economics of Migration*. London: Kegan Paul, 1947.

Jackson, J. A. *Migration*. London: Cambridge University Press, 1969.

Lee, E. S. "A Theory of Migration." *Demography* 3, no. 1 (1969): 47–59.

Peterson, W. *Population*. 3rd ed. New York: Macmillan, 1975.

Ravenstein, E. G. *The Laws of Migration*. New York: Arno Press, 1976.

Richmond, A. H. *Post-War Immigrants in Canada*. Toronto: University of Toronto Press, 1967.

Sauvy, A. *General Theory of Population*. London: Weidenfeld, 1969.

Schreiber, A. F., et al. *Economics of Urban Problems: An Introduction*. 2nd. ed. Boston: Houghton Mifflin, 1976.

Schultz, T. W. "Reflections on Investment in Man." *Journal of Political Economy* 70, Supplement (October 1962): 1–8.

Sjaastad, L. A. "The Costs and Returns of Human Migration." *Journal of Political Economy* 70, Supplement (October 1962): 80–93.

Todaro, M. P. "Income Expectations, Rural-Urban Migration and Employment in Africa." *International Labour Review* 104, no. 5 (November 1971): 387–413.

9

International

Migration

A SHORT HISTORY OF AMERICAN IMMIGRATION

The history of American immigration is customarily divided into four phases: colonial immigration and early settlement; the era of mass immigration; the period of restricted immigration; and the "new new" immigrants.

Colonial Immigration and Early Settlement (1607–1815)

This period lasted from the arrival of the first settlers in the seventeenth century to the end of the Napoleonic wars. Colonial immigration (1607–1776) began with the permanent settlement of the English at Jamestown in May 1607. From the same country and during the same period came the colonists who settled in New England. After twelve years in the Netherlands, the separatist Pilgrims sailed to America on the *May-*

flower and landed at Plymouth in December 1620. Within ten years they were followed by the Puritans, who held strong convictions about the need for reform within the established Church of England. Diversity of religious opinion was not tolerated in seventeenth-century England, hence these emigrations. Meanwhile, in 1619 a Dutch ship had brought the first "involuntary" immigrants to Virginia: twenty blacks for sale. As many as 200,000 slaves were subsequently brought to America, 90 percent of them going to the Southern colonies.

The early settlers were overwhelmingly English, with smaller numbers of Dutch, German, Scandinavian, Scottish, Irish, Swiss, and French settlers. Most of them had fled religious or political oppression or the feudal system, or were searching for adventure, or had "hopes of gaine." Profit and piety were, in differing proportions, the two most important motives for migration. The blacks remained the only involuntary migrants, and until 1660 or so they were treated very much like indentured servants; but a hundred years later the slave system was firmly established. The indentured servants themselves were a marginal category of immigrants, since they were not entirely free. Their passage to the colonies was paid for on condition that they work off the cost with a specific number of years of labor (often between four and seven). Ship captains would normally sell their contract with indentured servants to masters who would give the servants freedom after they had put in their required length of service. A number of indentured servants were convicts and had the not-so-difficult choice between the gallows and the colonies. In 1717 the English Parliament also decided to ease the overcrowding in the prisons by deporting felons to America; some 50,000 had been dumped on the colonies before the Revolution. When the American colonies won their independence, in 1783, about 3 million whites and 750,000 blacks lived in America. Independence was not everybody's liking: some 30,000 Loyalist settlers left for Canada.

Between 1783 and 1815 immigration brought not more than 250,000 people to the new nation. Wars and revolution disturbed both Europe and America and travel became unsafe, reducing the flow of migrants. The voyage to the United States was long and dangerous. The trip could take as little as twenty-seven days, but it might last four months if the winds were adverse. Some vessels lost large numbers of passengers; infant and child mortality on board were high.

Mass Migration (1815–1917)

When the world settled down to peace after 1815, a new influx of immigrants began. Within this long second phase several shorter periods can be distinguished. The first wave, between 1815 and 1860, brought approximately five million people to America's shores. The British Isles, Germany, and Scandinavia dominated the flow. An overwhelming push factor emerged in Ireland when famine struck in the 1840s. But in Germany, Scandinavia, and England (Scotland included), push factors were also at their height (see pp. 162–63) as political upheavals, changes in landholding systems, and the industrial revolution combined with a high rate of population increase to create powerful expulsive forces. The American Civil War (1861–65) suspended the flow temporarily, but thereafter it resumed. Between the 1860s and 1890s the Scandinavians, Germans, Italians, and Bohemians prevailed. From 1815 to 1890 the majority of immigrants came from Northern and Western Europe and the British Isles. During this period, which is usually called the era of "old migration," the total flow of humanity was just over 15 million. It was the "old" immigrants who crossed the prairies and tilled the virgin soils.

The same forces which had been so potent in Northern and Western Europe prevailed in Southern and Eastern Europe from 1890 to 1914 and thereafter. Although the European exodus continued unabated, the geographical origin of the migratory stream shifted to the Mediterranean countries and preeminently Italy, and to the Baltic and Eastern European states, led by Austria-Hungary and Russia. Most of these "new immigrants," who also numbered over 15 million, came from rural areas. This migratory flow was male-dominated and was essentially rural-urban. Because the majority of immigrants were illiterate, unskilled, and poor, they flocked to the developing industries. Large numbers of unskilled workers were needed in mining, manufacturing, and the building of cities and canals, roads, and railways. The new immigrants filled the gap. Like the Irish before them, they settled in the cities.

The "old" immigrants watched this influx of "new" immigrants with growing alarm. The new immigrants were easily identified by their divergent languages, customs, modes of dress, and, sometimes, complexion. Because their cultural habits were different from those prevailing in the host country, adjustment was often painfully slow. A thunderous public debate arose about the importance of cultural and ethnic homogeneity and the advisability of continued immigration in a society with a closed frontier. The restrictive immigration laws of the 1920s (see pp. 189–90) were the result.

Although most of the influx of this period was European, the flow had some Oriental and Mexican flavoring. The first Chinese actually came to America in 1820, but it was the discovery of gold in California in 1848 which brought them over in larger numbers. The Chinese worked in the mines, on the great transcontinental railroads then being planned and built, and in the laundry business. Although by and large the Chinese were hard-working and law-abiding people, they met with particularly cruel forms of prejudice and discrimination. In 1858 and 1868 the United States had signed treaties with China permitting unrestricted immigration, but the Chinese Exclusion Act of 1882 barred further entry.

In 1868, 153 Japanese came to (then independent) Hawaii. After 1885 more followed. Many worked in the sugarcane fields first and later branched out to other activities. By 1900 the Japanese composed about 40 percent of the Hawaiian population and they are still the second largest ethnic group in that state. From Hawaii many went to California, where they took jobs on railroads and farms, and in lumber camps, mines, canneries, and private households. Many developed prosperous farms on lands others considered marginal. They met with nearly as much prejudice and discrimination as the Chinese, and in 1908 the United States and Japan signed a "gentlemen's agreement" whereby the Japanese government refused to issue passports to Japanese who intended to work in America. It was a face-saving device for the Japanese and put an end to Pacific migration from Japan.

After 1846, when California entered the Union, a few long-established Mexican communities became part of the United States. After 1910, when revolution gripped Mexico, immigration from that nation increased. The building of railroads and the rapid agricultural expansion of the Southwest created a strong demand for unskilled labor. The majority of the Mexican immigrants remained in the rural southwest as farm workers, but a few migrated to the cities. Because of cultural, language, and ethnic differences, Mexican assimilation has always been slow and difficult.

Restricted Immigration

Once the gates were closed by the restrictive laws of the 1920s, the immigration flow was reduced to a trickle. The number of immigrants fell, but there was also a shift back to the earlier pattern whereby the majority of immigrants came from Northern and Western Europe. The new quota system heavily favored Northwestern Europe and the British Isles over Southern and Eastern Europe. However, the Northwestern European countries failed to use up their assigned quotas, while the nations of Southern and Eastern Europe were allowed to send only small numbers. (In postwar Russia the new communist government discouraged departures.) Between 1911 and 1920, in spite of World War I, 5.7 million people managed to come to the States. Immigration resumed after the war, but an economic downturn in 1920–21 stimulated fresh agitation for restriction. Between 1921 and 1930 immigration fell to about 4 million, a sharp contrast with earlier decades, when more than a million persons had entered annually.

The immigration figure for the Depression years is very low indeed. Only 528,431 people arrived between 1931 and 1940. But the net immigration figure is even lower, because during some of those crisis years the outflow actually exceeded the inflow. There was little change of law or policy during the decade. However, political immigration resumed in the 1930s as many refugees fled Nazi Germany. The refugee group, largely middle class and urban, included many professionals, business executives, and white-collar workers. No fewer than twelve newcomers were Nobel Prize winners.

During World War II very few people applied for immigration, but this changed once the war was over and American army personnel returned with foreign fiancées, wives, and children. Meanwhile, numerous European refugees and displaced persons found themselves without a home or even a valid passport—a situation that the United States helped remedy through *ad hoc* emergency programs such as the Displaced Persons Act of 1948. Then in 1968 the enactment of Public Law 89–236 greatly revised the criteria for admission to the country. Between 1931 and the early 1960s Northern and Western European nations again dominated the migratory stream, but the new law produced a major shift.

The "New New" Immigrants

As early as 1947 the well-known population expert Kingsley Davis stated:

> Demographically speaking, the potential migration pent up in today's world is enormous. Not only is the earth's population increasing at the fastest rate ever known, but the increase is extremely unequal between different regions. Generally the fastest growth is occurring in the poorest regions, the slowest in the richest. . . . The situation is analogous to atmospheric pressure. The human population of the earth is characterized by high and low pressure areas, and one expects an inevitable current from one zone to the other.[1]

In point of fact, new waves of immigrants, many of them from the developing countries, are now flocking to America and to the Western nations in general. The impact of these "new new" immigrants is already considerable and promises to be more so in the future. Between 1968 and 1978 about 10 million newcomers have arrived, most of them from nations that once had little representation on America's shores. In 1980, Asia and Latin America provided about 82 percent of the immigrants. If we take the twelve-month period from September 1979 to September 1980 as

[1] Quoted in B. M. Ziegler, ed., *Immigration, an American Dilemma* (Boston: D. C. Heath, 1953), p. v.

FIGURE 9–1

Immigrants to the United States
from Leading Countries, by County of Birth (1977)

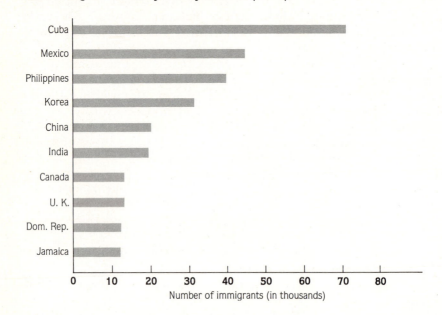

an example, we observe immigration from three sources: about 400,000 immigrants coming in under basic immigration laws; roughly 230,000 refugees from such areas as Indo-China and Cuba; and up to 1 million illegal immigrants from nations like Mexico and Haiti. There are now perhaps 12 million illegal immigrants in the United States. Meanwhile, in 1980 there were still about 14 million refugees in the world waiting to be resettled. The United States immigration laws are once more being reviewed; difficult choices lie ahead. Figure 9–1 lists the number of immigrants, by selected country of origin, entering the United States in 1977.

THE DETERMINANTS OF AMERICAN IMMIGRATION

What were the forces that induced millions of individuals and families to cross the seas and settle in the United States? As Chapter 8 indicated, both push and pull forces operated.

Historical Push Factors

Some of the migrants fled religious persecution and came to America to live in freedom. The Pilgrims and Puritans fled the oppressive laws prevailing in England. The Huguenots came from Catholic France, where their religious beliefs had made them outcasts; after the revocation of the Edict of Nantes in 1685, some 15,000 of them came to America while others went to such European countries as England and the Netherlands. Many German Mennonites had settled in the Volga and Black Sea region of Russia at the end of the eighteenth century, when Catherine the Great offered them immunity from military service and freedom of worship. With the end of the military exemption in 1874, the Mennonites emigrated in large numbers.

Still others came for political reasons. Russian Jews entered the United States in large numbers when the Czarist regime forced them to live in segregated areas and denied them education and entry into the professions. When massacres began in 1882, they emigrated by the millions. But most of the migrants came for economic reasons, driven by the twin pressures of population growth and large-scale shifts in the economy.

The European population had begun to grow rapidly after 1750, when the climate changed for the better, with a favorable effect on crops. Besides, the great epidemics ended, while the introduction of the potato by Sir Francis Drake in the late seventeenth century provided the rural population with more nutrition per acre of land than cereals. After 1800 medical and hygienic improvements also reduced mortality. With more children in each family surviving, the pressure on the land increased. The earlier stages of the demographic transition, with mortality falling and fertility on the rise, always involve rapid population growth (see pp. 141–44). Northwestern Europe and the British Isles went through these phases in the eighteenth and nineteenth centuries, while Southern and Eastern Europe experienced them later.

In the 1770s the belief spread that serfdom and its vestiges had to go, and that the land could be made more productive if appropriate agricultural reforms were enacted. After that time Europe's rural society underwent a transition from feudal or quasi-feudal agriculture to private enterprise farming. In each country a somewhat different landholding pattern prevailed; we will sketch here a highly simplified picture of the transition.

Although in many areas of Europe feudalism was already dead as a political system, much of it lingered on as a landholding system. In the older days of feudalism the political and socioeconomic unit was a village grouped around the landlord's house or castle. The lord provided the serfs with strips of farmland, implements, legal services, and military protection, in return for which the serfs paid with labor on the lord's land or in kind.

When the son took over the deceased father's holding, a fee had to be paid to the lord. Beyond the available land lay the common pasture, providing food for the livestock of lord and serf. The wasteland beyond the pastures supplied wood and sometimes peat for fuel.

Over the centuries, as the feudal system disintegrated and a money economy evolved, the lord's claim over the peasant's output was often replaced by obligatory cash payments. On the eve of the agricultural transition, a bewildering variety of landholding arrangements prevailed.

One category of farmers had bought or inherited unencumbered land. A second group, perhaps the largest, were the copyholders; they were hereditary tenants—former serfs and their descendants whose right to work their strips of arable land for the payment of money was inscribed on the court rolls of the manor. A third class consisted of tenants at will, who could farm the land as long as they and the landowners agreed on the terms. In the British Isles there existed still another group, called cotters, who owned small cabins; they cultivated very small plots, but had rights on the commons. Finally, there were the landless laborers.

In England landlords broke with the old system by raising the inheritance fee to be paid when an heir inherited the land; by raising the customary rents of the copyholders; by buying out copyholders, tenants, and cotters; and by resorting to enclosure. Enclosure consisted of putting up hedges or fences around the commons and wastelands, which the landlords then exploited as they saw fit; their objective was to consolidate their lands. Although enclosure was in direct conflict with established medieval practices, the landlords had the support of Parliament, which coincidentally was filled with landlords around 1800. Without a place to pasture their animals, of course, the villagers often could not make ends meet and had to sell their rights or holdings to the landlord. If the copyholders and cotters could be pushed off the land the landlords could divide their land into a few large, efficient farms and rent them out to enterprising tenant farmers willing to invest capital on the farm in exchange for a long-term lease. This arrangement permitted large-scale capital-intensive farming, which was highly profitable. Those villagers who were pushed off the land mostly migrated to the cities or overseas.

The story of Ireland is more dramatic. The Irish landowner was often an absentee landlord living in England who left the management to an agent whose ability was measured by the amount of money he extracted from the tenants. Some landlords let large tracts of lands to a middleman on a long lease. The middleman could carve the land into small units and sublet them as he chose. As the population increased, so did the rents. The demand for a plot of land became ever more frantic, land became like gold, and lords and middlemen split the land into smaller and smaller units. Then the people themselves divided the land yet again to give their grown-up children a means of living. The alternative to a plot of land was simply starvation. Also prevalent was the conacre system. A *conacre* was not a lease but a licence to occupy, and it was usually limited to one harvest, which the holder had to share with the owner. The conacre system was a kind of sharecropper setup whereby the owner manured the soil and prepared it for seed, while the hirer provided the seeds and did the planting and harvesting. At about the same time, early marriage had also become customary in Ireland, while mortality kept dropping. The consequences were disastrous.

In the early 1800s much of the Irish population lived on a diet of potatoes and milk. The potato was high yielding and easy to cultivate; all one needed was a spade. But the potato is a dangerous crop. In 1845 came that fateful day when the early risers noted a foul smell in the air: blight had struck the potato crop and the great famine began. Continuous land subdivision had created total dependence on the potato, and population density was high. For several years the blight struck again and again. Many tenants could not pay the rent; they were evicted and their possessions seized. A million and a half people died and two million emigrated. Ireland had become a cemetery. A more powerful push factor can hardly be imagined. During the great exodus there was so much disease and hunger on board that the ships carrying the emigrants were called "Irish fever ships" or "coffin ships."

The situation in Continental Europe was again different. The farm was often hereditary in the peasant family, but feudal dues still had to be paid. Most countries abolished seignorial land tenure after 1800, and a system based on individual ownership was usually put in its place. But while peasants became owners of their holding, in western Germany they had to pay the landlord a series of small money remittances in compensation. In Russia the state compensated the landlords, so the peasants had to pay the state over a number of years. Thus the peasants often started out in debt. The farm now had to be equipped, as the landlord no longer provided the tools, and the necessities of commercial farming and modernization required more investment. But the farmers were free to do with their land as they pleased. With mortality dropping, the number of surviving children grew. Farms were thus increasingly subdivided, and the point was quickly reached where an inherited plot could no longer sustain a family. The choice was then to migrate to the city, emigrate, or become a landless proletarian. Even those peasants who could make ends meet might be so saddled with debt that a few bad harvests could force them to sell their land.

In the eighteenth century and before, the principal industries—and the textile trades in particular—had been organized on a domestic basis. Such industries were tied to agriculture in that they were a subsidiary occupation to farming, providing employment in the slack season. Moreover the entire family, wife and children included, could participate, thus providing extra income. But with the Industrial Revolution and improved transportation, cheap city-made factory products could easily be brought to the village, and domestic industry declined. Many artisans lost their trade in the process. Now even more farmers were unable to meet their mortgage payments and had to sell out.

In the 1870s Continental Europe experienced further difficulties. The steamship brought cheap American wheat to Europe. Free trade prevailed, and city dwellers saw their living standard improve as they paid a lower price for their daily bread. But the European farmer was hard hit by a number of bad seasons between 1875 and 1896. A bad harvest was no longer counterbalanced by high prices, as cheap grain was brought in from America. In England entire farms were abandoned, while many Continental farmers were being gradually squeezed out. Some reacted by turning to dairy farming and the production of fruits and vegetables; others migrated to the cities or overseas.

In eastern Germany the peasants worked part of the land on their own behalf, and the rest obligatorily for the lords. By the land reform of 1811, hereditary peasants (copyholders) were allowed to become proprietors if they surrendered one-third of their land to the landlord, who would give up dues and labor services in return. Other tenants could take possession if they relinquished half their land. The lords usually managed to get the best land to begin with, and many of the freed serfs were not left with enough land to support themselves. So they faced a choice of laboring full time on the estates (the equivalent of accepting a lower social status) or migration. As in other countries, the reforms had made it possible for the peasant to leave the estate without the lord's permission, and many did.

Historical Pull Factors

Along with these powerful push forces, strong pull forces were operating. First, many newcomers eagerly sought the political freedom and religious tolerance which existed in America. While the American West was being opened up and cheap land was available, many farmers from Scandinavia, Germany, and the British Isles began to cultivate the new soil. Once the virgin fields were gone, the industries in the East and the Great Lakes region started to develop, and their voracious appetite for unskilled labor absorbed much of the mass immigration of 1880–1920. Much of the city-building was achieved with pick and shovel, and it was the immigrants, particularly the Italians, who wielded the tools.

The revolution in transportation reduced what E. S. Lee called the "intervening obstacles" between place of origin and place of destination (Chapter 8). The spoiled traveler of the 1980s who crosses the Atlantic in a comfortable plane will find it hard to imagine what an ocean voyage meant in the days of sailing. The journey was long, wearing, and perilous. Before 1860 it could take a few weeks when conditions were favorable, or several months when conditions were not. The food and water were often contaminated, and sea sickness, dysentery, and other diseases prevailed; it was not uncommon for a ship carrying 400 passengers to unload one-fourth or more of its human cargo in the ocean during the voyage. After 1815, however, the competition for the emigrant trade sharpened, lowering the costs. Ships brought timber, cotton, and tobacco to Liverpool, Le Havre, and Bremen, and had empty space on their return voyage because the cargo of manufactured goods took up less room. With the steamship came regular, reliable, and inexpensive transatlantic transportation. The trip from England or Western Europe now took ten or twelve days, during which food and water could be kept fresh and resistance to disease maintained, so that mortality fell. Even if sanitary facilities were not ideal, the shortness of the trip made it more bearable. And railways and ferries brought emigrants to their ports of departure, further easing the jolt of dislocation. In Sjaastad's terms, the costs of the migratory move, whether financial or psychological, were sharply reduced.

Still another pull factor was that more information about America was becoming available. In nineteenth-century Europe people were becoming increasingly literate, and newspapers began to publish accounts of the United States. More and more books and guides were published by travelers to America, addressed to a better-educated audience. A growing awareness of opportunities in America was also brought about by the so-called America letters from earlier emigrants. As postal services improved and more people emigrated to the United States, the flood of "Amerikay letthers" (as they were called in Ireland) rose. Settlers in America sent not only letters but money and prepaid tickets. The prepaid passage system expanded enormously before World War I. The letters described and often praised this unknown foreign country, telling of cheap land, good wages, low taxes, elected officials, freedom of religion, and an absence of class distinctions. The common man and honest work commanded greater respect than at home. The letters also mentioned toil, hardship, and disease, but the recipients were already so familiar with these that they were not that frightened. The letters did what television, movies, and newspapers do today in the developing countries: teaching people to be dissatisfied and provided them with the hope of a solution.

Twentieth-Century Push and Pull Factors

The push and pull factors of the twentieth century have hardly differed from those of earlier times. The rise of communism and fascism induced many people to leave Russia, Italy, and Germany for political reasons.

(Communism in Cuba has also prompted a heavy outflow more recently.) Although the Depression of the 1930s made the United States temporarily unattractive and for several years the return flow exceeded the inflow, after World War II many refugees and displaced persons looked for a home in the United States or Canada. The economic upturn of the American economy after 1945 resulted in a strong increase in employment opportunities, and people flowed in in large numbers, all the more so since the war had left the European economy in chaos. At present, the push factors in the third world countries are as strong as ever; if the Western world opened its frontiers completely, hundreds of millions would try to establish themselves in the high-income nations.

THE CONSEQUENCES OF AMERICAN IMMIGRATION

Production results from the effective combination of four major factors: land and other natural resources, labor, entrepreneurship, and capital. The proportion in which each factor is present can vary, but no output is possible without all of them. If, for instance—as was the case in early North American history—there is an enormous supply of land but a shortage of labor and capital, production will suffer. On the other hand, an increase in the supply of labor will improve the resource combination and thus raise per capita productivity. Under such circumstances, an increase in population is an economic blessing.

From the early colonial days until perhaps the first decade of the twentieth century, as we noted, the United States was indeed underpopulated. The frontiers had been continuously expanding, natural resources had been discovered, and abundant capital was available from American and foreign savings. Technology advanced and job opportunities multiplied as enterprising immigrants introduced crafts and set up new industries. Especially during the eighteenth and nineteenth centuries immigrants supplied much of the labor and technical know-how needed to develop the vast resources of a virgin continent. Besides labor power and technical skills, the immigrants furnished entrepreneurial and managerial skills, inventiveness and scientific knowledge.

Immigrants from the British Isles and Northern and Western Europe developed the farmlands of the West once the lands had been cleared by pioneers. Many immigrants brought with them financial means to equip and improve the newly bought farmlands. The great agricultural potential of the West was realized.

In the early days of America, a steady flow of European artisans established the first small industries, especially on the Eastern seaboard. In the nineteenth century, artisans, operators, overseers, and entrepreneurs, mainly from the United Kingdom, imported the technologies developed in the textile, shipbuilding, mining, iron, and steel industries. Immigrants from Central and Southern Europe provided the bone and sinew that the rapidly growing industries needed, while also supplying much of the muscle power required in the construction of the transportation and public utilities systems.

As industry expanded and immigrants gravitated toward the lowest paid and least desirable jobs, increased opportunities were created for the native workers and the "older" immigrants, who could move on to supervisory positions or jobs with higher pay and prestige. But as the land became settled and nonrenewable resources were consumed, America's capacity for absorbing immigrants was reduced. Nor is the level of production independent of the nation's environmental quality. Although it may be impossible to state exactly when immigration ceased to be a benefit, the report of the Commission on Population Growth and the American Future has stated again and again that there are no economic advantages to further population growth.[2]

A Note on Developing Countries

Although history does not necessarily repeat itself, there are always some analogies. The push factors fostering emigration which prevailed in preindustrial Europe now seem to exist in many less developed nations. Since the majority of the population in developing countries still lives on the land, the prevailing land tenure system is of utmost importance. Different types of land ownership prevail in different countries and may exist in combination in the same nation.

In many areas of the world, land is concentrated in the hands of a few owners. They may be absentee owners or they may let out the land to tenants through intermediate leases. In certain parts of Latin America, the Middle East, and Southeast Asia, for instance, a small quasi-feudal class of landowners still exists, while the land is tilled by tenants, sharecroppers, or farm laborers. Frequently, the tenants are permanently indebted to their landlords, who make loans at usurious rates. Furthermore, increasing population means a growing scarcity of land. As happened in Ireland and elsewhere, the frantic scramble for land pushes rents up enormously—they can rise to 70 percent of the value of the crop, leaving the rural populations with only meager subsistence. As the proportion of rent to total agricultural income goes up, the income distribution becomes ever more uneven.

[2] Commission on Population Growth and the American Future, *Population and the American Future* (Washington: Government Printing Office, 1972).

If land is communally owned, as in many parts in Africa, there is little incentive to improve it. First of all, the more energetic members of the group cannot acquire land at the expense of the more lethargic. Second, individuals cannot borrow on the security of land for productive improvements. Third, lots may be periodically reallocated by tribal or village authorities, and if there are common pasturelands, as there used to be in Europe, individuals have no incentive to limit the number of cattle they graze, because any benefit will be reduced by the overgrazing of others. Destructive erosion is often the result.

When peasants own the land themselves, the situation is not necessarily any better. The chief problem may be fragmentation of the land. More children are surviving, and the farmer (depending on the inheritance system) often leaves a parcel to every son, while the custom of giving land as a dowry to daughters may also produce fragmentation. When the land is subdivided among heirs, custom sometimes dictates that every heir should receive some of the choicest land. As a result, the individual farmer may end up with several pieces of land, of varying quality, scattered over an area. The cultivation of such holdings is wasteful in terms of labor and time.

Peasants in developing nations may revolt against the existing social order and press for land reforms. Or their inclination to migrate to the city or another country may be strengthened. Exhausted soils, high rents, oppressive indebtedness, fragmented holdings, severe overcrowding—all combine to create strong pressures for departure to countries where conditions are more favorable. A survey of the motives for immigration to the U.S.A. shows that historically they have been very similar from first to last. They are likely to remain identical in the near future.

AMERICAN IMMIGRATION POLICY: PAST AND PRESENT

The Beginnings of Restriction

The nineteenth century witnessed the triumph of classical liberalism, which advocates the free movement of humans, commodities, and capital. Governments were therefore little inclined to interfere with immigration. However, in 1882 the first attempt to regulate immigration was made with the Chinese Exclusion Act. In response to public pressure originating in the Pacific states, Congress suspended Chinese immigration for a period of ten years and also forbade the naturalization of Chinese. In 1892 the act was renewed for another ten years; in 1902 Chinese immigration was suspended for an indefinite period.

In 1882 a law excluding "convicts, lunatics, idiots and paupers" was also enacted. The law marked the first attempt to weed out undesirable emigrants; the practice continued as a basis for government policy until the 1920s.

Pressure for restrictive immigration soon became more broad-based. Even as the Statue of Liberty was being erected, in 1886, Americans began to doubt the wisdom of unrestricted European immigration. As more Southern and Eastern Europeans streamed in, the immigrants of older stock argued that people of such diverse cultures could not easily be assimilated. Others stressed that the new immigrants came primarily from countries governed by monarchs or dictators, which might endanger the democratic experiment in America. The American Federation of Labor feared that the low wages unskilled immigrant workers were willing to accept might undermine the standard of living of the American laborer. Finally, it was argued that the era of unrestrained expansion had come to an end with the closing of the frontier. The days had passed when the United States could absorb over a million immigrants a year.

The device the *restrictionists* wanted to use was the literacy test. Since many members of the "new" immigration could neither read nor write, a law providing for the exclusion of illiterates would at once be selective and restrictive. Presidents Cleveland, Taft, and Wilson had vetoed similar measures but in 1917, amid the passions of war, Congress passed the law over Wilson's veto. Literacy was now required of aliens over 16 years old as a condition of permanent residence. At the same time the head tax on immigrants was raised and the so-called Asiatic Barred Zone was set up. Under this arrangement inhabitants of Southeast Asia and China were denied entry as immigrants.

But this was not the end. World War I had stirred up nationalist feelings, generating a distrust of everything foreign. *Isolationism*—the desire for a complete separation from Europe—began to take hold. It is against this background that the restrictive legislation of the 1920s must be understood.

The End of an Era

On May 29, 1921, President Harding signed a bill that ended the era of practically unlimited immigration. Congress feared that wartorn Europe would send millions of its Southern and Eastern inhabitants to the United States—an event that, it was felt, would subvert the traditional American way of life. Immediately after the war, immigration had in fact resumed, and steamship companies reported a tremendous volume of immigrant travel in prospect. The highest estimate of the number of Europeans ready to move to America was 25 million. A climate of crisis prevailed in Congress, and the Quota Act of 1921 was enacted and signed by the President. Immigrants were now to be selected according to certain standards of acceptability. Moreover, immigration was to be restricted by a quota system setting a maximum number of entries per year. It limited the number of European immigrants to 3 percent of the number of that nationality living in the United States according to the census of 1910, with an annual maximum for all nations taken together of 357,000. The measure enacted by Congress was actually only provisional. In 1922 the act was extended for two more years.

The Quota Act favored immigration from Northwestern Europe, and was based upon the notion that individuals from Northern European countries can more easily be integrated into the American community than emigrants from Southern and Eastern Europe. The Johnson-Reed Act of 1924 established a yearly quota of 154,000 for the European nations. The nationality quota was lowered to 2 percent, and the basis for computation was changed to the census of 1890, favoring Northwestern Europe even more. The system was to be replaced in 1927 by a national origins plan. The irony of the 1924 act was that it favored the countries that had the fewest migrants to send, since they had already reached that phase of the demographic transition in which fertility drops. The countries of the Western Hemisphere were exempted. Orientals were for all practical purposes excluded.

After 1924 a committee worked for five years to establish what the ethnic composition of the American population really was. The committee's findings resulted in the National Origin Quota Act of 1929, stipulating that each European nation would annually receive a quota which bore the same ratio to the total quota of 154,000 as the number of people from that country, by either birth or descent, bore to the total American population in 1920. Thus the total quota was apportioned among the European nations according to their relative contribution to the total American population as enumerated by the census of 1920.

With the passage of the act, immigration fell sharply. The Northern and Western European countries never filled their quotas, whereas Southern and Eastern Europe lacked any significant quotas to fill. The era of unrestricted immigration had ended.

Still They Come:
Immigration Policy After 1930

While the Great Depression reduced the inflow, the Hoover administration ordered a stricter enforcement of the 1917 immigration act forbidding the entry of individuals likely to become a public charge. This policy was not abandoned until 1937. Most refugees from Nazi Germany who came after 1934 entered within the limits of the quotas.

After World War II there were two new problems to be faced. Returning American service personnel often wanted to bring European wives, children, or fiancées to the United States. The War Brides and Fiancées Act of 1946 relaxed the quota requirements for their benefit. Meanwhile the refugee problem had assumed unprecedented proportions. In response, the Displaced Persons Act of 1948, amended in 1950, provided for the admission of 400,000 persons over a four-year period.

During the administration of President Truman, Congress once again thoroughly reviewed the nation's immigration policy, then in 1952 it passed the Immigrant and Nationality Act, better known as the *McCarran-Walker Act*. The first section of the act, dealing with European immigrants, retained the national origins plan and its quotas, but introduced a method for allotting numbers within each nation's quota. Fifty percent of each quota was assigned to individuals possessing special skills and qualifications that America needed, and spouses, children, and close relatives of citizens and resident aliens had a priority for the remaining places. The rest of the quota went to nonpreference applicants.

The ban on Asian and African citizens was removed, so that they now became eligible for citizenship. Moreover, each African and Asian country received a quota of 100; and to provide for people of mixed origin a special Asia-Pacific quota of 100 was established. Because the bill was prepared after the outbreak of the Cold War, when fear of communism ran high, it broadened the grounds for exclusion on grounds of subversive activities, criminal records, and chronic diseases. Congress passed the law over the veto of President Truman. Indeed, passing an immigration act over a presidential veto seems to have become a congressional tradition.

Whatever its shortcomings, the act introduced the concept that immigration policy should be responsive to the nation's occupational needs. In the years following the McCarran-Walker Act it was increasingly argued that occupational skills and other special qualifications, rather than country of origin, should be used as the criteria for admission. President Kennedy initiated legislation to substitute general priorities for the national origins quota system. He explained his position in a book published after his death.[3]

In 1965 Congress enacted a law that abolished the quota system and welcomed immigrants according to their skills. Under the new act, which went into full effect in 1968, an overall quota of 170,000 annual immigrants was established for Eastern Hemisphere countries. No individual country was to exceed 20,000. First preference amounting to 20 percent of the quota places, went to relatives of United States citizens. The remaining 80 percent was assigned to professionals, to skilled and unskilled workers needed in the economy; and to refugees, displaced persons, and the like. A quota of 120,000 was set up for the Western Hemisphere,

---

[3] J. F. Kennedy, *A Nation of Immigrants* (New York: Harper & Row), 1964.

including Canada. Canadians and Mexicans may enter on a first-come, first-served basis. There were no ceilings for individual countries, and categorical preferences were omitted. Since 1968 the same preference system has been applied to applicants from the Eastern as from the Western Hemisphere. But in 1976 a congressional amendment placed a ceiling of 20,000 on Western Hemisphere nations.

As we saw earlier, a dramatic shift took place in the sources of immigration once these new regulations took effect. This is basically because in 1968 Congress lowered the "intervening obstacles" between third world countries and the United States. Subsequently, the Refugee Act of 1980 sought to establish a coherent refugee policy for the United States by raising the limit on refugee admissions to 50,000 annually for the first three fiscal years. Thereafter, the number is to be determined annually by the president in consultation with Congress.

CONCEPTS FOR REVIEW

Colonial immigration

Mass migration

"New" immigrants

Enclosure

Remittances

Chinese Exclusion Act

Restrictionists

Quota Act of 1921

War Brides and Fiancées Act

McCarran-Walker Act

QUESTIONS FOR DISCUSSION

1. Discuss the differences between the "old" and the "new" migration.
2. When commercial farming displaced the semifeudal landholding systems in Europe, large numbers of peasants emigrated to the United States. Why?
3. In what sense did the steamship encourage emigration from Europe to the United States?
4. A letter to the editor of the *Wall Street Journal* in February 1981 said the following: "The underlying assumption of the argument for increased immigration is that the U.S. is in some strange and wonderful way exempt from the limits that space and resources place upon population growth." Do you agree? Why or why not?
5. Why is it that millions of people from the less developed countries would risk their lives and fortunes to reach the United States?
6. Since 1965 the quota system of immigration has been replaced by a selection of immigrants according to skills. Discuss the advantages and disadvantages of this policy change.

BIBLIOGRAPHY

Bouvier, L., et al., *International Migration: Yesterday, Today and Tomorrow.* Washington: Population Reference Bureau, 1977.

Commission on Population Growth and the American Future. *Population and the American Future.* Washington: Government Printing Office, 1972.

Deane, P. *The First Industrial Revolution.* London: Cambridge University Press, 1967.

Divine, R. A. *American Immigration Policy 1924–1952.* New Haven: Yale University Press, 1957.

Habakkuk, H. J. and M. Postan, eds. *The Cambridge Economic History of Europe.* Vol. 6. Cambridge, England: Cambridge University Press, 1965.

Heaton, H. *Economic History of Europe.* New York: Harper, 1948.

Kennedy, J. F. *A Nation of Immigrants.* New York: Harper & Row, 1964.

Scott, F. D. *Emigration and Immigration.* New York: Macmillan, 1963.

Taylor, P. *The Distant Magnet,* New York: Harper & Row, 1971.

Ziegler, B. M., ed. *Immigration, An American Dilemma.* Boston: Heath, 1953.

10

Internal Migration

Internal migration represents the dynamic aspect of population distribution. As noted earlier, internal migrants are attracted to the sections of their nation with relatively high incomes and favorable employment opportunities. Migrants also prefer areas with mild climates and ample educational, health, and recreational facilities. A clean, quiet environment also has high drawing power.

In the United States, freedom to move anywhere within the country is a constitutional right. Large expanses of nearly uniform terrain and a more or less homogeneous culture have combined with the absence of political obstacles to make the United States a highly mobile nation. Typically, 20 percent of the population moves each year. But most of those who pull up stakes are actually not migrants, since they relocate within short distances and do not cross administrative boundaries.

Migration within a nation's borders usually takes two forms; it is either interstate and/or interregional, or rural to urban. The distinction is obviously somewhat arbitrary; much interstate migration is also rural-urban. However, the distinction between the two general types is a useful one.

A SHORT HISTORY OF INTERNAL MIGRATION

Settlement in the United States, which began along the Atlantic seaboard, with a population that was mainly agricultural, involved the colonization of new land. From colonial times onward, of course, there was a continuous westward movement. The native Americans were uprooted, and the migrants, some of whom had come from abroad, took over their land. The *westward expansion* accelerated after 1800, and was later aided by the building of a transcontinental railroad system.[1] By the 1890s, however, all the agricultural lands had been appropriated. While most of the westward trek had consisted of interregional migration, *rural-urban migration* developed simultaneously. Even in colonial days the cities may have grown faster than the nation's population as a whole. After 1800 this was certainly the case, and the trend persisted until the 1960s.

In fact, from about 1880 to the late 1920s, when the Industrial Revolution was accelerating, internal migration was mainly rural-urban. Industrial revolutions tend to be accompanied by a strong country-to-city drift, and America was no exception. Foreign as well as internal migrants flocked to the big cities of the Northeast and North-Central regions, where the most rapid industrialization occurred. In the rural-urban drift, which also involved a movement from the Midwest back to the East, many workers left the farms, where they were less in demand than before. After the turn of the century—and especially after 1920—men and women (as well as horses and mules) were increasingly replaced, on the farms, by tractors, trucks, and cars. With the new implements, the same amount of work could be accomplished with less labor. Thus, a powerful push factor prevailed, while the expanding manufacturing and commercial centers attracted the labor that the countryside no longer needed. When World War I reduced European immigration, and the restrictive immigration laws of the 1920s took effect, the demand for industrial workers from within the nation increased even further.

The industrial prosperity generated by World War I and the boom that followed the war had a powerful impact on the South as well as on the North. Fertility in the South had been high. Employment opportunities were few, while racial discrimination in hiring and education reduced pos-

---

[1] The American railroad system was born in 1830 in Maryland. Yet only in 1869 was the first transcontinental railroad completed.

sibilities for social advancement among blacks. Many young blacks could not afford to buy farmland; and even if they had money, white owners might refuse to sell to them. So blacks began to leave the Southern cotton belt in large numbers, especially after 1910. They went mainly to the manufacturing centers of the Northeastern and North-Central regions (in many cities, blacks settled in the central areas while whites moved out to the suburbs). Much of this migration was both interstate and rural-urban: from the rural South the blacks went to the industrial North. It also involved migration from a relatively uncomplicated environment to a much more complex one. Predictably, the migrants experienced numerous and often severe adjustment problems. And the poverty the migrants brought with them from the farms became an additional burden on the large urban centers.

The Depression decade of 1930–40 slowed down these migratory movements without reversing them completely. Total migration (irrespective of direction) fell during the entire period. Once the bubble of prosperity had burst, a major pull factor had evaporated. Some back-to the-land movement occurred: rather than asking for public assistance, some migrants went back to the home farm or undertook subsistence farming on abandoned lands.

Yet even during the Depression the drawing power of the cities did not completely disappear. After the inauguration of Franklin D. Roosevelt, in 1933, the federal government became heavily involved in public relief; through public works, it also became an employer of last resort. Since, to a large extent, benefit programs were available only in towns and cities, they spurred both poor white and black sharecroppers of the South to leave their rural homes and move to the cities. During the 1930s the Plains states were plagued by drought, again leading many small farmers to leave the land, frequently for the Pacific states. During the early 1940s, when the effects of the war effort were beginning to be felt, a revival of the cityward movement occurred.

As rural-urban migration resumed at full speed, so did the South-North movement. Until about 1970 the South remained a net exporter of people, many of them black, in part because of profound changes taking place in the rural South. Mechanization had first been achieved on the family farms of the Midwest. Only later did the large cotton, rice, and sugar plantations of the South follow. But despite mechanization, cotton production in the South did not fare well: the boom in synthetic fibers and the loss of foreign markets created serious problems. Many cotton belt farm workers were forced off the land. And small operators who did not have the capital to invest in mechanization joined the cityward exodus.

Another historic stream that continued until about 1970 was the Western migration to the Pacific states and, especially, to California. During the 1950s and 1960s this state welcomed an average of 1,000 migrants a day. Jobs in the aerospace industry, a benign climate, and attractive surroundings all combined to make this region particularly appealing.

As discussed in Chapter 5, the growth of metropolitan areas became particularly evident after World War II. Within a metropolitan area, however, people have tended to move away from the central cities into the suburbs. This intercounty migration has been in part responsible for the so-called metropolitan sprawl. It was especially the whites who moved out to suburbs, while the blacks from the South continued to move into the central cities of the Northeast, the North-Central states, and to a lesser extent the Pacific coast.

After 1970 a number of fundamental changes began to occur. First, the stream from farm to city became negligible. In 1970 only 4 percent of the population was still involved in farming, growing enough food for the remainder and a good deal available for export.[2] But if American farming has become highly productive, it is also very vulnerable. It depends on an unrestricted supply of gasoline, chemicals, electricity, farm implements, and spare parts.

Another shift in trend has been the reversal in the growth pattern of the metropolitan areas. Between 1970 and 1977, population growth in nonmetropolitan regions was actually higher (10.7 percent) than in metropolitan areas (4.4 percent), which were experiencing a relative decline. In the central cities there was, in that period, actually a net decline in population. Evidently, in the largest metropolitan areas some critical level of congestion had been reached, and some of the nonmetropolitan growth was apparently spillover. Since rapid growth took place in a number of nonmetropolitan areas immediately outside metropolitan areas, many people had obviously moved to lower-density areas to live, while commuting to work in the city.

In the 1970s the South-North tide was also reversed, as Figure 10–1 illustrates. With the exception of Florida, before 1970 the Southern states experienced net out-migration. But since 1970, the South has become a net importer of people. And it is not merely whites who are moving south; blacks have also joined the stream. The reasons for this new trend are not hard to guess. Congestion, pollution, and crime in the metropolitan centers of the Northeast and North-Central states have reached critical levels. Fiscal problems have led to cutbacks in municipal and local services. The industrial apparatus of the North has aged, and the railway system has deteriorated without being replaced with a reliable public transportation system. Militancy among trade unions has raised industry's wage costs substantially. These factors have impelled both industries and individuals

[2]To be classified as a *farm resident,* a person must live in rural territory on property that produces at least a small volume of agricultural products for sale.

FIGURE 10–1

Net Interregional Migration (United States, 1970–75)

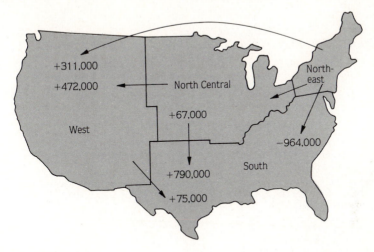

Source: J. C. Biggar, *The Sunning of America: Migration to the Sunbelt*, 34 no. 1 (Washington: Population Reference Bureau, March 1979) 11.

and families to leave. At the same time, the South's economy has been brought more in line with that of the rest of the nation. Modern highways, ports, and air terminals have lured industry, as has the accessibility of energy and water. Upgraded education and vocational-training have increased the supply of skilled workers. Moreover, taxes tend to be lower and trade unions less militant.

The South has advantages, as well, for individuals and families. Jobs are relatively plentiful, and many people are moving to the South in search of work. Because of the milder climate, housing and heating costs are low. Also, greater opportunities for year-round outdoor activities exist, while the racial climate has much improved. Finally, numerous retirees find that they benefit from the milder climate.[3] And older people find that their Social Security checks go further in the South and other Sunbelt states. (Similarly, in England and France older people move to the relatively warm southern coasts.) Many Sunbelt states have established health and recreational facilities specifically geared to the needs of the elderly.

The westward expansion still exists, but since 1970 the influx into California has tapered off somewhat. The most rapid growth now occurs in the Mountain states of the West; Arizona and New Mexico are now experiencing especially strong inflows.

[3] In the period 1970–75, 5 percent of the internal migrants were 65 or over.

TABLE 10–1

Percentage Distribution of United States Population
by Region, 1790–1977

Area	1790	1810	1830	1850	1870	1890	1910	1930	1950	1970	1977
Total United States	100.0	100.0	100.0	100.0	100.0	100.0	100.0	100.0	100.0	100.0	100.0
Northeast	50	48.3	43.0	37.1	30.8	27.6	28.0	27.9	26.0	23.9	22.8
North Central	n.d.	4.0	12.5	23.2	32.5	35.5	32.3	31.3	29.3	27.6	26.8
South	50	48.0	44.2	38.6	30.8	31.8	31.8	30.7	31.3	30.6	32.3
West	n.d.	n.d.	n.d.	0.8	2.5	5.0	7.7	10.0	13.3	17.0	18.2

Sources: U.S. Bureau of the Census, *Historical Statistics* (Washington: U.S. Government Printing Office, 1975), p. 22. U.S. Bureau of the Census, *Statistical Abstract of the United States: 1979* (Washington: U.S. Government Printing Office, 1979), p. 14.

Table 10–1, showing the evolution of the percentage distribution by regions in the United States, illustrates the trends outlined here. The relative importance of the Northeast has declined since 1790. The North Central region reached its peak around 1890. The growth of the West continues unabated, while the very recent upturn of the South is emphasized by a comparison of the figures for 1970 and 1977.

INTERNAL MIGRATION IN DEVELOPING NATIONS

In developing countries internal migration is mostly of two kinds. First, there is the movement to settle new territories as long as a frontier exists. Second, there is the rural-urban drift responding to a real or perceived change in opportunities.

As long as a nation still has unoccupied territories, or even marshlands that can be reclaimed, it has a frontier to which migrants can go. It often makes no difference if, in climate, environmental quality, soil fertility, and distance from markets, the frontier lands are inferior to the areas already settled. Brazil, for example, is attempting to gain land at the expense of the Amazon forest; the Chinese have encouraged the settlement of the western interior of their country; Indonesia is promoting migration from Java to other islands; and Israel has sponsored new villages in the Negev desert, once irrigation canals have been built.

But rural-urban migration remains the most important movement in

FIGURE 10-2

Regions and Divisions of the United States

* Pacific division includes Alaska and Hawaii.

developing nations. In Western nations and Japan, the sequence of development have had a common theme. Commercial farming was introduced first, and as agriculture became increasingly mechanized, it released surplus workers. Meanwhile, industrialization in the urban centers created new opportunities, so as the countryside pushed people out, the cities pulled them in. The cities served as a safety valve for rural population pressures and turned landless farmers and jobless artisans into an efficient urban labor force.

Not all developing nations repeat this pattern, however. The transformation of agriculture often lags, either because of the unproductive land tenure patterns (Chapter 9) or because many third world countries concentrate development funds in the big cities while neglecting their rural economy. Population often grows faster than was ever the case in the West (Kenya's population, for instance, grows at 4 percent per year and will double in eighteen years). The cities themselves frequently expand before any movement toward modernization has taken place. The cities, in fact, are primarily administrative centers set up by the colonial powers, and/or shipping centers for raw materials or crops from local mines and plantations. This makes them very different from the manufacturing and commercial centers of Europe and North America, which grew as a result of internally generated modernization and diversification.

Rapid urbanization, resulting mainly from a strong rural-urban drift, is now under way in many developing countries. Frequently, however, the urbanization does not mirror genuine modernization as it did in the West. Rather, the increasing density of occupation of arable land provides a strong incentive for people to leave the countryside. The disparity between numbers and agrarian resources is intensified by the government's comparative neglect of the countryside, which results in rural stagnation. At the same time, governments tend to devote their scarce resources to improve life in the urban areas, and the cities thus become relatively attractive. A flight from the land is inevitable.

At present about 39 percent of the world's population is urban. There is no indication that the rate of urbanization is slackening, either for the world as a whole or in the third world. Between 1970 and 1975 the net countryside to city flow in the developing countries amounted to 73 million people. In these countries the biggest cities are also the ones with the highest growth rate. Teheran, for instance, grew from 200,000 inhabitants in 1900 to just under 4.5 million in 1976. According to one source, by 1986 one-fourth of the entire Iranian population may be living in the capital city.[4]

The growth of the metropolitan areas has been spurred by the fact that, for a number of reasons, they are attractive to business and industry. Since most workers have little training and few skills, employers need a large pool of workers to choose from. Moreover, in the smaller cities and towns, public services are often inadequate. Blackouts are frequent, the water may be polluted, roads are low-grade, and telephone services unreliable. Delivery of mail is slow. Hotels are often of poor quality, while schools for the children of managers and engineers may be third-rate or nonexistent. Houses may be in short supply, and culture and entertainment close to zero. It is only in the metropolitan areas, that is, that business, and business executives, can find the facilities they need.

CONCEPTS FOR REVIEW

Interregional migration   Westward expansion
Rural-urban migration   Farm resident

[4]D. Behnam and M. Amani, *La Population de l'Iran* (Paris: Committee for International Coordination of National Research in Demography, 1974), p. 40.

QUESTIONS FOR DISCUSSION

1. In the twentieth century millions of people left farms to establish themselves in the cities. Discuss some of the push and pull factors at work.
2. Why has rural-urban migration in the United States for all practical purposes come to an end?
3. The Sunbelt now experiences net immigration. Explain some of the factors that make this region attractive.
4. In what sense is rural-urban migration in many third world nations different from the rural-urban migration which took place in the Western nations and Japan?

BIBLIOGRAPHY

Bairoch, P. *Urban Unemployment in Developing Countries*. Geneva: International Labor Office, 1973.

Behnam, D., and M. Amani. *La Population de l'Iran*. Paris: Committee for International Coordination of National Research in Demography, 1974.

Biggar, J. C. *The Sunning of America: Migration to the Sunbelt*. Washington: Population Reference Bureau, 1979.

Goodrich, C., et al. *Migration and Planes of Living 1920–1934*. Philadelphia: University of Pennsylvania Press, 1935.

Shryock, H. S. *Population Mobility Within the United States*. Chicago: Community and Family Studies Center, 1974.

Thompson, W. S. *Research Memorandum on Internal Migration in the Depression*. New York: Arno Press, 1972.

11

The Composition

of Population

POPULATION PROCESSES AND POPULATION COMPOSITION

Population processes—fertility, mortality, and migration—determine the growth or decline and movement of a population. *Composition (or structure) of population* refers to the basic characteristics by which the individuals who make up the population can be differentiated; some of the characteristics are more important to demographers than others. Of particular interest are sex, age, race, marital status, education, religion, and profession. Because sex and age are the pivotal features, most of the discussion will be devoted to these two traits; race will be considered briefly. The demographic processes and population composition are intimately related. As we'll see in a later section, fertility, mortality and migration have an impact on population composition, while, on the other hand, the composition of the population affects the three processes.

SEX COMPOSITION

The Sex Ratio

The sex composition in a population is a basic characteristic that has direct impact on nuptiality and fertility. Sex, of course, is one of the most readily observable components of population structure. People may misreport their age, but they are less likely to misstate their sex. The sex composition of a population is conventionally expressed by a summarizing device called the *sex ratio,* the *masculinity ratio,* or the *ratio of males to females.* The ratio shows the number of males per 100 females (see pp. 31–32) and is written as

$$\frac{M}{F} \cdot k$$

where M = total number of males in the population
    F = total number of females in the same population
    k = a constant—in this case, 100

For instance, the sex ratio in the United States in 1977 is shown in the formula 105,240,000 males/111,092,000 females × 100 = 95. When the sex ratio is more than 100, males outnumber females. The American population in 1977 had more females than males, since the ratio for that year was under 100. In earlier times, though, over-100 sex ratios were typical of America, partly because more men than women immigrated (see Chapter 9). In 1910 the sex ratio was highest; there were 106 males for every 100 females. Since then the figure has dropped gradually, reaching a virtually balanced sex composition in 1949. Since 1950 the U.S. population has had more females than males.

In the populations of most Western countries, including the United States, the sex ratio at birth is about 105, which means that for every 100 girls about 105 boys are born. For American blacks the sex ratio at birth is about 103. The sex ratio tends to decline progressively for each age group because of the high male mortality. As Chapter 6 points out, females of all ages have more favorable survival rates than males.

Sex ratios constitute an important piece of demographic knowledge; if an imbalance exists between the sexes and is not recognized, incorrect interpretations of statistics on marriages and births can result. And, in particular, sex ratios below 90 and above 110 indicate the presence of highly unusual social, political, or natural factors that need to be taken into account.

Determinants of Sex Ratio

More male than female births is a feature of most mammals, including human beings. In advanced nations, where women generally have good health and few prenatal losses, sex ratios at birth hover around 105, as they do in the United States. In low-income countries, where prenatal losses are more frequent, sex ratios at birth are around 102. Since, ordinarily, more males than females are conceived, improved health care for pregnant women will result in a higher sex ratio at birth.

The prevalence of female infanticide is another determinant of the sex ratio. In the past, in societies that preferred boys and practiced infanticide, more girls than boys were put to death, which increased the sex ratio.

Furthermore, in a number of societies girls are given inferior food, medical treatment, and personal care. This relative neglect of female children usually results in higher female mortality and, ultimately, in higher sex ratios. It is partly for this reason that rather high sex ratios are found in such countries as Pakistan, India, Turkey, and Iran. In 1973, Iran had a sex ratio of 107.[1] Another reason is that female births are often underreported in third world countries.

In advanced societies the mortality differential favors females, as we observed in Chapter 6. This mortality differential tends to reduce the sex ratio. Especially when the proportion of aged people in a population increases (a problem to be discussed in detail in later sections), the sex ratio is bound to decline, because in such circumstances the proportion of surviving females grows steadily.

Wars that result in large numbers of male casualties also distort the sex ratio. It has been calculated that if the First World War had not occurred, the German sex ratio in 1925 would have been 98.8, whereas in fact it stood at 93.9.

Large-scale migrations affect the sex ratio in the area of origin as well as in the area of destination. In Canada and the United States the sex ratio was considerably influenced by pre–World War I immigration, which was preponderantly male. In 1911 the Canadian sex ratio reached a peak of 113. Frontier areas, mining districts, and the like are typically characterized by a high sex ratio, because such areas attract male more than female immigrants. In large cities such as Washington, D.C., where a good deal of clerical work is done, females tend to outnumber males, because more women than men are employed as office workers. In many developing countries, the high levels of rural-urban migration, which is heavily male, can distort the population structure of the cities. And considerable imbalance in the sex structure affects community life negatively, as it did in the

---

[1] The computation was 16,328,000 males/15,317,000 females $\times 100 = 106.60 = 107$ males per 100 females.

former frontier areas of the United States. Because for many adults a normal family life is not possible, prostitution and delinquency may become rampant.

Trends in Sex Ratios

For the world as a whole the sex ratio was estimated at 100 in 1975. For the developed countries the ratio was 94, and for the developing nations, 103. No sudden or drastic changes are anticipated. (The sex ratios are higher in the less developed countries, for the reasons stated earlier.) In the developed countries, the number of surviving members of male and female cohorts becomes equal at an earlier stage than in developing nations. The turning point for a country like Great Britain is about age 45; for developing countries it is around 60. The normal trend of the sex ratio in industrialized countries is downward. Boy and girl babies are equally well cared for. Because male mortality exceeds female mortality at all ages, the initial preponderance of males is gradually reduced until the sex ratio reaches unity, while at older ages females outnumber males in each cohort. In 1977, for instance, the United States sex ratio for the population aged 65 and over was just below 69.

TABLE 11–1

Sex Ratios (United States and Canada, 1850–1976)

United States		Canada	
Census Year	*Sex Ratio*	*Census Year*	*Sex Ratio*
1850	104	1851	105
1860	105	1861	106
1870	102	1871	103
1880	104	1881	103
1890	105	1891	104
1900	104	1901	105
1910	106	1911	113
1920	104	1921	106
1930	102	1931	107
1940	101	1941	105
1950	99	1951	102
1960	98	1961	102
1970	95	1971	100
1976	95	1976	99 (latest)
1979	95		

Sources: U.S. Bureau of the Census, *Statistical Abstract of the United States, 1980* (Washington: U.S. Government Printing Office, 1977), p. 28. 1971 Census of Canada, *Profile Studies, Demographic Characteristics,* 5 (Ottawa: Statistics Canada, 1976) 4.

Table 11–1 shows the trends in American and Canadian sex ratios since 1850. The figures for the two countries are comparable in that the highest sex ratio was reached around 1910, and for the same reasons. Between 1900 and 1913 heavy immigration from Europe, chiefly comprising of young males, helped push the sex ratio to high levels. After World War I immigration tapered off but remained more important in Canada (relative to the total population) than in the United States.

As stated earlier, the sex ratios are higher in the less developed countries. As the low-income nations move through the modernization process, their sex ratios are bound to fall, as they have done in the advanced nations.

AGE COMPOSITION

It is important for the social scientist to have precise information about the age composition of a population, because the action and reactions of a population differ according to the proportions of young people, adults, and the aged. Familiarity with the age configuration of a population is also necessary for sound demographic predictions. And information on the age structure of a population is vital to policymakers as well. Government programs involving schools, medical facilities, housing, employment and the like cannot be properly designed unless the age structure and its likely future evolution are known.

Median Age

A simple way to describe the age distribution of a population is to use an average. Some authors use the arithmetic mean for analysis. However, as we explained in Chapter 2, (pp. 28–29), the *median age* is more commonly employed because most population distributions are skewed. The median age of a population divides that population into two equal groups, half older than the median age half younger.

Like individuals, populations can grow older, but unlike them they can also grow younger. When a population ages, the median age rises; when a population is rejuvenating itself, the median age falls. Demographers define a population with a median of less than 20 as "young." A population with a median of 20 to 29 is called "intermediate," while a population with a median of 30 or over is designated "old," although "fully mature" would be more appropriate. For developed countries the long-term trend of the median age is upward, reflecting the aging process typical of all low-fertility, industrialized nations.

Table 11–2 shows the median age for the United States and Canada

TABLE 11–2

Median Age of American and Canadian Population, 1850–1978

	United States		Canada	
Year	Median Age	Year	Median Age	
1850	18.9	1851	17.2	
1860	19.4	1861	18.2	
1870	20.2	1871	18.8	
1880	20.9	1881	20.1	
1890	22.0	1891	21.4	
1900	22.9	1901	22.7	
1910	24.1	1911	23.8	
1920	25.3	1921	24.0	
1930	26.5	1931	25.0	
1940	29.0	1941	27.1	
1950	30.2	1951	27.7	
1960	29.6	1961	26.3	
1970	28.1	1971	26.3	
1978	29.7	1976	27.8 *(latest)*	
1979	30			

Sources: 1971 Census of Canada, *Profile Studies, Demographic Characteristics,* 5 (Ottawa: Statistics Canada, 1976) 22. U.S. Bureau of the Census, *Statistical Abstract of the United States: 1980* (Washington: U.S. Government Printing Office, 1980), p. 28.

between 1850 and 1978. For both nations the largest jump in the median age occurred between 1930 and 1940 (1941 for Canada) a period characterized by low birth rates and equally low levels of immigration. The postwar rejuvenation of population reversed the trend. Because of the drop in fertility that started in the early 1960s, the long-term trend in aging has resumed. In the United States, though, the diversity of population is reflected in different median-age statistics for different groups. Because of higher fertility levels, for instance, the black population has a lower median age than its white counterpart. In 1978 the median age for the black population was 24.3 while it was 30.6 for whites.

The developing countries have much lower median ages than the advanced nations, again because of different vital conditions. As a rule, high birth rates are accompanied by low median ages, and vice versa.

COMPARISONS OF AGE AND SEX COMPOSITION

Once the census data are known, age distributions are relatively easy to calculate. But to present all the data in detail may sometimes be confusing.

TABLE 11–3

Population of the World, Developed and Developing Regions,
North America and Europe; Distribution by Broad Age Groups, 1975

| Age Group | Percentage of Total Population | | | | |
	World	MDC's	LDC's	N. America	Europe
0–14	36.0	27.9	38.7	25.5	23.9
15–64	58.3	64.6	57.0	64.3	63.8
65+	5.7	7.6	4.4	10.2	12.3

Source: United Nations, *The World Population Situation in 1979* (New York: Department of International Economic and Social Affairs, 1980), p. 45.

To simplify matters, a population can be divided into three main age-structure categories: young (0–14), adults (15–65 years), and the old (65 and above). Table 11–3 gives the percentage distribution by broad age groups for 1975. (The data for North America include the United States and Canada.) It is clear that the more developed countries have a larger population of aged persons, with Europe having the most sizable apex, while the less developed nations have the largest base. If we define "aging" as an increase in the median age or in the proportion of the old (65 and over), then Europe is the "oldest" region in the world.

The maturation of the American population can also be seen by comparing the age distribution in three different periods in the twentieth century (Table 11–4).

A slightly more sophisticated quantitative representation of the population is by five-year age groups. Table 11–5, which compares the age composition of the Canadian and Mexican populations for 1976, is an

TABLE 11–4

Population of the United States by Age Group, 1900, 1950, 1977

| Age Group | Percentage of Total Population | | |
	1900	1950	1977
0–14	34	27	24
15–64	61	65	65
65+	4	8	11

Sources: U.S. Bureau of the Census, *Historical Statistics* (Washington: U.S. Government Printing Office, 1975), p. 15. United Nations, Department of International Social and Economic Affairs, *Demographic Yearbook 1977* (St/ESA/Stat/ser. R/4) (New York, 1978), pp. 202–03.

TABLE 11–5

Percentage Age Distribution of the Canadian
and Mexican Population, 1976

Age Group	Canada	Mexico
0–4	7.5	18.3
5–9	8.2	15.1
10–14	9.9	12.9
15–19	10.3	10.7
20–24	9.3	8.7
25–29	8.7	7.1
30–34	7.1	5.7
35–39	5.8	4.7
40–44	5.5	4.0
45–49	5.4	3.3
50–54	5.3	2.6
55–59	4.4	1.9
60–64	3.9	1.5
65–69	3.1	1.3
70–74	2.3	1.0
75+	3.3	1.6

Sources: Ministry of Industry, Trade and Commerce, *Canada Yearbook 1978–79* (Ottawa: Information Division, Statistics Canada, 1978), p. 158. United Nations, Department of International Social and Economic Affairs, *Demographic Yearbook 1977* (St/ESA/Stat/ser. R/4) (New York, 1978), pp. 200–01.

example. The Canadian population has the more mature age structure, while the high ratio of youths to adults in the Mexican population is striking.

The Population Pyramid

Both age and sex compositions can be represented by a special type of bar graph called a *population pyramid*. Population pyramids provide graphic statements of the sex and age distribution of a population for a given year. They are static representations of a population that, because of the forces of fertility, mortality, and migration, is itself always changing. A pyramid "freezes" this motion at a particular moment in time. The age-sex pyramid illustrates some of the procedures discussed in Chapter 2 in connection with the histogram. Fundamentally, the pyramid is a two-way, or bilateral, histogram with the X and Y axes reversed, so that frequencies are represented by the horizontal axis and class intervals by the vertical axis.

FIGURE 11–1

Age and Sex Distribution of American Population (1976)

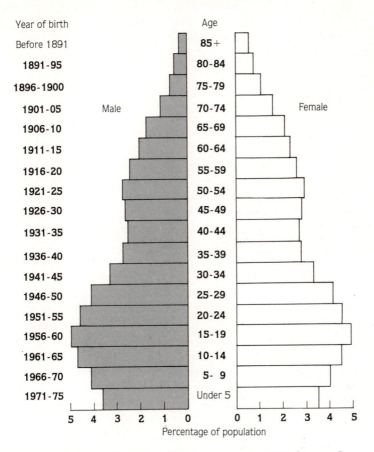

Source: A. Haupt and T. T. Kane, *Population Handbook* (Washington: Population Reference Bureau, 1978), p. 12.

Thus the population pyramid consists of two bar graphs (or histograms) placed on their sides and back to back (See Figure 11–1). The bars can be placed adjacent to each other, without any space between, to emphasize the continuity of the data. The length of each bar represents either the *total number* or the *percentage size* for each age or age category (it is common for each bar to indicate a five-year age group, although each bar may represent a single year, as in Figure 11.2). The youngest ages are at the bottom, the oldest at the top. The data for males are usually placed at the left, for females at the right. Since every year cohorts normally lose part of their number through death or emigration, each bar is usually shorter than the previous one, which gives the impression of a pyramid. A vertical comparison of the bars shows the relative proportions of each age or age group in the population, while a horizontal comparison shows the proportions of males and females in each age or age group. The population pyramid can be based on absolute numbers or on percentages the latter is more common.

Construction of the Pyramid

To build a population pyramid, we first draw a *horizontal axis* on which to plot the population either in millions (absolute figures) or in percentages (relative figures). The latter figure is obtained by dividing the age group by the total population and multiplying the quotient by 100. Ages or age groups are shown straddling the *vertical central* axis. As noted above, the size of each age group is then represented by a horizontal bar that extends from the central axis: the length of bar is proportional to the size of the age group; the width indicates the range of the age interval considered. As a result, the relative areas of the various rectangles are proportional to the class frequencies.

If we wanted to construct a population pyramid representing the population of the United States in 1978 *in absolute numbers* at intervals of five years, we could start with males, taking the 0–4 age group (under 5 years old) first. In 1978 the total number of this group was 7,855,000. The bar indicating this figure should have a length representing $7,855,000/5 = 1,571,000$. Then each of the single age groups (0, 1, 2, 3, 4 years) would be equal to one-fifth of the total of the five-year class. Although in this type of calculation the pyramid loses some precision, the general configuration remains correct.

The representation of age structure in the United States for 1976 (Figure 11.1) illustrates the point. The 1976 pyramid has a constricted base that reflects the decline in fertility in the early 1970s. The postwar baby boom is evident in the bulge in the age groups of elder teenagers and young adults (ages 10–34). The relatively small number of cohorts born during the 1930s now makes up the narrow middle section of the pyramid.

A population pyramid can show the history of a population year in, year out, over the last hundred years, including effects of wars, waves of in- or out-migration, fluctuations in fertility and mortality, and the like. The American population pyramid of 1976 shows no marked irregularities, but the French histogram of the same year does. The oldest age groups in Figure 11.2 have very low sex ratios, mirroring male losses in World War I estimated at 1,400,000. The pyramid also shows the deficient birth cohorts born during the two world wars as they move through the system. The effect on population of the two postwar recoveries is also evident, as

FIGURE 11-2

Population Pyramid (France, January 1, 1976)

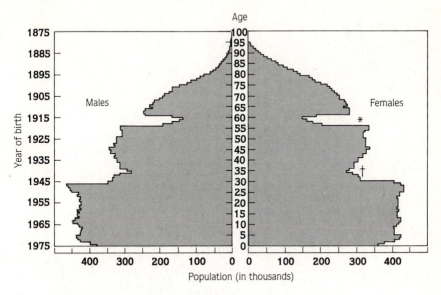

* Deficit of births because of the First World War (1914–18)
† Deficit of births because of the Second World War (1939–45)

Source: Ministère de l'Economie et des Finances, Institut National de la Statistique et des Etudes Economiques, *Annuaire Statistique de la France, 1977* (Paris: Imprimerie Nationale, 1977), Plate 1.

is the more recent decline in fertility that set in after the post-Second World War baby boom was over.

Classification of Pyramids

Several types of population pyramids can be distinguished. We will limit our discussion to the five more frequent forms (Figure 11–3).

The first cateogry of population pyramid, which looks like an ordinary triangle, may be called the *primitive* type, as it represents premodern fertility and mortality conditions. All populations before 1800 produce triangular pyramids, while a few developing countries still display this kind of age-sex profile. It reflects a population with relatively high vital rates and a rather low median age. The age-sex structure in the Netherlands in 1849 (Figure 11–4) fits this category.

The second variety of pyramid has a broader base than the first and

FIGURE 11-3

Five Most Frequent Forms of Population Pyramids

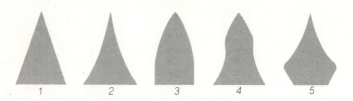

FIGURE 11-4

Population Pyramid (Netherlands, 1849)

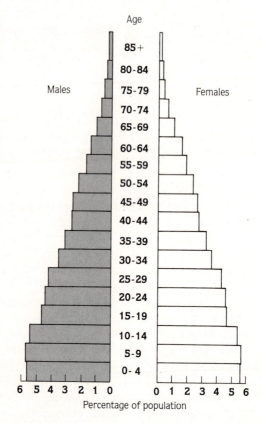

Source: Centraal Bureau voor de Statistiek, *75 Jaar Statistiek van Nederland* (S'Gravenhage: Staatsuitgeverij, 1975), p. 12.

FIGURE 11–5

Age and Sex Distribution of Iranian Population (1974)

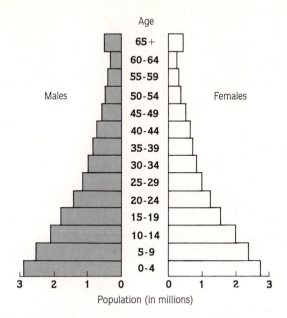

Source: *Iran Almanac 1977* (Tehran: Echo, 1977), p. 378.

is called *expansive*. The 0–14 age group is larger because this population is beginning to control mortality but not fertility, and the most impressive gains in mortality reduction are made in the younger age groups. The steeply sloping sides reflect the large proportion of younger people and the small percentage of aged people. The population structure of Iran in 1974 fits this description perfectly, as seen in Figure 11–5. The high sex ratio prevailing in Iran is also visible. The cut-off point is age 65, which is early for a developed nation but not for a developing one with relatively few inhabitants of 65 and over.

The third class of pyramids looks like an old-fashioned beehive or a Chinese lantern. Because the numbers in this age-sex profile are roughly equal for all age groups, gradually tapering off at the apex, this age-sex structure is called *near-stationary*. Many Western populations of the 1930s conformed to this pattern, as seen in the Swiss population structure of 1930 (Figure 11–6).

The fourth category of age and sex distributions is bell-shaped. It mirrors an older population in the process of rejuvenation. The recovery in the birth rate many Western nations experienced after World War II is apparent in the Canadian age-sex composition of 1951 (Figure 11–7).

FIGURE 11–6

Age and Sex Distribution of Swiss Population (1930)

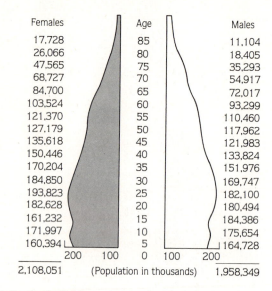

Females	Age	Males
17,728	85	11,104
26,066	80	18,405
47,565	75	35,293
68,727	70	54,917
84,700	65	72,017
103,524	60	93,299
121,370	55	110,460
127,179	50	117,962
135,618	45	121,983
150,446	40	133,824
170,204	35	151,976
184,850	30	169,747
193,823	25	182,100
182,628	20	180,494
161,232	15	184,386
171,997	10	175,654
160,394	5	164,728

| | 200 | 100 | 0 | 100 | 200 | |

| 2,108,051 | (Population in thousands) | 1,958,349 |

Source: F. Comlomb, *Quelques Aspects Actuels du Problème de la Population en Suisse et en Europe* (Lausanne: Librairie de Droit, 1943), p. 56.

The last category of population pyramids depict a fertility decline following a period of rejuvenation. The median age drops during the rejuvenation, then rises with the baby bust. This is the stage in which most Western nations and Japan found themselves in the 1970s. These populations may be said to have moved through the demographic transition. The age-sex profile of the United States shown in Figure 11–1 (page 213) depicts the smaller numbers in the younger age categories. This population profile is called *constrictive*.

Population Pyramids of Immigration

In Chapter 8 we noted that migrants are usually young. Population pyramids of immigrants reflect the age selectivity of migrant populations, and so tend to take the form of a cross, with low populations at the top and bottom and a disproportionately large middle section. The pyramid in Figure 11–8, showing immigrants reaching the province of Quebec in 1972, is typical in that the large proportion of young adults clearly stands out.

FIGURE 11–7

Population by Sex and Five-year Age Groups
(Canada, 1951)

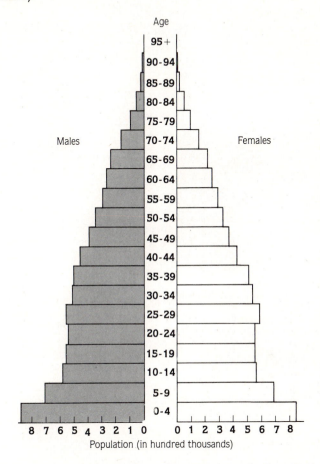

Source: Dominion Bureau of Statistics, *The Canada Yearbook 1952–53* (Ottawa: Cloutier, 1953), p. 218.

The Aged to Child Ratio

Another useful age index is the ratio of aged persons to children, or the *aged-to-child ratio*, which is used to illustrate the aging process in a rather dramatic form. The index expresses the ratio of aged persons to children and is stated as a percentage. It is computed as follows:

FIGURE 11–8

Foreign Immigration to Quebec by Age and Sex (1972)

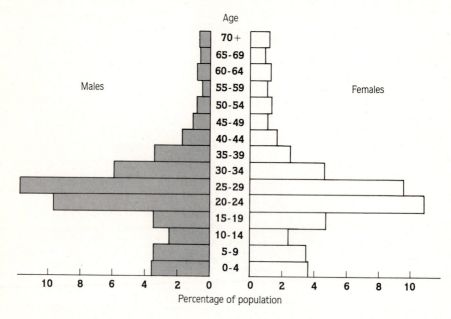

Source: Ministère de l'Industrie et du Commerce, Bureau de la Statistique du Quebec, *Annuaire du Quebec 1974*, p. 289.

$$\frac{P_{65}}{P_{0-14}} \times k$$

where P_{65+} = the number of people 65 and over
    P_{0-14} = the number of children under 15
    $k = 100$

Applying the formula to the data for the United States in 1977, we find $23,493,000/51,606,000 \times 100 = 46$. In other words, the 1977 population included 46 aged persons for every 100 children. The U.S. aged to child ratios since 1900 are shown in Table 11–6. The two biggest upward jumps are between 1930 and 1940 and between 1970 and 1977. The rejuvenation period is also seen in the negative percentage change of the 1950–60 period. By way of comparison, Austria has an older population than the United States, with a 1976 aged to child ratio of 66. Mexico, on the other hand, has a very young population, as shown by an aged to child ratio of 7.3 for the same year.

TABLE 11–6

Aged to Child Ratios (United States, 1900–77)

Year	Aged to Child Ratio	Percentage of Change
1900	11.9	
		+13.0
1910	13.5	
		+ 8.0
1920	14.6	
		+27.0
1930	18.6	
		+47.0
1940	27.4	
		+ 9.0
1950	30.0	
		− 0.7
1960	29.8	
		+16.0
1970	34.7	
		+33.0
1977	46.0	

FACTORS AFFECTING THE SEX AND AGE COMPOSITION

Mortality, fertility, migration, and such exceptional circumstances as war may be considered the main determinants of age composition. Mortality declined dramatically during the last two hundred years. In most Western nations, however, the reduction was gradual, making the effects on the age-sex profile hard to see. Since the 1950s the less developed countries have gone through a different evolution, adopting in a relatively short period the death-control techniques that the more advanced nations developed over the last two centuries. This large-scale transfer of health technology has resulted in disproportionately high reductions in death rates among younger age groups. As a result, the base of their population pyramids has become larger and larger, reflecting an ever-growing proportion of children and young teenagers. In Iran, for instance, the proportion of children under 10 grew from 32.6 percent in 1956 (first census) to 34.1 percent in 1966 (second census). The proportion under-20-year-olds grew from 49.7 percent in 1956 to 54.6 percent in 1966. Obviously, the Iranian population got younger between the two censuses.

Fertility is the second determinant of age and sex structure. Again, if fertility changes are slow, the effects on the pyramid will hardly be perceptible. Spectacular swings clearly show up, however. The low fertility of the Depression and the first years of the Second World War produced a visible dent in the United States pyramid of 1976 (Figure 11–1), while the notable postwar recovery of natality has resulted in a bulge. Pyramids of comparable populations show similar characteristics.

Migration is the third factor modifying the age-sex structure. Again depending on volume, immigration and emigration may produce bulges and dents in the pyramids of the receiving and sending countries. In both internal and international migration, adolescents and young adults tend to dominate, so the modifications in the age structure produced by migration occur in certain age groups only. The age structure of countries like Ireland and Sweden was modified in the second half of the nineteenth century, when millions left for America and Canada. The outflow was large relative to the populations of these areas. The American pyramid also changed moderately during the same period, when immigration was heavy.

Finally, special circumstances such as wars affect a country's population pyramid. France suffered perhaps 1,400,000 casualties during World War I, the effects of which are still visible at the summit of the French pyramid (Figure 11–2, page 215). Such heavy casualties are bound to produce a shortage of eligible males, reducing the marriage rate and the level of fertility. The low fertility level of the war years produced a deep symmetrical dent in the pyramid that is all the more striking because of the revival of fertility once the war was over. When the deficient birth cohorts born during World War I passed into the reproductive ages, natality declined again. The fertility of the cohorts born during the 1915–19 period was further lowered by the separations of spouses during the Second World War. Thus a second niche was created in the French histogram. A major war, as the pyramid shows, can send ripples, if not waves, through the sex-age profile of several generations.

DEMOGRAPHIC CONSEQUENCES OF AGE AND SEX STRUCTURE

It would be an exaggeration to say that a nation's age profile determines its institutions and way of life. However, any particular age distribution, no matter how it came about, establishes limitations on a nation's capabilities and may produce short-term changes in its social institutions. If the cohorts in the reproductive period are depleted, for instance, fertility is not necessarily reduced, but clear boundaries are set on the potential number of children that can be born. In other words, the age structure of a population (and the sex structure, too) is restrictive or permissive of social institutions without causing them to disappear or to thrive.

As we might expect, irregularities and even normal features of a nation's age and sex structure affect nuptiality, and the three main processes of mortality, fertility, and migration. Chapter 7 explained how a sudden increase in fertility can determine the prospects for marriage, for both men and women, some twenty years later. Because the baby boom was preceded by a period of low fertility, the female cohorts born during the early part of the boom found it difficult to find suitable mates a few years older (the marriage squeeze).

A population with a large proportion of young adults will usually have a higher birth rate than a population with a smaller percentage of people of reproductive age. The postwar baby boom cohorts have entered the reproductive age since about 1962. Throughout the 1970s and early 1980s the American population was still characterized by fairly large cohorts reaching the prime childbearing years. The prevalence of young adults is a factor that tends to raise the birth rates, even if the number of births per married woman is low. Hence the 1980 birth rate is 'deceptively' high.

Likewise, crude death rates are influenced by the age of the population (measured by either median age or the proportion of 65 and above). Just as the CDR is higher in a nursing home than in a prison, so death rates are bound to increase when a population grows older. Aging, an inevitable process in populations that have moved through the demographic transition, is the outcome of a decline in fertility—fewer babies are born, and the median age goes up. Because improvements in health care produce the greatest increase in survival among the young, a decline in mortality may offset a drop in the birth rate. Demographically speaking, there is no difference between saving a child's life and producing another one. However, most developed nations have by now reduced infant and child mortality to very low levels. At the same time, medical advances have prolonged the life of many older people. As a result, the proportion of high-mortality-risk people (65-plus) rises and, ordinarily, the death rate mounts as well. In 1980, for example, the crude death rates for Taiwan and Singapore were in the 5 percent range, while the figure for Luxembourg and Austria was 12 percent. It is not the differences in available health care that accounts for these variations in the crude death rates but the fact that in Europe the populations are older than in Asia.

Its population profile may also predispose a nation to emigration or immigration. When the European nations were in the earlier phases of the demographic transition in the nineteenth century, they sent waves of young adults to North America because so many young people were unable to find suitable employment at home. On the other hand, between 1872 and 1970 France allowed some five million immigrants to enter the country; the heavy casualties of World War I in particular transformed France into a nation that attracted immigrants in large numbers. Mexico and the Philippines are among the largest senders of migrants to the United States; both nations have exploding populations and large numbers of young adults looking for work. Canada is also receiving larger numbers of Asians, Africans, and Central Americans than before. Again, there is a strong push factor in areas of origin: a rapidly mounting proportion of young people and relatively few employment opportunities.

ECONOMIC AGE CATEGORIES

Another way of looking at the age composition of a population is in terms of producers and dependents. It is obvious that every member of a population is a consumer or at least a potential one, but not every individual is a producer. The relationship between the very young and very old nonproducing consumers on the one hand, and the adult active population on the other, has important economic implications. If relatively large proportions of the population are economically active, the maintenance and improvement of a given living standard is facilitated. Conversely, large proportions of dependents constitute a heavy burden on those who are actively employed.

It is customary to divide the dependents into two categories: those who are supposedly below working age, and those too old to work. The first group includes the population between age 0 and 14, and the second, those age 65 and over. The economically active population, then, is aged 15–64. It goes without saying, of course, that not all those aged 0 to 14 and 65 and over are nonworking dependents; some do in fact support themselves or contribute to their support. It is equally obvious that some of those in the 15 to 64 group cannot support themselves. Thus numbers for this group represent estimates of *potential* workers.

To evaluate a nation's dependency burden, we compute three ratios: the *old-age dependency ratio (OADR)*, the *youth dependency ratio (YDR)*, and the *total dependency ratio (TDR)*. The total dependency ratio is determined by computing the ratio of the number of persons in the age groups 0–14 and over 65 to the number of persons in the age group 15–64 multiplied by the constant, K, of 100. Thus the TDR may be calculated

$$\frac{P_{0-14+} \ P_{65+}}{P_{15-64}} \times k$$

For the United States in 1977 we obtain

$$\frac{51,606,000 + 23,493,000}{141,233,000} \times 100 = 53.2$$

The YDR and the OADR are calculated by the same method. The total dependency ratio, then, tells how many unproductive dependents there are for every hundred persons of working age.

A major demographic difference between the more developed and the less developed nations is that most less developed nations have substantially higher total dependency ratios than the advanced countries. Table 11–7 and Figure 11–9 present the three dependency ratios for the United States between 1870 and 1977. During the period the TDR tended to fall except after the two world wars—an exception explained by postwar changes in fertility. After World War I the YDR stabilized at 50, but the OADR rose slightly, so that the TDR was pushed upward. Between 1940 and 1960 both the OADR and the YDR rose substantially; as a result, the TDR increased sharply as well. After 1960 the OADR remained at 16, while the YDR dropped because of the baby bust; the TDR declined once more. When fertility declines, aging as a rule takes place, while a rise in fertility causes a population to grow younger. The dependency ratios reflect these occurrences.

The challenge that the developed countries must face in the years to come is an increase in the OADR. Now that life expectancy at birth is over 70 in all modernized countries, the old-age dependency burden is likely to become ever heavier. (This problem will receive more attention in Chapter 12.) The major dilemma of the developing nations, on the other hand, is a sharp rise in the nonproductive young. The YDR in low-income nations is usually twice as high as that in high-income countries. It might be argued that countries with high YDR's could partially solve this prob-

TABLE 11–7

Trends in Dependency Ratios (United States, 1870–1977)

Year	Total Dependency Ratio	Youth Dependency Ratio	Old-Age Dependency Ratio
1870	73	68	5
1880	71	65	6
1890	65	59	6
1900	63	56	7
1910	57	50	7
1920	58	50	8
1930	53	45	8
1940	47	37	10
1950	54	41	13
1960	68	52	16
1970	62	46	16
1977	53	37	16

Source: U.S. Bureau of the Census, *Historical Statistics* (Washington: Government Printing Office, 1975), p. 15. Computations by author.

FIGURE 11–9

Dependency Ratios (United States, 1870–1977)

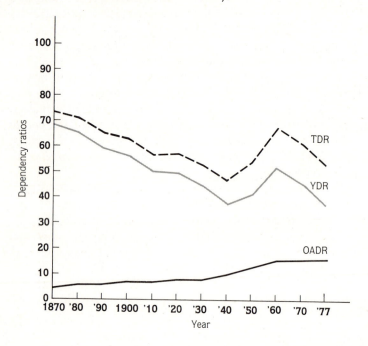

lem by introducing or reintroducing child labor, or at least by lowering the age of entry into the labor force. However, this proposition clashes with other ideals, such as compulsory education, improvement in the quality of the labor force and the elimination of the suffering historically associated with child labor. Besides, children, if put to work, are far less productive than adults. Although a high YDR may remain a challenge, the less developed countries do not have to worry about their OADR, at least for the time being, because their populations are young and the proportion of aged is still small.

RACIAL COMPOSITION

Countries with homogeneous populations, such as Austria and Norway, do not need to consider the ethnic composition of their populations. Other societies, of course—like the United States and South Africa—contain several racial groups. In population counts, racial groups must be defined, but because all-compassing, universally accepted racial classifications do not exist, the United States Bureau of the Census has traditionally taken the pragmatic approach of dividing the American population into a few loosely defined but easily recognizable ethnic categories, such as white and black, or white and nonwhite. Before the 1970 census, color was used to distinguish racial categories. The color group "nonwhite" include blacks, American Indians, Japanese, Chinese, and so on. Since 1970 the racial classifications used are a combination of color and nationality. In the 1980 questionnaire (short and long) a special question was asked on Spanish/Hispanic origin, because of the growing proportion of Mexicans in the American population.

Whites and blacks are the leading ethnic groups in the American population. In the late 1970s whites comprised about 87 percent of the population, blacks 11.5 percent, while American Indians, Mexicans, Orientals, and others made up the remainder.

Blacks make up the largest nonwhite group in the United States. In 1790 they numbered 757,208, or 19.3 percent of the population. After 1808 the importation of slaves became illegal, so that most blacks descend from persons who have been in the United States for almost two centuries. Their proportion of the total population has slightly declined, to about 11.5 percent, in spite of their high differential fertility. In total numbers blacks have increased to some 25 million as of the late 1970s. However, heavy white immigration, mainly from Europe, raised the proportion of whites. It is interesting to note that blacks are comparable, in at least one way, to the French Canadians, who grew by high natural increase, while English-speaking Canadians grew by a lower natural increase plus large-scale immigration.

If a society is composed of two or more racial groups at a different stage of the demographic transition, different fertility levels and rates of increase will prevail. In the end, the higher-fertility group will probably constitute a larger proportion of the total population. South Africa is a stark example of this. Because of higher fertility among blacks, the proportion of the black population increased from 67.5 percent in 1904 to 71.5 percent in 1977. That of the whites declined from 21.6 percent to 16.5 percent during the same period, even though there was a net immigration of at least half a million whites. The 1977 total population was approximately 23 million.

From the standpoint of racial composition, the Hawaiian Islands are unique in the United States, since Hawaii is the only state in which *all* ethnic groups are minorities. The Hawaiian race itself was depleted when visitors and immigrants introduced all known diseases and epidemics—including syphilis, tuberculosis, bubonic plague, and smallpox—to Hawaii.[2] Pure descendants of the old Polynesian race now represent less than 1 percent of the Hawaiian population. The subsidized importation of labor

[2]For details, see E. C. Nordyke, *The Peopling of Hawaii* (Honolulu: University Press of Hawaii, 1977), Chapter 2.

TABLE 11–8

Ethnic Groups in Hawaii, 1976

Ethnic or Racial Group	Percent of Total Population
Caucasian	27.7
Japanese	26.6
Filipino	10.2
Full/Part Hawaiian	17.7
Chinese	4.3

Source: C. Haub, *Hawaii Population Data Sheet* (Washington: Population Reference Bureau, 1980).

from China, Japan, and other nations to work on the sugar plantations created a racial mosaic unique in the world. Table 11–8 presents the main racial groups constituting the population of Hawaii in 1976.

CONCEPTS FOR REVIEW

Population composition
Sex ratio
Masculinity ratio
Median age
Population pyramid
Primitive population pyramid
Expansive population pyramid
Near-stationary population
    pyramid

Constrictive population pyramid
Aged to child ratio
Aging of population
Total dependency ratio
Old-age dependency ratio
Youth dependency ratio

QUESTIONS FOR DISCUSSION

1. Why is it that in certain less-developed countries sex ratios are relatively high?
2. In the United States and Canada, sex ratios were high around 1910. Explain why.
3. Over 50 percent of the Mexican population is under 20 years old (see Table 11.5). What are the reasons? Is this situation typical for other low-income nations?
4. What did the American population pyramid look like around 1800?

5. List the reasons why after World War II the American population pyramid was bell-shaped, while at present it is constrictive.
6. Explain: "When a country suffers many casualties during a war, a dent will appear in its population pyramid. It is quite likely that another dent will appear twenty or thirty years later."
7. Why might the crude death rate be higher in Florida than in Georgia or North Carolina?
8. Why do countries like Mexico, the Philippines, and South Korea send many migrants to the United States?
9. The total dependency ratio in the United States has fallen since 1960, while the old age dependency ratio remained stable. What forces, if any, are responsible for this trend?
10. In what sense are American blacks like the French Canadians?

BIBLIOGRAPHY

Bogue, D. J. *Principles of Demography*. New York: Wiley, 1969.

Coale, A. J. "How a Population Ages or Grows Younger." In *The Vital Revolution*, edited by R. F. Freedman. New York: Anchor Books, 1964.

Hawley, A. H. "Population Composition." In *The Study of Population*, edited by P. M. Hauser and O. D. Duncan. Chicago: University of Chicago Press, 1959.

Momeni, D. A. *The Population of Iran*, Shiraz, Iran: privately published, 1975.

Nordyke, E. C. *The Peopling of Hawaii*. Honolulu: University Press of Hawaii, 1977.

Pressat, R. *Demographic Analysis*. Chicago: Aldine-Atherton, 1972.

Sauvy, A. *La Population*. Paris: Presses Universitaires de France, 1970.

Shryock, H. S., J. B. Siegel, et al. *The Methods and Materials of Demography*. Vol. 1. Washington: Goverment Printing Office, 1973.

Thomlinson, R. *Population Dynamics*. New York: Random House, 1965.

Valaoras, V. G. "Young and Aged Populations." *The Annals of the American Academy of Political and Social Science* 316 (March 1958).

12

The Socioeconomic

Effects

of Population Change

Chapter 11 mentioned the problems associated with age structure, problems that both developed and developing countries must face. High youth dependency ratios (YDR's) are at present a major obstacle to rapid economic progress in the less developed countries. Aging, on the other hand, is likely to become a growing topic for discussion in the more developed nations. Inevitably the "graying" process will involve significant social, economic, and political changes. The following sections will review some of the issues at stake.

THE ECONOMIC IMPACT
OF A RISING DEPENDENCY RATIO

Youth Dependency Burden
and Economic Development

High-fertility, low-income countries are burdened with a large proportion of young dependents. To be sure, the industrialized nations faced somewhat similar problems in the earlier stages of their development, but relatively high mortality and low fertility held rates of natural increase and dependency ratios below levels now prevalent in some Asian, African, and Latin American nations. In countries like the United States and Canada, moreover, the constant inflow of productive young workers from abroad has also helped to keep down the dependency ratio.

Table 12–1 shows the three dependency ratios for eight selected countries, using the latest data available. The high total dependency ratios (TDR's) and youth dependency ratios of the developing countries stand out.

As stated earlier, many developing nations introduced Western health technology after 1945. Mortality dropped, especially in the younger age groups, and the rate of natural increase rose, resulting in a jump in the youth dependency ratio as well. This rather sudden increase in the propor-

TABLE 12–1

Total, Youth, and Old-Age Dependency Ratios
for Selected Countries per Hundred Persons Aged 15–64

Area	Total Dependency Ratio	Youth Dependency Ratio	Old-Age Dependency Ratio
Developing Nations			
Iran (1976)	92.1	85.3	6.8
Mexico (1978)	98.2	91.7	6.5
Morocco (1973)	95.7	90.9	4.9
Philippines (1976)	84.3	79.1	5.3
Developed Nations			
Canada (1977)	51.1	37.7	13.4
France (1977)	55.6	34.5	20.6
Japan (1977)	48.4	34.5	20.6
United States (1977)	51.1	36.5	16.6

Source: United Nations, Department of International Economics and Social Affairs, Statistical Office of the United Nations, *Demographic Yearbook 1978* (New York, 1979), pp. 148, 154, 156, 158, 162, 164, 168.

tion of unproductive dependents has had two effects. To understand fully the impact of a changing dependency ratio in developing countries, we have to examine each effect.

The Transitional Effect.   During the first fifteen years after the drop in mortality, the increment in population consists almost entirely of non-productive young dependents. Although imported health measures may save the lives of some productive workers, too, no major changes can be expected in the size of the labor force. With a relatively stable workforce, total output is not likely to grow, but that output will have to be shared among more members of the population. Inevitably, per capita output (or income) will be affected negatively; it will be smaller than before the increase in the proportion of dependents. This will be true both at the level of the family and at the level of the nation as a whole. This is called the *transitional effect.*

When the transitional effect is over, we find a YDR that is relatively high. The case of Iran is relevant: between the two censuses of 1956 and 1966, the population of under-15-year-olds increased from 42.2 percent to 46.1 percent. The economically active population (15 years and over) declined from 47.5 percent to 46.1 percent, and this at a time of increased female participation in the labor force.

This new situation will affect the proportion of the national income that can be saved and invested.[1] It is families (or individuals) especially who save, although corporations and even governments also save. As mortality is reduced and more children survive, families become larger; with more surviving dependent children per family, the basic consumption requirements of the family increase. A larger percentage of the family income will have to be spent on food, clothing, and other consumer items. This suggests that a smaller proportion of the income can be saved since, as the economic textbooks tell us, disposable family income is either consumed or saved. Saving is a residual activity, because whatever is consumed cannot be set aside for later use. Totaling the number of families with more surviving, income-consuming dependents will yield the aggregate.

The Quasi-Permanent Effect.   On the national level, the capacity to save is ordinarily reduced by the rise in the proportion of young dependents. This is termed the *quasi-permanent effect.* Most studies of saving patterns suggest that saving and family size at any given income level are inversely related. We must add, however, that all of those studies have been carried out in developed nations. Yet it is reasonable to assume that in the less developed countries similar patterns prevail, although perhaps

---

[1]*Investment* here means the building and accumulation of productive equipment that increases the productivity of labor. Investment is identical to capital formation.

FIGURE 12–1

Effects of Increased Rate of Population Growth
on Economic Growth

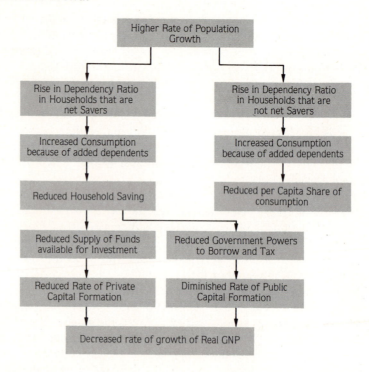

to a lesser extent because of the greater participation of children in economic activities.

With regard to public saving, a high dependency ratio reduces the government's powers either to tax or borrow from the public in order to finance schools, transportation systems, power plants, irrigation projects, and the like. The government may even have to subsidize basic items such as food, in order to keep part of the population from extreme misery. This is common practice in a number of low-income nations.

While high dependency ratios tend to reduce per capita savings, the investment requirements are usually increased (see the next section). Figure 12–1 summarizes the relationships discussed.

Population Growth and Capital Investment

In developed and undeveloped nations alike, population growth increases the capital requirements, or the stock of productive equipment necessary if current productivity levels are to be maintained. To understand the impact of population growth on capital requirements, we must introduce the concept of *capital-output ratio*—the relationship of the value of a nation's total capital stock to the annual output that it produces jointly with labor. If, for instance, the constant capital-output ratio is 3, then in one year's time $3 of capital will produce $1 of output. If the *marginal* or *incremental,* capital-output ratio is also 3, then a $3 addition to the capital stock will produce $1 of increased output. Numerous observers believe that in the developed nations the capital-output ratio is close to 4, while in the developing countries it is nearer 3.

As a population grows, it needs more houses, farm buildings, schools, hospitals, roads, bridges, and so on. Furthermore, since population increments eventually result in growth of the labor force, factories, workshops, machines, and tools of all kinds must be in adequate supply if productivity levels are to be maintained.

Let us suppose that a given population grows by 1 percent. If existing living standards are to be maintained, the total national product should also grow by 1 percent. This increment in output requires an expansion of the capital stock. With a capital-output ratio of 3/1, 3 percent of the national income has to be saved and invested to obtain the 1 percent addition to the national product. It is not uncommon for the population of a developing country to grow by 3 percent, as does Iran's at present. In Iran, then, an expansion of the capital stock of 9 percent is required merely to prevent a drop in the standard of living. With the possible exception of the oil countries, saving 9 or 10 percent represents a major effort. Yet this is often what is needed merely to keep pace with current rates of demographic increase.

But simply staying even is not what most developing nations want. Rather, they wish to increase per capita output and income, which implies a *deepening of capital stock*—in other words, equipping each member of the labor force with more tools of various kinds. It also necessitates the development of human skills and work capacities, which, in turn, requires the construction of schools, colleges, and technical institutes. Additions must also be made to the existing infrastructure: more transport means that more roads are needed; more production means that more electricity must be generated; and so on.

Investments that increase per capita output and income are sometimes called *economic investments,* while the sum of all commitments necessitated by increased population are defined as *demographic investments.* Population growth tends to alter the composition of total investment activity to the advantage of demographic investments. Economic investments can be thought of as a residual activity that ordinarily contracts as the rate of demographic increase expands. Obviously, a rapid increase in numbers is a serious obstacle to improving a nation's living standards.

An Alternative View

The problems discussed above can also be examined within the framework of the successive stages of the economic and demographic transition. When a population's death rates drop while the birth rates remain high, that population initially tends to grow younger. Then a vicious cycle is set in motion. A high rate of population growth impedes saving and investment, and thus the modernization of agriculture and industry. Economic progress becomes more difficult to attain, and so it is harder for people to get jobs. Furthermore, a reduced national treasury is less able to provide schooling. The number of youthful dependents goes up, lowering each family's ability to save. The cycle continues, and the higher the rate of population increase, the more difficult it becomes to break the spiral.

A successful economic and demographic transition would combine an increase in the level of production and consumption with a decline in mortality and fertility. In the early stages, foreign technology would be applied to several sectors of the economy. Per capita output and consumption would rise, while mortality would drop as a result of better medical care. A healthier work force would be more productive. Because of the increased survival of children, the dependency burden would become heavier, too, but with the introduction of effective population policies and family planning (to be discussed in Chapter 13), fertility would eventually drop, reducing the average family size and dependency. As incomes kept rising, saving and investment would steadily expand, and high levels of production and consumption would eventually be attained. With continued economic development and modernization, mortality and fertility would drop to levels that no longer endangered economic progress.

The experiment may fail, however. Let us suppose that technology from abroad is applied in a developing country in combination with foreign investment or some form of international assistance. Production and consumption begin to rise. Public health measures, including improved nutrition standards, lower mortality rates among children and young parents. Family size and dependency increase. In a society still basically agrarian, however, a rise in income may induce people to marry earlier. Suppose now that the nation's population begins to grow more rapidly than does production. Per capita output begins to drop and, with fertility remaining high, mortality may eventually begin once more to rise because of growing malnutrition. As population pressure proves stronger than economic growth, the standard of living is again reduced and production and consumption fall, while mortality and fertility remain high.

A useful model initially developed by Richard Nelson summarizes the so-called *population trap*, as it may occur in a less developed country that fails to make the economic and demographic transition (Figure 12–2). In this simplified model the levels of per capita production (including food

FIGURE 12–2

Low-level Income Trap

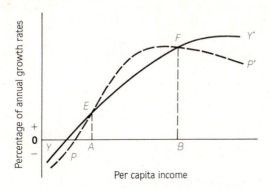

Source: R. R. Nelson, "A Theory of the Low-Level Equilibrium Trap," *American Economic Review* (December 1966), 894–908.

and other items) are measured on the *horizontal axis*.[2] The *vertical axis* indicates the percentage rates of growth of population and total output. The *PP'* curve depicts the rate of population growth, while the *YY'* curve shows the rate of income growth. Thus the figure illustrates the percentage rates of growth in population and in total output at different levels of per capita income.

Let us now suppose that we are at point *A*, which corresponds to a very low per capita income level, close to subsistence. Both output and population are growing at, say, 0.5 percent per year, with no change in income per capita. Suppose further that for some reason—for instance, an injection of outside aid and/or a sudden rise in the price of one of the nation's main export crops—per capita income rises to a level higher than *A* but lower than *B*. Because we are in the early stages of economic development, population begins to grow faster than production. The growth rate of production (or income) also rises, since a higher per capita income allows more saving and expenditure on productivity-increasing investments. Yet because of the sharp drop in mortality, the rate of population growth begins to exceed the rate of growth in output. Between *E* and *F*, the population growth curve *PP'*) is higher than the output growth curve (*YY'*).[3] This, then, is the "trap area," because per capita income is gradually pushed back to the level prevailing at *A*.

---

[2] The value of a nation's output is equal to the sum total of all incomes, because every dollar's worth of final product yields a dollar's worth of income for someone. Therefore it is common practice in economics to equate a nation's output with its income.

[3] The rate of population growth has an upper physical limit of around 4 percent.

The per capita income that *A* represents can be thought of as an equilibrium position to which the system always tends to return. To the left of *A*, mortality increases as per capita income falls below subsistence. Hunger and malnutrition may prevail. Eventually the increased mortality is likely to result in a contraction of the population that would reduce agricultural density while improving the ratio of people to land. Because, in this basically agrarian society, social and economic opportunities would improve for those who survive, per capita income increases and the system returns to *A*.

The model also indicates the importance of effective fertility-reducing population policies. Family planning policies that are successful in curbing fertility pull the population curve downward, thus reducing the trap area.

FIGURE 12–3

Percentage of Population 65 Years and over
(Selected Industrialized Countries, 1941–76)

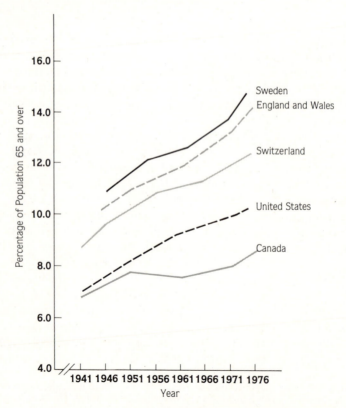

Source: L. O. Stone and S. Fletcher, *A Profile of Canada's Older Population* (Montreal: Institute for Research on Public Policy, 1980), p. 9.

AGING: A PROBLEM FOR DEVELOPED NATIONS

In the decades to come, the population of the Western world, the Soviet Union, Eastern Europe, and Japan, with their high life expectancies and low fertility and mortality levels, will experience further aging. Although all industrially developed nations are experiencing an upward shift in their entire age distribution, a number of countries, such as Sweden and England, are ahead of the United States. This is shown in Figure 12–3.

America's population has been growing older for quite a while, but the pace is likely to accelerate, especially in the next century. Table 12–2 shows the increase in the older population between 1900 and 1980.

Reasons for the Aging Population

The latter part of the nineteenth century and the early part of the twentieth were characterized by both high birth rates and a large volume of births. Since around World War I, however, the crude birth rate has been falling although with some ups and downs. (A major rise occurred during the baby boom after World War II.) A decline in the birth rate tends to lower the proportion of young persons in a population. The aging of the large cohorts born in 1890–1920 accounts for recent increases in the 65-plus population. Because of the relatively low fertility during 1920–40, the rate of increase in the 65-plus population will slow down after about 1985. By the year 2010, however, the baby boom cohorts will begin to enter the ranks of the 65-plus population, which will push the rate of increase of the elderly population upward. Once the baby boom cohorts begin to die off, the baby bust cohorts joining the 65-plus population after the year 2025 will cause the rate of increase in the elderly population to drop again.

The second factor in aging is that, between 1930 and 1980, medical

TABLE 12–2

Number and Percentage of Those 65 and Over
in Total United States Population, 1900–1980

Year	1900	1910	1920	1930	1940	1950	1960	1970	1980 (est.)
Number (in thousands)	3,099	3,986	4,929	6,705	9,031	12,397	16,675	20,085	24,523
Percentage	4.1	4.3	4.6	5.4	6.8	8.1	9.2	9.8	11.0

Source: J. S. Siegel et al., *Demographic Aspects of Aging and the Older Population in the United States*, (Washington: United States Bureau of the Census, 1978) pp. 3, 9.

advances and higher living standards increased life expectancy at birth by about ten years. Mortality at all ages has fallen—including the mortality of the elderly themselves. As a result, the aged population itself is aging, too: within the 65-plus population, the proportion of those over 75 is increasing. Thus there is a greater concentration of the very old in the highest age group. Because life expectancy is longer for women than for men, the sex ratio in the 65-plus population is low and declining (Chapter 11).

The third cause of aging is that between 1901 and 1930 some 18.6 million immigrants entered the United States. Their age on arrival generally ranged from 18 to 35. By now all of them have joined the 65-plus population.

The Dependency Load and Society's Burden

Assuming that fertility will be approximately at replacement level while life expectancy at birth will increase slightly, Spengler and Clark have projected the following shifts in age distribution and dependency ratios (Table 12–3). The projections also assume a net immigration of about 400,000 persons per year.

The implications of the coming shift in age composition can best be understood in terms of dependency ratios (Table 12–4). In the near future the total dependency ratio will actually fall. The sharp drop in the TDR in the near future (until the year 2000) basically results from the entrance of the tail of the baby boom into the labor force. The relatively small cohorts born after 1915 are now beginning to enter the 65-plus popula-

TABLE 12–3

Projections of Population by Percentage
of Broad Age Groups (United States, 1975–2050)

Age Group	1975	2000	2025	2050
	Percentage of Total Population			
0–17	31	27	25	25
18–64	59	61	59	59
65+	10	12	16	16
Median Age	28.8	34.8	36.9	37

Source: R. L. Clark and J. J. Spengler, "Changing Demography and Dependency Costs: The Implications of Future Dependency Ratios and Their Composition," in B. R. Herzog, ed., *Aging and Income* (New York: Human Sciences Press, 1978), pp. 62–63.

TABLE 12–4

Estimated Dependency Ratios (United States, 1975–2050)

Year	Youth to Aged Dependency Ratio Po–17/P18–64	Old Age Dependency Ratio P65+/P18–64	TDR = YDR + OADR
1975	53.1	17.9	71.0
2000	44.2	19.0	63.2
2025	42.5	27.3	69.8
2050	41.8	27.2	69.0

Source: R. L. Clark and J. J. Spengler, "Changing Demography and Dependency Costs: The Implications of Future Dependency Ratios and Their Composition," in B. R. Herzog, ed., *Aging and Income* (New York: Human Sciences Press, 1978), p. 68.

tion, while the baby bust is reducing the youth dependency ratio. The sharp rise in the old-age dependency ratio and the TDR that will take place in the intermediate future (2000–50) is the effect of the baby boom cohort's move through its retirement years.

Table 12–4 projects that the ratio of the aged to the working population will rise. Since this ratio, however, is compensated for by a decline in the ratio of young people to workers, there should not be a dramatic increase in the total burden, as some alarmists would suggest. As a matter of fact, between 1980 and 2000 the demographic setting for an improvement in living standards is favorable, since the tail of the baby boom will join the labor force. The entire baby boom will experience the most productive phase of its life during a time when there will be relatively few dependents, whether younger or older. But as the proportion of the elderly increases, society will have to devote more resources to health care services. Older people tend to need more medical services—for example, their average length of stay in a hospital is twice the national average. On the other hand, educational expenditures at the elementary and secondary level, where attendance is mandatory, may drop as the number of students falls. For higher education, the participation rate is the crucial variable; this rate may be expected to rise somewhat in the years to come.

Social Security and Retirement Age: Some Possible Solutions

Raising the Age for Full Benefits.   Since the proportion of elderly is increasing, the ratio of pensioners to workers will rise, and per worker Social Security costs will increase. The question has been raised whether the Social Security system—or, rather, the Old Age Survivors and Disability Insurance portion of the program—will be able to provide adequate retirement benefits for an aging population.

In the United States, Social Security benefits have been financed through a payroll tax levied in equal portions on the employer and the employee. Since the passage of the Social Security Act in 1935, benefits have increased and so have the taxes. The financing of benefits is essentially a *pay-as-you-go* scheme: all contributions to the plan are used to pay current beneficiaries, with a small trust fund to smooth out short-term shortfalls and surpluses. But in the face of the coming demographic shifts, especially after the year 2000, the present system cannot be maintained without alteration. While in 1975 there were 30 beneficiaries for each 100 workers, in 2030 there could be as many as 45 beneficiaries per 100 workers. Various solutions are available.

First, the payroll tax could be increased. A danger here is that the contributory working population may react by reducing its family size even further in order to maintain present living standards. Society may then be caught in a vicious cycle of higher taxes, lower fertility, fewer workers, and so on.

A second solution would be to reduce the real benefits of the scheme. As the proportion of the elderly increases, however, they may gain more political clout, which could be used to resist such measures.

A third solution would be a shift from pay-as-you-go to general revenue financing. The claims of the current beneficiaries would be met out of public funds from various revenue sources. Financing Social Security out of general revenues would make the system less vulnerable to the shifting ratios of beneficiaries to workers paying Social Security payroll taxes, but might necessitate an increase in other taxes.

A logical solution would be to delay the age at which full benefits can be received until say, 68. Extending the age of entitlement would ease the burden on future taxpayers. Because of the extension of life expectancy at birth, a gradual postponement of old-age benefits by two or three years need not be thought of as inequitable. For example, the age of entitlement could be raised by two months a year from 1985 or 1990 onward until age 68 is reached. Such a scheme should be carried out in the next three decades, before the baby boom generation enters its retirement years. This solution, in combination with some general revenue financing, may be the only way to avoid intergenerational conflict. Any sudden increase in the age at which Social Security benefits are paid would impose a heavy burden on a small portion of the population—that is, on those who had counted on being able to retire at 65.

Gradual Retirement After 65.   No matter how the benefits retired people enjoy are financed, it is the economically active part of the population that generates the national product, and so it is always the workers who provide for the nonactive elderly. At the same time, many private and public retirement systems are seriously underfunded and may prove unable to meet their obligations in the future.

There is an obvious case for making greater use of the labor of retired people. Public opinion polls have shown that a relatively large proportion of the retired or unemployed 65-plus population would like to be working, at least part-time. Many retirees have accumulated valuable experience and become highly skilled in their work. Moreover, retirement often reduces their standard of living, whereas continued moderate activity may have an excellent effect on their health and enthusiasm.

The concept of retirement at 65 is, in the developed countries at least, more than forty years old. In the United States, in 1930, life expectancy at birth for the two sexes taken together was 59.7 years. Forty years later it stood at 70.9 years. In the early 1980s an individual reaching 65 can expect to live another fifteen years or so. And as life expectancy has been going up, of course, the health of the elderly has improved. A 60-year-old man or woman today may be in as good condition as the 50-year-old of only a few decades ago. Furthermore, the physical demands that most jobs make on the labor force have been cut back. Under these circumstances there is no reason to assume that all members of the labor force should or would wish to retire at 65.

Another important consideration is the prolongation of the period of instruction. Along with the increase in life expectancy at birth, the number of years young people spend in school has shot up too. In premodern societies, where most people live on farms, economic activity starts early. Children help on their parents' farm or work for others when still quite young. But this pattern changes in a society undergoing rapid social and economic transformation. As education becomes compulsory and child labor is abolished, entry into the labor force occurs at a later age. In the modernized society, the period of instruction and training becomes even longer, and consequently the age at which people enter the job market is even higher. One could argue that this prolonged educational period, which after all requires considerable investment, should be compensated for by a longer active period.

At present the pensionable age is perhaps too rigidly defined, and a mandatory retirement age of 65 will probably make even less sense in the future. Common sense suggests two solutions. Now that life expectancy at birth is over 70 in all modernized nations (and will probably keep on rising), the retirement age could simply be raised to 68 or 70 or be tied to the average life span. A second solution would be a phased-in retirement scheme: instead of forcing people out of their jobs at 65, 68, or whatever age, a more gradual transition to retirement could be planned, the employee's workload being progressively lightened. Many peasants, artisans, and laborers slowly cut down on their work activity as their potential drops. Why not try such a solution for every worker? Allowing the worker to retire gradually, with workload and hours reduced over a period of years, would probably be a wiser management of human capital than the existing system. Of course the administration of such a plan might raise some difficulties. People who worked part-time would have to receive partial payment of their pension, to compensate for the loss in earnings resulting from their lighter workload. However, the real difficulty may be in getting society to accept the concept—once that has happened, administrative problems could be handled.

Since older people generally prefer to retire from unpleasant occupations, such jobs might be redesigned to make them more agreeable. Private and/or public retraining programs could help the elderly find work in less demanding or different positions.

In the United States the *Age Discrimination in Employment Act,* as amended in 1978, eliminated mandatory retirement in the federal government and prohibited it for most employees in the private sector before the age of 70. It was not the economic argument, however, but concern for the human rights of older workers that prompted this legislation.

Demographic Aging and Social Problems

Some researchers, like the French demographer A. Sauvy, have expressed a pessimistic view of the implications of aging. The young, he says, are noted for their energy, enterprise, and capacity to learn new things, as well as their ability to adapt and innovate. Older people excel in experience and patience, but have less vitality and willingness to react to challenge and change and tend to be less creative than the young. As a result of the coming shift in age composition, the whole society may become unprogressive, even backward-looking, unwilling to try anything new, and creative activities may become stagnate. Moreover, as older people predominate in the highest social positions, the young may be subjected to pressures to conform to the patterns of thought and behavior of their elders. Instead of "striking out in the wilderness," the young will become submissive, unimaginative, and unadventuresome. Social and political decadence may be the final outcome.

Sauvy, like several other French writers before him, succumbs here to *demographic determinism* [4]—to the concept that a nation's social and political life is determined primarily by the demographic makeup of its people. In particular, the case for demographic causation of enterprise, innovation, progressiveness, and creativity is not very strong. Nondemo-

[4] I have discussed the problem in my book *History of Population Theories.*

graphic factors such as a nation's institutional framework, its cultural traditions, and other variables are much more important. Progressiveness deserves special mention. If by "progressiveness" we mean the willingness to introduce changes, it would seem that the world's most conservative societies are the ones with the youngest, not the oldest, age structures. The Iranian population, for example, with more than 50 percent under age 20, is extremely young. Yet the revolution that began in 1978 seems to imply a return to the past. In contrast, the older populations of the Western world and Japan seem more progressive.

Creativity is another issue: is it a function of age? Research on eminent scientists has shown that productivity and working habits do not change noticeably with age. Nobel Prize winners in theoretical fields like physics and chemistry typically produce their prize-winning work in their late thirties, while those who excell in applied fields are usually in their forties. Clearly, the most significant creativity is to be found in early-middle-age groups, and it is precisely those age groups that are least likely to increase or decrease in number in the decades to come. We will have more old and fewer young people but about the same number of people in the middle groups as we do now.

SOME IMPLICATIONS
OF ZERO POPULATION GROWTH

A decline in fertility results in a shift in the age structure. If the decline continues, eventually a *zero population growth rate* will occur. It is important to recognize, though, that the implications of the *absence of growth* differ from the likely outcomes we have been discussing of a *changing age structure*. If the present fertility decline continues in developed countries—and the rate of natural increase keeps dropping—a zero rate of growth will become inevitable, and the days of the numerophiliacs will be over. Depending upon the behavior of fertility, however, this may not happen in the United States until after the year 2000.

The quasi-stationary population that is likely to emerge in the future will be characterized by low mortality and fertility levels, the latter being voluntarily kept low. The birth rate will probably be in the neighborhood of 13 ‰, while the death rate will have risen to a level just about matching it. Because of the increasing proportion of older people, mortality is bound to increase, even if health conditions continue to improve. In the quasi-stationary population that may emerge in the United States, life expectancy at birth for both sexes taken together may reach 77 years. The median age will probably be around 37 years. Some 16 percent of the population may be older than 65, while about 25 percent will be younger

than 17. This leaves 59 percent of the population as potential labor participants. In other words, the age pyramid will have become almost rectangular, with nearly equal numbers in each age group until age 70.

The advent of a quasi-stationary population entails both advantages
and disadvantages. The following sections will briefly survey some of them.

Advantages of a Quasi-Stationary Population

The first benefit of a quasi-stationary population is that a relatively
large fraction of the population will be of working age. For one thing, as
fertility declines the youth dependency ratio will drop too. In the quasi-
stationary population to come, approximately 60 percent of the population will be able to work. The old-age dependency ratio will rise, but at a
relatively low rate. At the same time, with low fertility prevailing, mothers
will be less tied to the home and can enjoy greater opportunities to pursue
professional interests. Educational facilities—including refresher courses—
should be at least as good as at present; mothers whose skills have become
rusty while raising children should be employable again. As a result, the
ratio of employed labor to the population of working age is likely to become very favorable. Therefore, the conditions for a satisfactory per capita
output exist.

Of course, obstacles from other sources may intervene. Trade unions
may bargain successfully to bar older workers from the labor force, or
obtain a shorter work week. There may be energy crises, troubled international relations, and so on. From the purely demographic viewpoint,
however, there is no reason to fear that, in a quasi-stationary state, there
will be a scarcity in the potential labor force—especially if we prolong the
economically active period by a few years.

The second benefit of a quasi-stationary population will be that, given
a low youth dependency ratio, families will be in a better position to save.
Consequently, the capital-formation potential of the low-fertility, stationary population will be relatively high.

Third, the demographic investments in a quasi-stationary population
are zero. All available investable funds can be used for economic investments, which increase the capital-labor ratio in the private sector and the
per capita amount of public amenities. Other things being equal, the potential per capita growth of output should be higher in a quasi-stationary
than in a growing population. But other things, of course, may *not* be
equal. It is also possible that part of the increase in productivity will be
consumed in the form of leisure.

The fourth advantage of zero population growth is that a whole set
of problems related to population expansion will stop getting worse. For
example, the rate of increase in consumption of depletable raw materials

will drop. Environmental pressures in general will at least not intensify. Social and political turbulence inspired by the large proportion of young adults in the population is likely to diminish.

Disadvantages of a Quasi-Stationary Population

The first disadvantage is that vertical mobility is likely to slow down. A growing population, if accompanied by a flourishing economy, definitely induces promotion and upward mobility. Suppose, for instance, that there are ten thousand highly desirable positions in a country, and that in an average organization or corporation it takes about thirty years to make it to the top. If the population grows at 2.3 percent per year and doubles in thirty years, some twenty thousand desirable positions could exist by the time an individual and his cohort reach the top. In any given organization or corporation, however, the slowing down of the rate of expansion because of demographic stabilization reduces the number of new openings created at the executive level, as long as power and position are at least partly determined by length of service. Older people will, by right of seniority, occupy the preferred jobs. Because death will no longer create many openings, the most desirable positions will be occupied by older persons, who will stay in those jobs until they retire. This relatively static job structure, associated with a stationary population, reduces access to executive positions. This may also negatively affect work incentives, and could sharpen *intergenerational conflict.*

But the problem is not without solution. One way to alleviate the difficulty would be to weaken the relationship between age on the one hand and reward and position on the other. At the present time, many income differentials are determined by convention rather than performance. Inequities in the earnings structure could be decreased to the point where work incentives would no longer be adversely affected. It might also be necessary to reorganize public and private managerial hierarchies so as to permanently include a sufficient proportion of people below 40 and 50—certainly not an impossible innovation. To some extent, the problem may take care of itself. Whatever is scarce has value: if the younger, more adaptable and dynamic people are in short supply, some organizations may be eager to hire them under attractive conditions. This will make the young more ready to move from firm to firm. Those organizations that lose their valuable younger employees because of inflexibility will be forced to adjust.

It will be interesting to see what impact (if any) such changes would have on migration. A decrease in status mobility may lead more people to switch jobs—and perhaps migrate—if they assume that the limits to occupational mobility are less confining elsewhere. On the other hand, the shortage of opportunities for promotion may lead to less internal migration, especially of professionals and executives. Some neighborhoods would then become more stable, with people feeling greater attachment and commitment to their communities. In itself, this would be a social benefit.

A second problem associated with a quasi-stationary population is that of *interoccupational balance*. When a population grows, the labor force grows as well. When each cohort is followed by a larger one, the number of annual entrants exceeds the outgoers. This tends to make the economy flexible and adaptable, for it is generally the young entrants who seek out the new industries and occupations. But in a quasi-stationary population the quantity of annual entrants in the labor force will approximately equal the number of withdrawals. The cohorts of younger people seeking jobs will no longer be as important, relatively speaking, as in an expanding society, and so new trades and occupations may have difficulty finding an adequate supply of labor. Nonetheless, transfers of labor remain necessary in a technologically dynamic society. The maintenance of an optimum interoccupational balance will have to depend upon those who are migration-prone and those who leave the declining industries. Carefully selected foreign immigration may be of some help, while the increased participation of women in the labor force may also provide relief. Information about expanding work opportunities should be made more readily available. More retraining courses will probably become necessary. Finally, the trade unions should be discouraged from interfering with inter-industry mobility.

A final economic problem related to a quasi-stationary population is that the demand for certain items will cease to grow, while the demand for some other goods and services will actually decline. With fertility dropping to replacement levels, the demand for baby products and youth-related items is bound to shrink. The demand for soft drinks, blue jeans, and the kinds of music that symbolize the youth market will decline. A predominantly middle-aged society, however, will witness an expanding demand for other products, ranging anywhere from color TV sets to prune juice.

But American and other Western business leaders will have to adjust to the fact that markets will no longer automatically expand because of population increase. (The building industry and education are especially likely to suffer. The slump in primary education has started already.) Since the nineteenth century, continued population growth has always sustained our expectations. A society with a stationary population will require a different ideology, one of stability rather than growth. Since throughout most of history population grew very slowly or not at all, however, we do not have to adjust to an entirely new situation. Rather, we must abandon some recently acquired habits as, in a sense, we return to the old ways.

CONCEPTS FOR REVIEW

Transitional effect

Quasi-permanent effect

Capital-output ratio

Deepening of capital stock

Demographic investments

Population trap

Aged population

Pay-as-you-go financing

Age Discrimination in Employment Act

Demographic determinism

Zero population growth

Intergenerational conflict

Interoccupational balance

QUESTIONS FOR DISCUSSION

1. Many if not most less developed countries have experienced a rising youth dependency ratio in recent decades. How did this trend affect their level of economic well-being?
2. A nation's population is rising by 3 percent per year. Its capital-output ratio is 4/1. The country saves and invests 16 percent of its national income. What does this mean for the growth of per capita income?
3. Discuss the difference between "economic" and "demographic" investments.
4. Explain how a successful population policy which lowers fertility can reduce the population trap.
5. List three reasons for the aging of the U.S. population which has taken place since the 1970's.
6. Aging will put the social security system under heavy pressure. Discuss four policy measures which might help solve the problem.
7. "Retiring at age 65 is a relic of a bygone age." Do you agree? Substantiate your position.
8. "Older people are less creative than young people, therefore the aging of the American population will cause society to be arteriosclerotic, unprogressive, and unimaginative." Argue for or against.
9. Discuss and evaluate; "With zero population growth such problems as energy shortages, water shortages, congestion, and pollution will stop getting worse."

BIBLIOGRAPHY

Clark, R. L. and J. J. Spengler, *The Economics of Individual and Population Aging*. Cambridge, England: Cambridge University Press, 1980.

Daric, J. *Vieillissement de la population et prolongation de la vie active*. Paris: Presses Universitaires de France, 1948.

Day, L. H. *What Will a ZPG Society Be Like?* Washington: Population Reference Bureau, Vol. 33, No. 3, June 1978.

Espenshade, T. J. and W. J. Serow, eds. *The Economic Consequences of Slowing Population Growth.* New York: Academic Press, 1978.

Herzog, B. R., *Aging and Income.* New York: Human Sciences Press, 1978.

Myrdal, G. *Population, A Problem for Democracy.* Cambridge, Mass.: Harvard University Press, 1940.

Nelson, R. R. "A Theory of the Low-Level Equilibrium Trap." *American Economic Review* (December 1966): 894–908.

Overbeek, J. *History of Population Theories.* Rotterdam; Rotterdam University Press, 1974.

———. *The Population Challenge.* Westport, Conn.: Greenwood Press, 1976.

Roe, A. "Changes in Scientific Activities with Age." *Science* 60, no. 3694 (15 October 1965).

Sauvy, A. "Les Conséquences du vieillissement de la population." In *La France ridée,* edited by G. F. Dumont et al. Paris: Librairie Française Générale, 1979.

Sweezy, A. and A. Owens, "The Impact of Population Growth on Employment." *American Economic Review* 64, no. 2 (May 1974).

13

Population Policy

DEFINITION, GOALS, AND ETHICAL CONSIDERATIONS

Although the concept of a *population policy* specifically designed to modify demographic behavior is of fairly recent origin, in the past some attempts were made to increase fertility levels among specific groups of people, the oldest known endeavors being the Lex Julia (18 B.C.) and Lex Popae (A.D. 9) enacted under the Roman Empire. In the sixteenth and seventeenth centuries a number of European nations tried to raise their populations by such measures as the encouragement of immigration and the granting of fiscal privileges for large families. But it was in the twentieth century that some fascist countries ventured upon more comprehensive programs to raise fertility levels. By the 1930s Germany, Italy, and Japan had already gone through the earlier stages of the demographic transition. Especially in Germany and Italy, fertility had fallen to a relatively low level, hampering a national need for the large reserves of manpower required for world domination.

In the developing countries, during the 1960s and 1970s, it became increasingly clear that fertility levels, if allowed to prevail for a sufficiently long period, would imperil the quality of life of present and future generations. Obviously, more had to be done to bring existing fertility levels in line with rapidly declining mortality. But in the early 1980s most population policies, insofar as they existed at all, still lacked clear goals and strong convictions.

Population policy itself is usually defined according to one of two viewpoints. One school argues that population policy includes all direct and indirect measures that intentionally or otherwise, may influence the characteristics or processes of a population. This broad definition embraces measures—such as the promotion of literacy, the enhancement of the status of women, and the provision of services for children—that are usually undertaken for health, social, or humanitarian reasons. In other words, this definition comprises government activities that, although perhaps justifiable, go beyond programs for influencing the population size and makeup of a nation.

The other school of thought has argued that only measures explicitly intended to affect the size and composition of a population are part of population policy. H. T. Eldridge, for instance, has defined population policy as "legislative measures, administrative programs and other governmental action intended to alter or modify existing population trends in the interest of national survival or welfare."[1] Writers like Eldridge recognize that many aspects of public policy influence demographic phenomena. Nevertheless, they view population policy as positive action deliberately taken to alter a nation's demographic variables. Most demographers now prefer this narrower definition. Eldridge's definition also emphasizes the fact that population policies ought to be part of broader socioeconomic policies promoting a nation's survival and welfare. In other words, population policy should be considered as a means rather than an end. Increasingly, population policies are designed to speed up the process of economic development or to enhance the quality of the environment.

The Goals of Population Policy

Population policy is related to other policy areas and should be integrated with them. In the narrower sense, population policy may be viewed as efforts to affect the size, structure, and distribution of a population. A population policy, for example, may have such goals as the reduction of mortality and the extension of longevity. It could be argued, however, that

---

[1]H. T. Eldridge, "Population Policies," *International Encyclopedia of the Social Sciences*, vol. 12 (New York: Macmillan, 1968), p. 381.

such measures are to be thought of as health policies rather than population policies, since their purpose is to improve the health of the population rather than to change such quantitative characteristics as size or age structure.

Currently, most population policies deal with fertility, because the most pressing problem in developing nations is that of excessively large families. A few other countries feel that their birth rate is too low and are attempting to raise it. Countries like the United States and Canada periodically alter the number of immigrants allowed to enter each year, and these upward and downward adjustments remain an important element of population policy. In addition, population redistribution programs within nations fall within the scope of population policy. Developing nations in particular are now attempting to change the geographic distribution of their populations.

POPULATION POLICY
IN THE LESS DEVELOPED COUNTRIES

The Ethics of Population Policy

Policy involves making choices—sometimes very difficult choices. Usually several options are open to policymakers, and often they must take a negative approach and ask, "Which policy involves the fewest number of evils?" If population policy implies the modification of demographic behavior, then, the question may be raised whether such steps can be justified on ethical grounds. If we lived in an ideal world in which the reproductive decisions of couples produced an optimum population maximizing the community's welfare, no population policy would be needed.

Unfortunately, we do not live in such blissful universe. Often couples do have the freedom to decide on family size, but such decisions are usually made without reference to the rights and interests of others. Yet the reproductive choices of couples *do* affect the freedom and wellbeing of the remainder of the population. Our quality of life in society, our educational and employment opportunities, the rewards we obtain for our work, the political stability we enjoy, the amount of recreational space at our disposal—all these and more are largely determined by demographic processes, which in turn reflect individual reproductive decisions made at some point in the past.

Implicit in this discussion is the concept of *external diseconomies* or *negative externalities* discussed in Chapter 8. The concepts refer to actions undertaken by one individual that result in uncompensated costs to others.

A well-known example of such external diseconomies is pollution, which often occurs because producers shift part of their production costs to others. If, for instance, a factory releases untreated smoke into the air, surrounding houses have to be painted more often, and those living nearby also may have to have their clothes cleaned more frequently. Thus the factory displaces part of its production costs onto others. Furthermore, the social costs of production exceed the private costs. Because the individual producers can shift part of their production costs to others, they are able to produce a greater volume of output than if they had been held responsible for *all* costs of their actions—including those of treating the smoke.

Obviously, couples can also transfer part of the costs of reproduction to others, since they are not held responsible for the social implications and expenses of their reproductive decisions. The concept of diseconomies is therefore central to the justification of government intervention. In our example of pollution, the environment will become cleaner only if the authorities force the manufacturers to "internalize" the "externalities" or to settle all costs of production. Similarly, individual reproductive decisions must not be allowed to handicap the wellbeing of present and future generations. If couples were somehow forced to pay a greater share of the full costs of reproduction, they might end up having fewer children.

Family Planning Programs

A first step toward nationwide fertility reduction would be to set up an effective *family planning* program. Family planning as an ideology does not attempt to modify the motivations of couples but merely urges them to have the number of children they desire. In other words, it aims at eliminating unwanted births. Even the "desired" number of children, however, can be disastrously high; in developing nations, it is often close to four and above. In Iran in 1977, the number of children the average family wanted was about five. Yet as a first step, family planning is probably still the best approach. If its benefits to the health and welfare of mothers and children are emphasized, its political acceptability can be greatly enhanced. It may also be argued that family planning services enlarge a couple's options and thereby their freedom to decide.

Supplying the full range of fertility-control services implies basically three things. First, it means providing the broadest possible selection of birth control techniques, including oral contraceptives, IUD's, and condoms. Abortion and sterilization services can also be made available. Abortion, whether legal or illegal, is one of the most ancient and widely practiced means of birth limitation. Today, the annual number of abortions in the world has been estimated at 40 million. In nations where it is still illegal, it often becomes a clandestine operation performed by unqualified practitioners and results in the maiming and killing of millions of women. If performed under proper medical conditions, preferably during the first three months of pregnancy, the operation is less dangerous to women than normal birth. Male and female sterilization (vasectomy and tubal ligation) are now safe methods also, requiring only a minor surgical intervention with no known side effects.

The second requirement for a comprehensive family planning program is an adequate delivery system by which couples can obtain the services they need. Such a system might include family planning clinics (mobile or otherwise) and sterilization centers, the distribution of educational materials such as booklets and films, and the use of paramedics in villages to provide contraceptives and information. Whenever possible, the existing commercial distribution network—drugstores and even the small general store in the village—should be used to supplement whatever facilities the government provides. Commercial outlets can be used even if the government subsidizes contraception. Thus contraceptives can be provided free to the commercial sector, which then can sell them at an agreed-upon price covering the dealer's costs and a reasonable profit. This might be cheaper than selling these devices in special government-operated establishments.

The third requirement for a successful family planning program is accelerated research to develop more effective and cheaper contraceptives. When birth control technology improves, the psychological and monetary costs of contraception fall, removing two major obstacles to the use of birth control.

The per capita costs of providing the full range of family planning services in a developing country have been estimated at $1 a year. Costs *per user* are actually higher, but only a fraction of the population is at risk, so it evens out at $1 per capita (as estimated by the United Nations Fund for Population Activities). Excluding mainland China (whose per capita costs are not known), the costs of universal provision of family planning services would be around $2 billion per year. If half this sum could be provided by the developing countries themselves and the remaining half by the international community, only $1 billion would be needed in the form of international aid—a relatively modest sum compared to the world's $434 billion armaments bill in 1977. At the moment only about $250 million is devoted annually to family planning.

It is sometimes said that if family planning efforts fail to yield quick results, such efforts should be discontinued. This view may in fact not be correct. To change people's attitudes about such fundamental matters may take years. A restructuring of the mind has to take place—by definition, a slow process. To bring about ultimate change may require a substantial initial effort that at first seems to produce no visible results.

Altering Deep-seated Pronatalist Attitudes

Once the family planning benefits are provided, an environment must be created conducive to the use of the available services. This implies a number of institutional reforms designed to alter people's demographic behavior.

The creation of a new low-fertility environment must begin with the recognition and removal of the *pronatalist incentives*—inducements to increase the birth rate—prevailing until recently. In the past, death rates were high, sometimes leveling temporarily above the birth rates. Life expectancy at birth was short. Each society had to mobilize its reproductive potentialities to the full, to keep up with the high mortality. Those societies that failed to ensure high levels of reproduction disappeared.

Practically all communities that have survived have done so because, over thousands of years, they evolved a complex system of values, customs, and policies that promote marriage and the bearing and raising of children. The custom of early marriage, for example, lengthens the period during which it is likely that women will become pregnant. The practice of arranged marriages, still customary in some third world countries, ensures that almost everybody does in fact get married early. Furthermore, the extended family relieves parents of some of the costs of raising children. The linking of sexual roles and parental functions has also been a powerful incentive to marriage, because parenthood has been, and in many countries still is, implicit in the very definition of femininity and masculinity. And the fact that no career alternatives to marriage, homemaking, and childrearing were open to women again encouraged universal and early marriage.

Although it may seem that individuals themselves make reproductive choices, such choices are voluntary in a limited sense only. Legal and cultural pronatalist pressures are so embedded in the human consciousness that people often do not even notice their presence. From birth, children are indoctrinated with these customs and values and eventually internalize them. But now that mortality is declining, the whole pronatalist framework that has allowed humans to survive so far has suddenly become useless, even burdensome and obstructive, in the attainment of the good society. A lifting of the existing reproduction incentives must rank high in an antinatalist population policy, if such a program is to be successful.

A large part of the world's population still lives with pronatalist values and norms that reflect the death rates of the past. If modifications in demographic behavior are to be brought about, substantial changes in attitudes toward marriage and childbearing are essential. The media will have to play an important role in the process. Hong Kong, Taiwan, and Singapore have already experimented successfully with the media. Films, radio and television, posters, leaflets, exhibits, and newspapers can all be used to dramatize the realities and implications of rapid population growth, to provide information about contraceptive practices, and to promote the benefits of a small family. Population-related information should also be taught in the schools. If political and religious leaders, national celebrities, and others were to endorse the new population ethic, the effect on public thinking would be considerable. A prime minister announcing his vasectomy in public would work wonders. If the preferences of couples can be changed successfully, parents would produce and even prefer smaller families. Conformity between fertility performance and fertility preference would be maintained, and the diseconomies that provoked the manipulation of taste in the first place would disappear.

Raising the Minimum Age of Marriage

Early marriage is a typical arrangement encouraging fertility. Since in many Asian and African countries marriages are often still contracted when the marriage partners are young, raising the legal age of marriage for young women to at least 18 and that of young men to 20 would significantly reduce fertility. Such a measure would shorten the period during which women are likely to conceive and would, in addition, give women more time for training and education, which are themselves inversely associated with fertility. In countries such as Iran, Pakistan, and India the parents often decide upon the marriage partner for the girl. A simple but effective legislative change would be to confer on women of all ages the legal right to refuse to marry a partner chosen for them by their parents or other family members. Thus young women could not be forced into marriage and would be allowed to wait until they had met a man they loved.

Prohibition of Child Labor
and Establishment of Compulsory Education

If the costs and benefits of an additional child have some effect on fertility decisions, the number of desired children would obviously drop with any increase in the costs and/or any decline in these benefits. Making child labor illegal, and setting up a system of compulsory primary education, would be two ways to bring this about. If children have to be sent to school, they cannot be hired out for gainful employment until, say, their early adolescence. Not only do they contribute less to the family income by working fewer hours on the family farm or elsewhere, but they still must be provided with food, clothes, shelter, books, and so on. Such a shift in costs and benefits might induce parents to want fewer children.

The Role of Women

The classic role assigned to girls and women has been that of marriage and parenthood. Having no genuine alternatives, women had every inducement to get married and to do so early. If the existing pronatalist machinery is to be dismantled, then all laws, customs, and regulations promoting sex discrimination must be eliminated. In particular, appropriate property laws, inheritance and divorce laws, and regulations giving women the right to vote and to share with their husbands in decisionmaking, must be enacted. Schools and institutes of vocational training must be opened to girls, whose chances of admission should equal those of men. There are still too many nations in which women's chances for education and training are inferior. Schools and public information programs should explain to girls that being the mother of a large and poor family benefits neither her nor the nation, and that alternatives exist.

All available data indicate an inverse relationship between education and fertility, and there is no doubt, either, that women who work tend to have fewer children. One obvious reason is the indirect, or opportunity costs—foregone social activities, relinquished salary, and so on—associated with each additional child. Childrearing consumes time and money. An extra child may tie a woman to the home for at least four more years, during which she may have to quit her job and give up chances for promotion. The higher the level of education, the larger the salary the woman is likely to earn, hence the more substantial the opportunity cost of the added child.

As soon as an antinatalist institutional structure has been set up, it is time for the next step: the adoption of financial incentives and disincentives designed to encourage couples to limit family size.

A Note on the Value of Children

To be effective, population policy must be based on some understanding of reproductive behavior. A number of social scientists have tried to explain such behavior in terms of cost-benefit analysis, asserting that parents somehow compare the psychological and economic benefits of an additional child with its psychological and economic costs. If the advantages exceed the inconveniences, parents will try to have another child, whereas if costs exceed advantages, they will not. However, those who have worked with this concept know that it looks simpler than it is. Besides, the demand for children is not the only variable at stake. People seek sexual gratification for its own sake; thus, reproduction is also a byproduct of human sexuality. Of course, contraception can be used, but birth control has its psychological and financial costs, too. So a couple not only balances the advantages of an additional child against the drawbacks, but also weighs the emotional and monetary costs of contraception against the benefits it confers. Here, then, is the rationale for family planning programs: they widen a couple's options and reduce the psychological and financial costs of fertility inhibition.

With all its shortcomings, the cost-benefit framework provides some useful clues as to what kind of population policies might be effective. In many developing nations, for instance, children have real economic value while the costs of raising them are relatively small. In predominantly agricultural societies young boys can help on the farm or work for small wages that are turned over to their parents. Girls can help their mothers with household chores, take care of younger children, and perform other tasks. As those children get older, they often continue to work for their parents, who count on their sons to provide them with a minimum of material security when they are old. Thus to have many children, especially sons, is economically rational.

In developed countries children no longer have economic value, while the costs of raising them are high. This explains in part why families have become smaller as the development and modernization process has continued. Couples do go on having children, of course, but in the Western countries the primary motive may be that children provide companionship, an outlet for feelings of love and affection, the opportunity for play, diversion from the stress of work, and so on.

Societal inducements that favor childbearing, and societal barriers that discourage it, can modify the perceived costs and benefits. In many developing nations such factors still encourage procreation. An intelligent population policy, using the cost-benefit framework as its point of departure will attempt to modify the couple's perceived costs and benefits so as to modify reproductive behavior in the desired direction.

Incentives and Disincentives

We may define *incentives* and *disincentives* as conditions that induce certain types of behavior at the expense of other types. Suppose we want families not to exceed a target number of, say, two children. We can then reward those parents who comply with the norm and penalize those who do not. The incentives may consist of monetary rewards such as cash, tax rebates, bonds, and bonuses, or goods and services like food, housing, and medical services. Incentives and disincentives, promising as their application may be, do have their problems, too. Some are politically sensitive, others are difficult to implement, and all of them require the allocation of scarce administrative talents and financial resources. Besides, they are easier to handle in a modern, urbanized society in which most people are employed taxpayers, than in the less developed countries with vast, populous rural areas. A government must measure the price of implementing them against the much greater price of not doing so. In spite of their disadvantages, however, benefit-cost ratio of incentive programs is likely to be high. A common argument against the use of disincentives is that they may punish the children as well as the parents. Yet the absence of disincentives may result in a larger number of births per family, which often penalizes all the children and may even increase their mortality risk.

Positive Incentives.   Positive incentives, or rewards for correct fertility behavior, are usually given prominence over penalties, or negative incentives. The reward can be declined if the couple insists on continuing its traditional fertility behavior. In other words, the couple gains an option when a system of positive inducements is adopted.

Among proposed positive inducements is an annual bonus to be given to men or women who have postponed marriage for another year. If, for instance, the legal minimum age of marriage for women has been fixed at 18, a woman would be entitled to a first disbursement on her nineteenth birthday if she were still unmarried. The idea is, of course, to reduce the reproductive period of the woman. The additional year or years before marriage can be used for training or education; the bonus will help defray its costs. One drawback, to be sure, is that rewards will also be given to people who would not have gotten married in any case—but all bonus schemes have the drawback of rewarding people whose behavior is not actually motivated by the promise of payment.

A second possibility is an allowance paid to married couples for each year of nonpregnancy. The premium could be paid at the end of each year or after a two- or five-year period. Or the payments could be deposited in a blocked savings account to be released at the end of the woman's reproductive period. It is likely, however, that most recipients would prefer annual disbursements. A major difficulty inherent in this type of plan is the administration, and administrative know-how is a scarce commodity in all developing nations.

A third proposal involves rewards to individuals who agree to be sterilized, vasectomy of the males being the obvious procedure. The compensation could be given in cash or kind—if the latter, perhaps a transistor radio or a bag of rice. Such schemes can also be tried at the community level. A village can be offered a water pump, a well, or a cash award if a given percentage of the qualified men accepts a vasectomy. The proposition would create group pressure, but not every eligible man would have to accept sterilization.

If the plan is tried on an individual basis, it is possible to pay a flat rate or a graduated one for every sterilization. In a vasectomy project, for example, sterilization could be denied to men not having at least two children. Fathers of two offspring would then get the highest compensation, if they agreed to the operation. Fathers of three would get a smaller reward, and so on. Such a plan would encourage those most likely to have many more children to accept permanent sterilization.

Surveys show that parents often want numerous children—especially sons—because they are a guaranteed source of income and help in old age. Parents of larger families are thus often better off in old age than heads of smaller households. To neutralize this particular advantage, a special pension could be paid to those couples willing to limit their offspring. If support were given to those couples restricting their families to two or three children, and not to other couples, all parents would be placed on equal footing. The parents of the larger families could rely on their sons, while parents of smaller families would qualify for government support. In a variant of this plan, all people reaching a certain age would be eligible for support, but the parents of small families would qualify for higher benefits.

It has also been suggested that parents should be rewarded at the time of retirement or at the end of the childbearing period if they have not exceeded a specified number of children. The economist Ronald Ridker has proposed giving a bond, which would mature at the end of the woman's reproductive period, to all couples willing to limit the number of children to two or three. If the couple has more than the specified number of children, the bond becomes automatically void. The implementation of the scheme would not tie up too many administrative resources, since only two contacts with administrative authorities would be needed: first, when the couple accepts the bond and, second, at the end of the childbearing period. The advantage of such deferred payment schemes is that they reach the parents directly while leaving them free to decide upon their own contraceptive methods. However, there is some evidence that recipients prefer immediate disbursements to future compensation, even if the bonds are actually more valuable than cash awards would be.

Disincentives.   Disincentives penalize those who have more than a specified number of children. Suppose that a nation officially proclaims a family of more than n children to be socially undesirable. It may then set up a number of social and financial arrangements to dissuade couples from exceeding the nth child. An advantage of negative incentives is that they cost the taxpayer little, while some programs may actually add to tax revenues. But they will obviously be a great deal less popular than the positive ones.

It has been argued that disincentives might penalize the poor rather than the well-off, because low-income groups are usually the slowest to restrict their progeny. There is also the danger of punishing children rather than the parents. Such dilemmas are real, but governments must take into account the immeasurably greater burden of uncontrolled population growth.

A first disincentive might be a tax on children at orders three or four and above (the birth order of a child is defined by the number of children already born to the mother). The first two or three children might not be taxed, but for each additional child parents would have to pay a given percentage on their combined adjusted gross income. The tax would be effective until the age of retirement. The tax, justified as it might be, runs the risk of arousing too much political opposition to be acceptable. In the developing countries, moreover, many couples who would be subject to such taxes would probably be too poor to bear the expense anyway. Besides, the costs of collecting such levies might simply be too high.

As another disincentive, housing-allocation and school-admission policies can be structured to favor small families. In Singapore, for instance, families with only two children enjoy priority over larger families in qualifying for public housing. If a nation's educational facilities are limited, the children of small families, or the first two children of any family, large or small, could be given priority in school admission. The latter proposal seems fairer and would still have some effect.

There are still other approaches. Income tax laws can be revised to limit the number of exemptions for children to only the first two. Maternity benefits can be allotted only for the first two or three children. In Singapore, where 80 percent of all births take place in government-run hospitals, delivery fees rise steeply after the second child, though such fees are waived if one of the two parents accepts sterilization. Many more disincentives could be designed, but such measures must be adapted to different environments. What succeeds in one country may well fail in another.

Coercion.   If governments fail to act in time (and many do), coercion will ultimately become unavoidable. Not many examples exist as yet, but the future is likely to see direct limitations on family size as well as sanctions to enforce them. Biologist G. Hardin has recommended one kind of coercion or rather voluntary compliance that would be mutually agreed upon by the majority of the people affected. We accept compulsory taxes, says Hardin, and we all accept the notion that an individual can have only one spouse at a time, and so on. We institute coercive measures, in other words, to escape far worse alternatives. So if necessary, couples can also be limited to, say, two births.[2]

In mainland China a mild form of coercion exists already. Births are planned by neighborhood production teams for each five-year period. The

---

[2]G. Hardin, "The Tragedy of the Commons," in A. C. Enthoven and A. M. Freeman, *Pollution, Resources and the Environment* (New York: Norton, 1973), pp. 11–12.

reproductive intentions of couples are coordinated with the planned birth quota passed down by higher authorities. If necessary, couples are persuaded, in group discussions and through peer pressure, to limit their families. For instance, a couple may be "advised" (under considerable pressure) to extend the interval between the first and second child.

Another proposition likely to be adopted in the future in some countries is obligatory sterilization after the nth child. It goes without saying that incentive systems are preferable and much easier to live with then coercive methods. But by remaining inactive many governments have missed the opportunity to solve their population problems painlessly.

At present most existing population control programs show little commitment or conviction, and even less imagination. More optimistically, it is still possible to argue that population policies aimed at accelerating recent trends have a very good chance of success. Once the powerful forces of modernization and economic development have begun, such policies are like swimming with the tide.

Population Redistribution Programs

The manipulation of migration patterns is a legitimate aim of population policy. Policymakers in developing countries increasingly take the view that redistribution policies are necessary, mainly to prevent further congestion in metropolitan areas. The following policies are some of those used to modify current migration patterns.

First, there are policies whose goal is to stop the flow of migrants at the source. *Agrarian reforms* that redistribute land tend to anchor people to the land and so may help reduce rural-urban migration. Unfortunately, it is usually the older generations who benefit from land reforms; younger men and women may continue to migrate to the cities. *Community development,* or the upgrading of rural areas, whereby the villages are supplied with the amenities available in the larger cities, is another well-known method. Such a program might provide low-cost housing, roads, schools, health centers, drinking water, and electricity. The establishment of small manufacturing centers would help generate local employment.

A second policy is to establish new *growth poles,* or growth centers, to create job opportunities in nonmetropolitan cities and towns. If firms can be induced to establish themselves outside the large urban centers, a more balanced distribution of the population may be achieved. Smaller cities with growth potential would have to be selected and provided with the kind of infrastructure (highways, railways, ports, hydroelectric facilities, telephones, and so on) that the metropolitan centers already enjoy. Because companies tend to cluster so as to enjoy the so-called economies of agglomeration (pp. 59), the incentives offered must be very strong to compensate them for the loss of benefits from a metropolitan location. Such incentives might include free or very cheap land, a reduction of government red tape on new business ventures, and special tax advantages. The implementation of such decentralization policies tends to be very expensive, however. The creation of new growth centers may also simply accelerate rural-urban migration by creating a new flow of migrants to the intermediate-size cities, without reducing preexisting urban flows.

A third approach consists of resettling migrants in any existing frontier areas. If a nation still has lands with very low population densities, and if it has the capital as well as the administrative capacity to carry out such ventures, the measure may be worth considering. For example, Indonesia has attempted for years to transfer individuals and families out of densely populated Java; in the 1960s and 1970s sponsored migrants were transported free of charge from Sumatra, where they were provided with a simple dwelling, a plot of land, and some tools, as well as food for twelve months. But such programs are costly, and they require heavy investment in the area of destination.

A fourth kind of redistribution policy encourages urban residents to return to their rural homelands, or simply prevents migrants from leaving their community or from entering the city. But such policies are either ideologically unacceptable to most governments or beyond their administrative ability. Yet since the 1970s mainland China has been able to check rural-urban migration through a set of administrative controls on migration, including restrictions on travel permits and access to ration cards; freedom of movement has been impeded to a degree unknown in other nations except in times of war. Indonesia has tried to reduce the growth of its capital, Djakarta, by various measures limiting immigration. Migrants who come to Djakarta have nine months to find a job; if at the end of that period they are still unemployed, they must return to their place of origin. Legal residents of the capital must buy an identification card that enables them to live and work in the city.

POPULATION POLICY
IN THE DEVELOPED COUNTRIES

Needless to say, some of the above considerations apply to less developed and industrialized countries alike. However, in the developed countries fertility seems to move ever closer to replacement levels and has fallen below it in a number of them, including the United States. As a result, much of the need to reduce aggregate birth rates has evaporated. At present, moreover, there is probably no solid case for encouraging population growth or fertility above replacement levels. Such a consensus would seem to call for "neutral" social policies—policies without a specific pronatalist bias.

But what should be done if fertility in a developed nation drops below replacement levels and stays there? Although this question is still somewhat theoretical, it may well become an issue in the near future. Presumably, population policies should then aim at raising fertility to replacement levels without encouraging large families. Since first children are usually born as a result of the spontaneous will of the couple, material inducements would not be necessary. They should be substantial for the second child, however, and very generous for the third, but low thereafter. Another plan would be to provide couples under a certain age (say 30) with a generous *marriage loan* that bears no interest. When the first child is born, 25 percent of the loan could be forgiven. The same would hold for the second child, while the remaining 50 percent would be forgiven if a third child was born.

Since working women tend to be less fertile than nonworking women, some of the following measures might also be contemplated:

1. Public nurseries, or day care centers, could be provided at low cost, to enable working women to have moderate-sized families. If they know their children will be well taken care of, working women might be more willing to have a second or third child.
2. Employers might be given tax concessions, if they agreed to employ women on more flexible conditions (especially working hours) than is common at present.
3. *Maternity grants* and related provisions might be improved. A working woman could be given her full salary for a period before and/or after the birth of her child, perhaps up to three months' time.

THE POLICY DEBATE ON IMMIGRATION

As was pointed out in Chapter 9, immigrants contributed immensely to the growth of the United States. But now the United States has more than 220 million inhabitants, many of its nonrenewable resources are already depleted, and the environment is under heavy pressure. Although much of the earlier enthusiasm for encouraging immigration has evaporated, immigration swells the population by some 400,000 people each year. Furthermore, the distribution of immigrant settlement is typically unbalanced. In both the United States and Canada, foreign immigrants prefer certain metropolitan centers and certain states. Filipinos who come to America tend to settle in Honolulu, for instance, while Mexicans flow to California, Arizona, and New Mexico.

Rethinking Our Immigration Policies

To permit a small flow of highly trained immigrants will probably continue to make sense, since it provides the nation with talents not otherwise available. Some immigration of close relatives of American citizens and residents is also desirable. Finally, the United States and other high-income nations may periodically allow specific categories of political refugees and displaced persons to enter for humanitarian reasons. But the whole idea of systematic immigration will probably become increasingly questionable as we move toward the twenty-first century.

The writer G. Hardin, for example, feels that current immigration policies are outdated. He assumes that at present population levels, every person places some burden upon the ecosystem. Immigration hastens the environmental degradation for which posterity must pay. Conventional ethics, he says, ignores the claims of posterity. Large-scale immigration means being generous with posterity's possessions. Our posterity-blind ethic ought to be replaced by an ecological ethic that pays attention to posterity.

In his discussion of legal and illegal U.S. immigration, which together add up to some 600,000 persons per year, Hardin compares the nation to a lifeboat with limited capacity. The relatively few prosperous lifeboats in this world are surrounded by a larger number of relatively poor ones, with many needy persons jumping out of the "poor" lifeboats to get into the "rich" ones.[3] If all the destitute are aboard, the capacity of the rich ones will be strained and all passengers will drown. "Complete justice, complete catastrophe," says Hardin. Both the nation's available space and its carrying capacity have finite limits that can be approached only at great peril. Thus, even if only a small portion of those who apply are taken aboard, the safety margin may be eliminated. Besides, what criteria should we apply to those who are allowed to enter? And what can we say to those who are not?

Hardin proposes that the prosperous nations simply arrest systematic immigration, which will allow them to preserve a small safety factor. Those passengers in the prosperous lifeboats who feel guilty about being fortunate should have the option to leave, yielding their place to others. Since the population of the developing nations is about twice that of the developed countries, while their rate of increase is more than double, a sharing of territory would simply be suicidal. Hardin recognizes that his approach is still taboo, which explains, he says, why those who question the wisdom of present immigration policies are immediately accused of selfishness, isolationism, bigotry, and racism.

A purely demographic argument also seems to militate for restricting

---

[3] At present, illegal immigrants from Haiti actually swim to the American coast when the boats carrying them come close enough to the shore.

immigration now, but for being a bit more expansionist in a few decades. During 1944–61 large cohorts of babies were born, many of whom have already entered the labor market, while others are still in school. Fertility in the United States dropped after the early 1960s and the cohorts born in subsequent years became smaller. In the near future, then, the youth dependency ratio and the total dependency ratio will be relatively low. As a result, the investments needed to carry the increase in population will be small, creating the proper demographic and economic conditions for a spurt in economic growth. However, around the year 2010 the first cohorts of the baby boom will begin to retire. By 2030 the age pyramid will be sharply constrictive, unless present fertility conditions change again. With a relatively small workforce and a relatively large number of elderly, the Social Security System will be under enormous pressure, to say the least. As noted earlier, the choice may then be to reduce support to the aged or increase the tax burden on the employed. Most immigrants are young adults, so continued immigration now means an influx of people born during the baby boom period, which will worsen the situation after the year 2010. By this reasoning, it would make more sense to reduce immigration now to a small flow; then, just before or at the very moment when the baby boom cohorts begin to retire (around 2010), the influx of productive young workers could be increased. The tax base would be broadened, the old-age dependency ratio would drop a little, and more favorable conditions to support the aged would be created. This proposition, however, relies on a kind of long-term view rarely adopted in policy recommendations.

Illegal Migration

The problem of illegal international migration is steadily worsening and therefore receives increasing attention. Although direct quantitative data are fragmentary and often unreliable, it seems obvious that most of the illegal international migration follows the same direction as the legal current; from low-income to high-income nations. In both the United States and Europe illegal migration usually consists of individuals crossing the border without official permission. In other cases individuals enter as tourists, visitors, or students and then remain. In America most illegal aliens— probably around 80 percent—are Mexicans.

It often pays employers to hire illegal aliens, who are unlikely to demand job rights such as overtime pay or unionization. They will accept relatively low wages and poor working conditions. Illegal immigrants are often concentrated in occupations requiring few skills, so it is the blacks, the Hispanics, women, and teenagers who bear the brunt of illegal immigration, since their job opportunities and wage levels are the most affected. Moreover, all available data indicate that unemployment among these four categories far exceeds the national average. Illegal immigrants also place an additional burden on the taxpayer insofar as citizens or permanent residents lose their jobs and must receive public welfare support.

In the United States no comprehensive action has been undertaken to stem the tide. In Europe, however, several nations, including West Germany, impose stiff fines of up to $25,000 on employers who hire, temporarily or permanently, a foreign worker who does not have a work permit. In Denmark such employers may even be imprisoned for up to six months. Imposing penalties on the employers of illegal migrants makes a great deal of sense, because if no employment is available the major inducement to migrate is neutralized. France also punishes individuals or groups that recruit illegal migrant workers and bring them into the country; they are subject to fines of from $2,000 to $50,000 and to imprisonment of up to five years. France imposes equally severe penalties for forging fictitious documents like residence permits, visas, and Social Security cards. In Belgium, Germany, and France the migrants themselves are subject to expulsion for not complying with the conditions of admission and residence the law provides. Such measures would go far in discouraging the illegal traffic in migrants between Mexico and the United States. It will be interesting to watch in which direction the United States moves as the problem assumes ever-more-alarming proportions.

CONCEPTS FOR REVIEW

Population policy
External diseconomies
Family planning
Pronatalist incentives
Minimum age of marriage
Antinatalist institutional structure
Positive incentives
Nonpregnancy bonus
Disincentives

Antinatalist coercion
Agrarian reforms
Community development
Growth poles
Marriage loan
Maternity grant
Lifeboat theory
Illegal immigration

QUESTIONS FOR DISCUSSION

1. "In a democratic society people should, under all circumstances, have the freedom to procreate." Discuss this as objectively as you can.
2. "Family planning as an ideology has as its goal the elimination of unwanted births. Since this will not solve the problem of rapid population growth in less developed countries, family planning is useless and should be abandoned." Do you agree? Substantiate your argument.

3. "Lowering fertility levels in less developed countries involves changing human beings." Discuss and evaluate.
4. Discuss some of the methods by which pronatalist values and preferences can be modified in a developing nation.
5. Up to a point, the more years of schooling a woman has, the smaller her family tends to be. List the reasons for this inverse relationship.
6. Since in less developed nations investments in such areas as rural development and irrigation projects are badly needed, can one justify large-scale expenditures on family planning and population policies? Explain.
7. Provide the government of a typical less developed country with a comprehensive program of sanctions and incentives which respects human dignity but brings down fertility levels.
8. How would you advise a developed nation in which fertility has fallen to such low levels that it is threatened with extinction?
9. It has been said that present immigration policies which result in several hundreds of thousands of entries per year are outdated. Do you agree? Why or why not?

BIBLIOGRAPHY

Berelson, B. "Beyond Family Planning." *Studies in Family Planning* (February 1969).

————. *The Great Debate on Population Policy.* New York: Population Council, 1975.

Blake, J. "Coercive Pronatalism and American Population Policy." *In Aspects of Population Growth Policy,* edited by R. Parke and C. W. Westoff. Washington: U.S. Government Printing Office, 1972.

Brown, L. R. *In the Human Interest.* New York: Pergamon Press, 1974.

Davis, K. "Population Policy: Will Current Programs Succeed?" *Science* 158 (November 1967).

Demeny, P. "Welfare Considerations in U.S. Population Policy." In *Aspects of Population Growth Policy,* edited by R. Parke and C. W. Westoff. Washington: U.S. Government Printing Office, 1972.

Eldridge, H. T. "Population Policies." *International Encyclopedia of the Social Sciences,* Vol. 12. New York: Macmillan, 1968.

Hardin, G. *Stalking the Wild Taboo.* 2nd ed. Los Altos, Calif.: Kaufmann, 1978.

————. "The Tragedy of the Commons." In A. C. Enthoven and A. M. Freeman, *Pollution, Resources and the Environment.* New York: Norton, 1973.

Heisel, D. F. and E. Brennan, "Policies for Dealing with Illegal/Undocumented International Migration." Paper presented at Annual Meeting of the Population Association of America, 26 April 1979, Philadelphia.

Lorimer, F. "Issues of Population Policy." In *The Population Dilemma,* 2nd ed., edited by P. H. Hauser. Englewood Cliffs, N.J.: Prentice-Hall, 1969.

Spengler, J. J. "Population Problem, In Search of a Solution." *Science* 166 (December 1969).

Stycos, J. M. "Population Policy and Development." *Population and Development* 3 (March/June 1977).

ACKNOWLEDGMENTS

Figure 2–10 from *The Demographic Basis of Canadian Society,* by W. E. Kalbach, and W. W. McVey (Toronto: McGraw-Hill, 1979) p. 55.

2–11 Adapted by permission of The University Press of Hawaii, from *The Peopling of Hawaii,* by Eleanor C. Nordyke, copyright 1977 by East-West Center.

6–1 A. Haupt, T. T. Kane, *Population Handbook* (Washington: Population Reference Bureau Inc. 1978) p. 29, courtesy of Population Reference Bureau.

6–2 Ministry of Industry, Trade and Commerce, *Canada Yearbook, 1972* (Ottawa: Information Division, Statistics Canada, 1972), p. 259.

6–3 I. Taylor, J. Knowelden, *Principles of Epidemiology,* 2nd ed. (Boston: Little, Brown, 1964), p. 22. Copyright 1964, reprinted by permission.

6–4 Reprinted from R. Ram, T. W. Schultz, "Life Span, Health, Savings and Productivity," in *Economic Development and Cultural Change,* Vol. 27, No. 3, April 1979, p. 401, by permission of The University of Chicago Press.

6–5 Netherlands Bureau of Statistics, *Statistical Yearbook of the Netherlands 1978* (The Hague: Staatsuitgeverj, 1979), p. 60.

7–3 Statistics Canada, *1971 Census of Canada, Profile Studies, Fertility in Canada*, Vol. 5 Pt. I (Ottawa: 1976), p. 5.

7–4 Statistics Canada, *Canada's Population, Demographic Perspectives* (Ottawa: 1979), p. 5.

7–9 Geoffrey McNicoll and Si Gde Made Mamas, *The Demographic Situation in Indonesia* (Honolulu: Papers of the East-West Population Institute, No. 28, 1973), p. 21. Reprinted by permission.

7–10 A. Haupt, T. T. Kane, *Population Handbook* (Washington, D.C.: Population Reference Bureau, 1978), p. 12, courtesy of Population Reference Bureau.

7–17 Westinghouse Health Systems, *Mexico, Summary Report* (Columbia, Md.: October 1978), p. 1.

10–1 J. C. Biggar, *The Sunning of America: Migration to the Sunbelt*, Vol. 34, No. 1 (Washington, D.C.: Population Reference Bureau, March 1979), p. 11, courtesy of Population Reference Bureau.

11–1 A. Haupt, T. T. Kane, *Population Handbook*, (Washington, D.C.: Population Reference Bureau, 1978), p. 12, courtesy of Population Reference Bureau.

11–2 Ministère de l'Economie et des Finances, Institut National de la Statistique et des Etudes Economiques, *Annuaire Statistique de la France, 1977* (Paris: Imprimerie Nationale 1977), Plate 1.

11–7 Dominion Bureau of Statistics, *The Canada Yearbook 1952–53* (Ottawa: Cloutier, 1953), p. 218.

11–8 Ministère de l'Industrie et du Commerce, Bureau de la Statistique du Quebec, *Annuaire du Quebec 1974*, p. 289.

Index